A 5 $4.00

The Paris Edition

The Autobiography of

WAVERLEY ROOT

1927-1934

*Edited and with an Introduction
by Samuel Abt*

NORTH POINT PRESS
San Francisco   1987

Contents

Introduction

Waverley Root began this book in self-defense. In 1971 and 1972, he contributed to the *International Herald Tribune* a series of articles about life in Paris in the late 1920s, specifically life on the Paris Edition of the *Chicago Tribune*. After the articles were published and became what scholars would call "source material," he wrote somewhat huffily: "Imitation is, we are told, the sincerest form of flattery, but I could have done without flattery in this case. I suppose I should feel grateful to those who admired my stories so ardently that they could not refrain from passing them on to the public before I got around to doing so myself."

What bothered him most, he confessed, "was to see good articles spoiled by inept writing; I would have preferred outright plagiarism." And so he began work on his memoirs from his arrival in Paris in the spring of 1927 and his landing a job with the Paris Edition until that paper folded in the fall of 1934. "I had signed on with the poorest-paying paper in Paris," he writes in his memoirs, "—one of the luckiest things that ever happened to me."

Like many people, said the American writer Mary Blume in a profile of Root early in 1982, he planned to remain in Paris for a few weeks. Like many people, he stayed. Life in Paris then was cheap and easy and funny. "Nobody was thinking serious thoughts except about literary manifestos," he says in the memoirs. "There were a good many loafers in Montparnasse whose conversation dealt largely with the great books they were going to write or the great pictures they were going to paint as soon as they finished their beer—unfortunately the beer never ran out. These practitioners of the *dolce far niente* were usually pleasant and often picturesque company. . . ."

Root was not one of these loafers. He talked himself onto the *Chicago Tribune*, one of three American papers published then in Paris. The others were the *Paris Times* and the *Paris Herald*, the European edition of the

New York Herald Tribune, which in 1934 swallowed up the *Chicago Tribune*. From a reporter making $15 a week at the start, he rose to become news editor of the paper at its end. He saw the paper from all levels, including at a distance: for two years he worked in the London office of the *Chicago Tribune*'s Foreign News Service. Late in his life, he set down all the daffiness and dedication.

"We worked on the Paris Edition because it was a club and a cult, because we liked each other, because we loved putting out the paper," he explains in his memoirs after telling stories of Colonel McCormick and the less-than-impeccable limousine, of the Paris Edition's disappearing sports editor, of Louisette, the staff mistress, of Lindbergh's flight to Paris, and the *Paris Herald*'s scoop when it reported that Admiral Byrd had made it too. Root writes about both the Right Bank, where the Paris Edition had its building, and the Left Bank, where it had its readers. Whichever Bank, his love for Paris shines through.

Except for the time in London, which he hated, he remained in Paris until just before the Nazis arrived, when he returned to his native New England. Born in Providence, Rhode Island, Root grew up in Fall River, Massachusetts. He owed his first name, which was frequently misspelled, to his Aunt Millie's fondness for the Waverley novels of Sir Walter Scott—Root was named for his uncle, her son Waverley. Root followed family tradition by attending Tufts College, where he wanted to study English literature. Finding the English department not up to his standards, he switched his major to psychology and talked the college authorities into letting him give undergraduates a course in contemporary literature from Meredith to Joyce.

After graduation he moved to Greenwich Village in New York and wrote book reviews and short stories that he later described as *New Yorker* short stories before the *New Yorker* was there to publish them. At eight o'clock on a spring evening in 1927, Root decided to visit Paris. At noon the next day he was on a transatlantic steamer with a tin suitcase and a typewriter. After World War II, he lived in France for the rest of his life, working as a free-lance writer and editor and as a correspondent for the *Washington Post*. Along the way he had also worked in Paris for the Copenhagen *Politiken*, the United Press, Time-Life, and the Mutual Broadcasting System. Late in his life, he was the dean of the foreign press corps covering French politics and diplomacy. He was an officer of the Legion of Honor in France, a reward, he liked to say, for annoying the U.S. State Department by supporting General Charles de Gaulle during the war.

Despite his many years abroad and his fondness for French-speaking wives (he had four), he remained a Yankee. "I've never felt in the least expatriate, the Americanism is just bred in the bone. I've never felt in the least non-American. I think unless you change countries very young, the roots are always important. Not only your own personal roots but the generations before you." His family came to America in 1635.

In his eightieth year, Mary Blume described him as "a burly, pink-faced man with a fine, square white beard that rests on his off-white turtle-neck sweater and gives him a rather nautical air. He claims he used to sit around the port in his beloved Ile de Ré wearing a fisherman's hat and waiting for tourists to offer him ten francs for a photograph. None did, but Root does have the sort of calm and confident face that invites strangers to approach." He confirmed this: "I have the kind of face, apparently, that provokes being asked questions. I never went to a strange city that I wasn't asked street directions, sometimes in a language I didn't know."

Root had been a journalist for thirty years and the author of half a dozen books, including *The Truth About Wagner*, *Are You Ready for World War III?*, and *Winter Sports in Europe*, when, in 1958, he became a world authority on food with the publication of *The Food of France*.

The way he told it, the book came about almost by accident. "After nearly thirty years in France, I'd gathered quite a good little restaurant guide," he explained. "But there's only so much you can say about restaurants. So I began adding little footnotes, anecdotes. Pretty soon the footnotes were the interesting part, and I threw out the restaurants." The book, which divided France gastronomically by the fat—butter, oil, or lard—used regionally, was acclaimed, and Root was, as he said, typecast. "Since I got myself typecast and have had to write about food, I write on the subject seriously because I think you have to document anything you're writing about. But I try to write about a lot of things other than food in the food articles, between the lines."

The Food of France was followed by several books in which he combined gastronomy and erudition, including *The Food of Italy* and *Italian Cooking*. He finally did write a guide to restaurants, the *Paris Dining Guide*, a paperback.

His monumental dictionary, *Food*, which appeared in 1980, he subtitled "An Informal Guide." This was changed by his publisher to *An Authoritative, Visual History and Dictionary of the Foods of the World*. Root disliked and mistrusted publishers, whom he periodically attacked in print as parasites and thieves. He almost never had the same publisher twice.

Food took nearly ten years of work. Selections were periodically published in the *Herald Tribune* with a note that the complete work would be published soon. The word "soon" was dropped after several years. As they say in the trade, Root wrote long—at one point he reported that the book seemed to be a million words long and that he was working on a one-hundred-fifty-thousand-word abridgment, of which two hundred thousand words were already written. A former agent still recalls with horror a contract he won for Root to write a children's guide to Switzerland; the final manuscript came in at two hundred thousand words, at least one hundred seventy-five thousand more than the publisher felt any child wanted to know about Switzerland. The book was never published. (These memoirs originally ran more than seven hundred pages, and Root crammed words onto the typewritten page.)

Root was an eater but not a cook, and was inordinately proud that he had never furnished a recipe for any of his books. "I did cook once," he admitted, "but I had no choice." That was during his World War II days in Vermont, where he did what he described as hackwork: ghostwriting books and condensing material for newspaper syndicates. "I was snowed in alone for five months. I cooked a lot of chicken, because I had a lot of chickens."

Toward the end of his life, he put aside his food writing to concentrate on his memoirs. He wanted to celebrate what his widow, Colette Root, refers to as "the crimes of his youth" on a newspaper that he agreed was "one day a work of genius and the next a ghastly mistake." Not a sentimental man, he found himself feeling nostalgic as he remembered the Paris of his youth. "I have a horrible impression now that maybe the praisers of things past have always been right," he said. "At least it seems to me that life then was much more carefree."

Playfully, Root said he would call his memoirs "I Never Knew Hemingway"—a gibe at all the authors of memoirs about Montparnasse who said they had known Hemingway. As he reveals in the memoirs, he too knew Hemingway, if indirectly. That was the way Root and I knew each other—indirectly.

When he was a stringer for the *Washington Post* and a frequent contributor to the *International Herald Tribune*, he often visited the offices of the *Tribune* at 21, rue de Berri, just off the Champs-Elysées, where I began working in 1971. Somehow we never met. I worked on the copydesk then, handling hard news, and knew and admired his copy only in its published form. Then, in 1981, I became editor of the paper's Weekend section, a weekly outpouring of feature, cultural, and travel articles. Like many people in Paris, I had heard that Root was writing his memoirs and thought that parts would fit well in the section.

He had then spent years confined to his apartment on the rue du Cherche-Midi, not far from the center of Montparnasse, because of a slipped disc in his back. The *Tribune* had moved its office to an antiseptic and charmless building in suburban Neuilly that Root never visited. He went infrequently to restaurants and I did not presume to visit him at home. Since neither of us seemed to like talking by phone, we communicated exclusively by mail. His letters were filed away, although no copies of mine were kept.

In the first of his letters, he sounded themes that ring throughout his book and continued to mark his life as a free-lance writer:

"I enclose an article on the Ile de Ré, which I hope will not be too long for you (I cut out as much as I left in). One of my difficulties . . . is that my style, for better or for worse, is somewhat leisurely. I need space in which to turn around. . . .

"Well, yes, the crass question of money gets in my way, though for the *Herald Tribune* I am always ready to stretch a point. But most of what I write is based on research, which takes time, and in any case on the attempt to arrive at the best possible language (you should see some of my first drafts, so marked up as to be almost illegible). It's a different job from sitting around the rim of a desk and turning out copy, which I used to be able to do as fast as I could type, with little need for correction. This takes time too, and when it takes more than . . . the payment accounts for, it just isn't possible unless I am ahead of the game on something else.

"My memoirs (covering only 1927 through 1934) were completed some time ago, but I withdrew them from the publisher since his ideas of how to edit them did not coincide with mine. The trouble with trying to extract passages from them is again length; it would be difficult to find sections that would fit in the space you would have available. . . . Here again the question of money intervenes. . . . For instance, the chapter on Henry Miller . . . If I publish this separately, I could get $2,500 for it from a general magazine. . . .

"About the interest in the Paris of the 1920s and 1930s—it seems to come in waves. I am conscious of this because everybody who wants to write anything about that period seems to come to me, as one of the last survivors, for information. At the moment, the demand seems to be calm; but every ten years or so it perks up again."

A few weeks later but still in November 1981, Root wrote that he was not yet ready to consider publishing some of his memoirs in the *Tribune*. But, he added, he had a counteroffer:

"I have something that might be interesting. . . . The *Washington Post* ordered from me quite a long time ago an article on how publishers cheat authors nowadays. They never printed it. . . . I think they got cold feet when they saw it. After all, they also publish a weekly book review section, which depends wholly on publishers' advertising. Example: I have sold ten books in the last fourteen years: total revenue from advances, a little over $4,000 a year; total revenue from royalties, about $1.50. My food dictionary is selling in New York for $13, in Los Angeles for $19, in Ann Arbor for $25; my share, nothing. *Eating in America* is selling not only in the original hardback edition, but has just gone into its second printing in paperback; my share, nothing. The villain in the picture is the conglomerate that owns the publisher; the machinery, to simplify it, is to remainder a book as soon as it comes out—that is, sell it to a cut-rate house at a price on which the publisher makes more than selling the book normally through bookstores, while the cut-rate house can still sell it at bargain prices and make money. The author gets nothing on remainder sales."

A few months later, he continued to withhold the memoirs but could say: "I hope to be able to keep contributing to the *IHT*, if only for sentimental reasons. After all, I have been associated with the paper, though intermittently, in its various avatars since April 1927—fifty-five years."

Two months after that, in March 1982, Root allowed us to publish one of his chapters in a shortened form and seemed pleased enough with the result: "Since the . . . piece worked, would you like to exercise your technique on any other chapters?" he asked. Our letters, exchanged about once a month, began to turn personal on his side as he talked about his interest in tennis—"I lacked the killer instinct. I could take anybody to 5-5 in the fifth set, after which I was clobbered"—and even a trip he had taken decades before with, as he would have put it, a woman not his wife. It also revealed the broadness of his interests and friends:

"Gertrude Norman, my companion on this trip, was, incidentally, the closest friend of the Spanish-Hungarian girl I mentioned in the piece you ran on James Joyce. While Ilona was the mistress of Giorgio Joyce, Gertrude was the mistress of François Gruber, who at one time offered me one of his paintings, which, foolishly, I didn't take. I have no idea what Grubers are worth now; he doesn't get cited at auctions because he died young, at thirty-three I think, from the asthma that was already afflicting him when I knew him, leaving very few paintings behind, of which three are in the Museum of Modern Art here, knocking the spots off everything else in the same room. Before dying, he married the daughter of Henri Bernstein, the playwright. . . . Gertrude was in Paris on a Guggenheim scholarship, and like all the other Guggenheim beneficiaries I knew at the time, did nothing to justify the scholarship (she was supposed to be studying music), but was saved by the war, which permitted her to report to the foundation the loss of a nonexistent trunk containing all her notes. I chose her to keep me company on the ride south because I thought she was the one girl my wife would not suspect of dalliance en route. On this I turned out to have been wrong."

The *Tribune* had published in a series of articles his chapter on Robert McAlmon when he wrote again in August: "I'm happy to hear that people liked the pieces you ran. I've had a few pleasant reactions too, one from an editor on the *London Observer*, who is coming to see me Monday. . . . Any further chapters? Sure." In October 1982, he again sent a personal note: "I am getting out of my apartment for the first time in four years (less three weeks) . . . to spend a month or so on my old stamping grounds on the Ile de Ré. . . . I shall eat John Dory there. Also lobster. Also oysters. And put on weight, dammit."

A few weeks later, from the Ile de Ré, he returned the corrected proofs of another chapter and added: "Don't be sure that nobody ever put on weight eating oysters. The ones I have just had for lunch were cooked in a rich cream sauce. Add to that that the chef here is both a saucier and a pâtissier (not to mention the lusciousness of the breakfast croissants), and the chances of my returning to Paris several pounds heavier are high."

Then, on October 30, he sent a short note from his Paris apartment: "Definitive report on the Ile de Ré and the thinning qualities of shellfish: I have gained three kilos." He signed it, "Weightily yours, Weighverley Root."

That night, age seventy-nine, he died in his sleep. His wife later told me that this note was the last thing he wrote.

As he says in these memoirs, life on the Paris edition of the *Chicago Tribune* could be fun, especially compared with working at a *Herald* catering to "lobster-palace Americans," as Colonel McCormick called them. "I fear that as a newer, brasher, and livelier paper, we were less inhibited by scruples and delivered more low blows than the *Herald*," Root writes. "As befitted so venerable a newspaper—it was founded in 1887—the *Herald* was more decorous. That must have been the quality that inspired Ezra Pound, in his frequent postcards to me, to describe it regularly as 'the dead-and-stuffed *New York Herald*.'"

If he felt disdain for the *Herald* before it bought the *Tribune*, Root remained fond of the paper thereafter, especially once it had merged in 1966 with the International Edition of the *New York Times*. (In a list of best newspapers, he once put the *New York Times*, the *Washington Post*, and the *Los Angeles Times*, continuing, "If a fourth name were to be added to this list of American newspapers of high quality, I would nominate the *International Herald Tribune* of Paris.")

In the 1970s when he wrote this, he still would have known his way about the paper's offices and indeed could have pulled up a chair on the copydesk and set to work. The boisterousness in the city room, the camaraderie of the staff, the general contempt for the business office, the sense of achievement that everybody from editors to printers felt—all these would have been familiar to him from the Paris Edition. Root would have recognized even the way copy was sent to the composing room: by force of gravity, through a chute attached to a hole in the floor; when the chute became plugged, a heavy piece of metal was dropped after a warning cry. That is exactly how it was done on the Paris Edition.

Then, late in March 1978, the *Herald Tribune* became computerized and the world that Root knew disappeared. Gone were the offices on the rue de Berri, sold to a developer while the paper moved to the air-conditioned premises it needed for its computer. Gone were most of the printers and all the pressmen, because the paper no longer needed them with an electronic printing process that relied on rented presses elsewhere in Paris. Gone was the sense of community around the copydesk because now people had to sit apart, separated by their consoles, and could no longer chat or sometimes even see each other. Gone was the noise of the city room, replaced by the quiet tapping of editors who resembled nothing so much as airline reservation clerks, and gone too was the linotype noise of the composing room, where printers now sliced sheets of paper and pasted them to pages.

The newspaper had come a long way from the *Tribune* and the *Herald* that Root described as relying for their circulation on Americans in France, particularly in Paris. Now the paper was printed by satellite transmission around the world and more than half its readers were not Americans. France remained a major market, as the business office put it, but the paper took pains to de-emphasize this coverage lest it be thought of internationally as "an American paper in France."

Root's hated business department had grown beyond his direst imaginings and now included such appendages as a promotion department and a marketing department. The promotion people sponsored balloon races and thought up such eye-catching activities as an elephant polo match. The marketing people produced surveys that plumbed the readers' up-market tastes—lobster-palace Asians and Europeans now. There was a person in charge of public relations and another to organize conferences and another to keep track of airline travel by executives using free tickets bartered with airlines for free advertising.

The world had changed and journalism with it: Instead of allowing Communists to sit in the Paris Edition city room and hear the news about Sacco and Vanzetti, editors now worked behind shatterproof glass doors with an electronic code to hinder terrorists. The day had arrived when a high editor of the paper, asked in a brainstorming session how he would spend a hypothetical windfall of one million francs, announced that he would not spend any of it on the editorial department. Instead, he said, he would give the money to the circulation department to improve its services.

What would Root, or anybody else who worked on the Paris Edition, have thought of that?

The Paris Edition

¶

An International Sport

¶

About eight o'clock one evening in April 1927 it occurred to me that I was out of a job, that I had a little money, and that I had long wanted to go to France. At noon the next day I was aboard the S.S. *President Harding* steaming down the Hudson, outwardbound. I had no definite plans. If anyone had asked me how long I expected to be away, I suppose I would have said a few weeks, possibly a few months. I stayed thirteen years, and it took a world war to send me home.

The desire to see France had been planted in my soul by Dr. Courteny H. Bruerton, one of my French professors at Tufts. Dr. Bruerton was the enthralled victim of a permanent love affair with France. After his last class each June he boarded the first available ship for France and each September he returned on the last ship that would get him back in time for his first class. He was a bachelor, with a life uncomplicated by conjugal obligations; I was able accordingly to spend a good many evenings in his quarters playing chess. When we tired of chess, he would bring out some of his apparently inexhaustible collection of photographs of France and comment on them lovingly.

I hungered for the land of Gothic cathedrals and Renaissance châteaus, and I do not recall that I was discouraged even when he told me how he stood at the window of his hotel in the rue des Beaux-Arts in Paris and watched the art students returning from the Bal des Quat'z-Arts in the early morning, carrying their naked models on their shoulders. When I inspected the same scene some years later, I decided that if Professor Bruerton had really viewed this spectacle from his hotel window, he must have used a telescope. I suspect that he really descended from his room and watched the parade from the sidewalk across the street from the Ecole des Beaux-Arts, as I did.

Alas, the Gothic cathedrals and the Renaissance châteaus lived up to their billing, but the naked models did not. They were naked all right, and they were transported to their destination on the shoulders of the students all right (in imminent danger of falling, for their mounts were a trifle unsteady), but there were a few details that Dr. Bruerton had neglected to brush in.

One was that a girl who has spent a long night in revelry is apt to have lost a good deal of bloom by morning. I suppose these mistreated creatures would have looked gritty by morning even if they had been beauties to start with; but, as they were carried by, it occurred to me that satiny skins and enticing curves are not really essential for modeling and, indeed, that for the purpose of educating the artist's chalk, unexpected bumps in the wrong places might be more useful than symmetry. Perhaps Bruerton had watched from his hotel window after all.

The art school models, in any case, had not afflicted Professor Bruerton with disdain for the female form. One morning in the twenties, walking along a side street running off the Grands Boulevards, I turned into an alcove in which would be displayed, I knew by experience, photographs of the nymphs who provided the entertainment in the little theater behind it, at minimum expense to the management for costuming. My view was blocked by a back that looked familiar. I tapped on it. "Dr. Bruerton, I presume?" I asked, with a certain lack of originality. *"J'adore la plastique,"* he stammered, startled into the only language in which such explanations are elegant. Well, I adore *la plastique* myself, and he need not have been embarrassed before a former student, no longer a member of a body he was honorbound not to corrupt. I had become old enough and imprudent enough to see to my corruption myself.

The crossing of the Atlantic on which Professor Bruerton had launched me was the first of eleven that I made by ship; it was also the best, in spite of having been the most primitive. More exactly, it was the best because it was the most primitive. As the luxury liner developed, so did the habit of protecting passengers from unseemly contact with the sea by aligning their steamer chairs behind barriers of heavy glass, of which the deck steward might deign to open a pane or two at times of flawless weather—or he might not. By 1938, when I crossed on the floating museum called the *Normandie*, I could easily envisage a hapless passenger, once engulfed in its gilded interior, spending the whole voyage in an attempt to thread his way through the labyrinth of carpeted corridors, brilliantly decorated salons, and siren bars to some point where he might get a glimpse of the water, and never making it.

The *President Harding* was a sturdy no-nonsense ship designed to get from one side of the Atlantic to the other, and with no prejudice against letting the passengers know it. It had been acquired from Germany as part of the World War I reparations, a reasonable assumption being that the *President Harding* had been rebaptized (from the *Vaterland*, I think) before the Teapot Dome scandal.

With the ship the United States had inherited most of its German crew, including, unfortunately, the cooks. Food apart, the voyage was pure enchantment. There may have been frills in first class, and perhaps in second, but not in third class, in which I was riding. There was even "steerage" on the *President Harding*, but it was empty west to east. It served only east to west, for immigrants traveling to the United States to make their fortunes; those who succeeded returned to Europe to visit or to stay, but not in steerage. Later, when I had enough money to choose my class, I continued to travel third.

One was conscious of weather at sea in the waterborne days and conscious also of the powerful presence of the ocean. I often stayed on deck until late at night. As it grew dark, the black water seemed to rise about the flanks of the ship until I felt that I could dip my fingers into it if I put my arm over the side. It was on this first Atlantic crossing that I saw an iceberg gleaming majestically white in the distance; a whale spouting a few rods from the ship; flying fish skimming just above the waves; and several times porpoises leaping along beside us, happy for our company. I never saw any of them again, except the porpoises.

The *President Harding* was mercifully devoid of prearranged amusement for the passengers. The first day out a young man from the YMCA, probably given free passage for this purpose, appeared on deck with a large medicine ball, which he urged us to throw around. There were no takers. After a while he wandered forlornly away and was never seen again. For exercise, if anyone wanted it, there was shuffleboard or the traditional walk around the deck, so many circuits to a mile. The *President Harding* must have been split into classes horizontally, not vertically, as became the rule later, for we could walk all around the ship bow to stern, and back again on the other side, without being blocked anywhere by forbidden high-priced territory. A few resolute souls took advantage of this opportunity and strode away around the course, passing, at more or less regular intervals, the chair on which I was taking the only exercise that seemed necessary, breathing deeply.

The great charm of ocean travel in those days was its complete detachment from the world and its worries. From the moment you lost sight of land, you belonged to a self-sufficient universe within which nothing could go wrong. You experienced, suddenly, a great lightening of heart, a feeling of complete liberty, unthinkable on land, where you could move in the direction of trouble and were frequently forced, by one form of pressure or another, to do so. At sea you were being moved inexorably toward your destination with no possibility of exchanging it by the exercise of volition. It proved pleasant to give volition a rest. No matter what disaster might occur behind you, on land, you could do nothing about it; you were therefore relieved of all responsibility. If some private disaster arrived to friends or family, you were unlikely even to know about it. There were no ship-to-shore telephones in those days. There was of course a radio ("wireless" then) housed in a makeshift shack tacked perilously to the starboard side of the top deck, from which it spat crackling Morse, but it was difficult to imagine anyone's taking so unprecedented a step as to dispatch a message to it.

The radio did bring us daily news from land, the only breach in our isolation, but hardly a broad one. It provided half a dozen items of information, inserted by the ship's printing shop in a blank space left for that purpose in the preprinted papers that had been put aboard at New York, filled otherwise with marvelously dull material, to be doled out to us daily, which we read with inattention. This publication was called, I think, the *Inter-Ocean Times*, and I might have inspected it more carefully if I had been endowed with the gift of prophecy, for it was published by the *Chicago Tribune*, for which, a few weeks later, I would start working for a stint of eight years.

So perfect was every detail (except one) of my first entry into France that I might have been inclined to suspect the Ministry of Tourism and the Ministry of Information (i.e., Propaganda) of having worked out the scenario together to captivate foreign visitors, if there had been any such ministries in those unself-conscious days. It began with the landing at Cherbourg, in those days a tiny fishing port into which the *President Harding* could not possibly have been squeezed. We were discharged into a tender, which made its way through an opening in a breakwater into a small, sheltered harbor whose three sides were lined by walls of low gray stone buildings, delightfully foreign.

Our train lay ready to take us to Paris when we left the tender. My porter deposited me in one of its compartments, in a wagon whose design owed nothing to the American day coaches to which I was accustomed—again, of course, delightfully foreign. At that moment anything different and foreign was bound to be charming, the charm of adventure.

A moment of crisis had now arrived: I had to tip the porter. Throughout a long life of traveling and tipping, I have never, in any given circumstances, been capable of determining how much I should tip. I have solved this problem by tipping too much, which I prefer, stupidly, to tipping too little. In this case I tipped at random, possibly too much but certainly not too little, for the porter smiled, thanked me politely, and left.

A second porter entered, followed by two American girls, who had mistakenly entrusted their luggage to him. They were even more ignorant than I was about tipping. They conferred lengthily, in whispers, though it was hardly likely that the porter understood English, examining with anguish the strange pieces of paper that had been given them in exchange for dollars, in a fruitless effort to divine how much they might be worth. They decided finally to hand to their porter three or four times the amount that had satisfied mine. The porter, an acute psychologist, had their number. He shook the banknotes in their faces, roaring at them ferociously. I admired his art. He even managed to work up an angry purple tint to suffuse his features. The girls understood no word of his tirade, but its general meaning was not difficult to grasp: They had been niggardly. The girls gazed at him in dismay, and one said to the other, "How much more should I give him?"

"Don't give him anything," I told them. "You've already given him far too much."

They paid no attention to me. Neither did the porter, to whom I was now directing a few well-chosen insults, admiring myself for being able to abuse somebody in a language that I had never spoken before, though

7

I had been reading it since high school. My billingsgate did no harm to French-American amity, in the unlikely case that the porter felt any, for he ignored me and succeeded in his purpose. The girls, quaking with terror, doubled their already excessive tip. I suspected that the porter was prepared to try for the triple, and I stood up. I have broad shoulders and he was a little man. He retreated into the corridor, still grumbling, an honest worker outrageously exploited by overbearing foreigners, and disappeared.

I did not allow this encounter to prejudice me against France. Quite possibly the porter voted with the opposition, or he was secretly in the employ of some foreign power seeking to sabotage the French tourist industry. In any case I knew that such incidents were not specifically Gallic. Shortly before leaving New York I had been told the story of a Bavarian immigrant who had come to the United States to work in the kitchen of a German restaurant. He left his ship wearing a too-small Bavarian hat pushed together like an accordion on the downbeat, and a costume that, although it did not actually include lederhosen, looked as if it did. He found a taxi at the curb just outside the dock. Doffing his hat politely to the driver, he said, "Plizz," the only English he knew except "Denk you," and held out a card on which was written the address of the hotel where he had been told to go. "OK, buddy," said the cabbie, "hop in." He hopped in and covered a distance that brought him to his hotel with several dollars on the meter, a fantastic sum in 1920. It took several days before he discovered that the hotel was only four blocks from the dock. The knowledge rankled, for several years indeed, and then he got a job as a chef on a German liner. Every two weeks he docked at New York, and every two weeks he put on a crushed hat and a comic foreign costume, sought a taxi, and took off his hat to the driver, held out his address, and said, "Plizz." To the honor of New York taxi drivers, it may be reported that most of them took him directly to his hotel, but every once in a while he was treated to an extensive tour of New York and would reach his destination with a fare of several dollars staring at him from the meter. He would then say softly to the driver, "Will you take a quarter or shall I call a cop?"

Fleecing the foreigner is an international sport.

The train trip from Cherbourg to Paris was an overnight ride in 1927.

The two girls went to sleep, sitting upright, for we were in an ordinary compartment. Sleepers existed in France, but they were reserved for crack trains and this seemed not to be one. I was too excited to sleep anyway, and what I saw through the windows was too beautiful to be missed. It was a night of full moon, and we were rolling through Normandy in apple blossom time. Enthralled by the snowy beauty of the orchards, I couldn't close my eyes, nor did I want to. The heady happiness of being in France continued to keep me wakeful even after we left Normandy and began passing more towns than orchards. At dawn I could see that we were now gliding through a trench, parallel to a dirty gray stone wall, against which there appeared suddenly a magic word in great red letters: PARIS.

It was six o'clock in the morning when we were deposited at the Gare St. Lazare, which I would consider later a lugubrious spot, gloomier and grimier than it had the right to be—but it did not strike me that way then. I emerged from it into a scene also carefully designed to enchant me. A street sweeper was coaxing debris into the running water of a gutter with a large, thoroughly foreign broom made not of straw but of twigs (they must be efficient, for they are still used to sweep Paris streets).

A man passed herding half a dozen goats; a woman called from an upstairs window, and he and the goats turned into an open doorway. I could hear them clattering up the stairs on the way to deliver milk on the hoof. I crossed the streets to the first hotel I saw, took a room, and ordered breakfast—the standard Continental fare, coffee and croissants—to which, with the assurance of a seasoned traveler, I added a half-bottle of Barsac. Victoria Lincoln, the historian of Lizzie Borden and before that a fellow student at the Bradford Matthew Carlton Durfee High School of Fall River, Massachusetts, had confided to me at a youthful age, not without mirth, the complete guide to France: "The French are gay people, fond of dancing and light wines." So I knew that in France I could drink wine. I had neglected to learn, however, at what time of day it was drunk, so I ordered wine for breakfast and the waiter brought it without cracking a smile. I suppose he had met Americans before.

I was still too excited to sleep. I went to explore, and once more luck took me by the hand. I had no knowledge of the geography of Paris, but if I had known the city I couldn't have selected a better first-view route than the one chance offered me. Turning right at random, I found myself in a few minutes in front of the somewhat garish Opéra, whose broad avenue beckoned me on. The end was barred by a somber wall pierced with three openings. I walked through one of them and gasped, thrust all unprepared into the middle of one of the grandest vistas in the world. I found myself standing between the two wings of the Louvre, near the small arch of the Carrousel, surmounted by the four horses Napoleon had stolen from Venice. I was gazing into an immense expanse, through the green formal flowered gardens of the Tuileries, across the place de la Concorde with its sky-pointing obelisk, by another green patch—the chestnut trees and gardens of the Champs-Elysées—and up its avenue to the mighty Arch of Triumph crowning its hill. It drew me like a magnet.

Beyond the Arch there was another broad avenue clasped in green whose name rang a bell for a young man who had read much about Paris: the avenue du Bois de Boulogne (the avenue Foch today). I followed it to the Bois itself, where automobiles were rare but horse-drawn carriages common. Here and there through the trees, dressed in the tender green of spring, I glimpsed horseback riders on the bridlepaths. I must have veered to the left in my wanderings, for presently I came upon the Seine. I followed it back toward the center and discovered the Eiffel Tower.

There was nothing to do, of course, but to go up it. From its third platform, the highest, I had spread out before me the prodigious panorama of Paris. Straight ahead, at the end of a broad strip of green park, was the formal elegance of the Ecole Militaire; behind was the fake Moorish architecture of the Trocadero. In the far distance, high-perched on the Butte Montmartre, I could see the shining white dome of a building incongruous also, in a different fashion, which I recognized as Sacré Coeur. Domes and towers that I could not yet identify rose here and there from the general level; they promised a metropolis where magnificence was normal.

I descended to the second platform for lunch. The Eiffel Tower has evolved in the same direction as ocean liners. The *President Harding* exposed its passengers to the weather, but its successors put them behind glass. Today the restaurant of the Eiffel Tower shelters its diners behind sturdy walls, but in 1927 they were allowed to battle with the wind. The tables were placed against the outer railings, their paper tablecloths held in place by metal clamps, without which they would have taken wing and soared off over Paris. This was my first full meal in France, eaten in the open air of a lovely spring day, in the middle of this unmatchable setting, and the food seemed nectar and ambrosia. I would learn later, when I had become accustomed to the Paris norm, that the food of the Eiffel Tower was only run-of-the-mill French cooking, honest but not distinguished.

Replete and refreshed, I continued my walk up the Left Bank. Easily identifiable, behind a vast empty space, was the Invalides, with its gold-trimmed dome. I passed an impressive structure where I was destined to spend a good deal of time during the next half-century—the Foreign Ministry—and the classic columns rising deceptively before the blind wall of another building of which I would also become a habitué, the Chamber of Deputies. (Across its bridge I could see the ordered stateliness of the place de la Concorde, and beyond that the Madeleine.)

There was a small, elegant, eighteenth-century structure that I did not yet know was the headquarters of the Legion of Honor. I passed the French Academy, bearing its heavy dome like Atlas the world. Across the river now was the long wall of the Louvre, and on my side the Mint, and then the grilled openings in a wall of masonry that gave a truncated glimpse of one side of the Ecole des Beaux-Arts. On the river side of the quais the parapets of the Seine offered their much-pictured bookstalls. At the place St. Michel I crossed the bridge onto the Ile de la Cité and found myself face to face with the first Gothic cathedral of my experience. I entered Notre Dame and bathed in the mottled light of its ancient glass.

The Latin Quarter, Montparnasse, and St. Germain des Prés, not to mention Montmartre halfway across Paris on the Right Bank, remained to be discovered, but I could absorb no more. My heart was full and my feet were tired and I had not slept the preceding night. I took a bus to my hotel and went early to bed, unutterably content.

II

¶

I Never Knew Hemingway

¶

The first question asked, inevitably, of anyone who lived in Paris during the 1920s and 1930s, at least if he moved at all in the culture-conscious circle that came to be synonymous with the name of Montparnasse, is: "Did you know Ernest Hemingway?" The invariable answer, whether it is true or not, is "Yes." Nobody wants to admit that he was on the spot and did not know Hemingway.

Well, I was on the spot and I did not know Hemingway. Or more precisely, I knew Hemingway, but he didn't know me.

This was not an isolated case. As I look back to that period I am surprised by the number of people I did not know, although I was up to my neck in the artistic controversies, especially the literary controversies, of the time. But this was chiefly through the columns of the Paris edition of the *Chicago Tribune*, with people I never met in the flesh.

Moved by curiosity about the extent of my ignorance, I took the trouble of counting, in the index of George Wickes' *Americans in Paris: 1903–1939*, an excellent and unjustly ignored book, the number of people mentioned, leaving out a few whom I had reason to believe did not frequent the major Montparnasse artistic cafés, the Dôme, the Select, and the Rotonde. There were 322 players in his cast of characters, of whom I could claim only 15 as friends. There were 9 others with whom I had frequent contacts, 26 whom I saw occasionally, and 24 of whose presence I was constantly aware whether or not they were aware of mine. This adds up to no more than 74, as against 248 actors on this scene about whom I knew little or nothing.

There were several reasons for this. To begin with, during my first few weeks in Paris I was conscious of nobody; the impact of Paris was so great that I was incapable of identifying mere human beings. I was blinded by the brilliance of a city that presented itself like a rapid succession of explosions of light too bright to illuminate the objects on which it fell, demanding exclusive attention to itself, like fireworks. I wandered through Paris in a dream, incapable of paying attention to people—I was soaking up the city like a sponge and with just about a sponge's capacity of comprehension.

After I had finally found my footing and become capable of distinguishing individual trees through the disorderly luminance of the forest, I was handicapped in making acquaintances in the colorful quarter of Montparnasse by the fact that by then I was working. The society of Montparnasse was not dedicated to remunerative effort. It was centered on the café terrace, and the personal relationships that were built up there were the products of long hours of café sitting. I didn't have the time for this, and what little time I did have occurred at odd hours. Except for a few weeks at the beginning of my apprenticeship on the Paris edition of the *Chicago Tribune*, I worked on its night staff, from 8:00 P.M. to 2:30 A.M. Before work was too early, after work was too late. I dined about 7:00 at Gillotte's, the bistro across the street from our Right Bank office, where we all ate together. This meant I had to leave my Left Bank headquarters, handy to Montparnasse, no later than 6:30. At that hour the Dôme, the Select, and the Rotonde were only just beginning to fill up. By the time I got back, 3:00 A.M. at the earliest, but more often 4:00, the cafés were not slowing down, but I was.

Even my daytime hours were restricted by a long-standing peculiarity of mine: I have seldom held only one job at a time. Not long after I began to work at the *Tribune* I acquired, I no longer remember how, a loose attachment with an organization that imported musicians from the United States and handled English-language publicity for them. In the early thirties I was to find myself performing on the side what should have been a full-time job, when I became Paris correspondent of the leading paper of Scandinavia, the *Politiken* of Copenhagen, and as though this were not enough, I was also a regular contributor to the "Periscope" section of *Newsweek*. This left me very little time for café sitting.

In running through Wickes' index I noted that a majority of the people he listed could have been described as workers only by the charitable, while some of the more diligent workers of the quarter did not get in at all. The most conspicuous omission was Alexander Calder, who arrived in Paris about the same time I did, or a little before, and was a tireless worker. He never gave the impression of being hurried or harassed or even of having anything in particular to do that would prevent him from chatting with you, but actually he never stopped creating. I don't think he was fully happy except when he had some object of art in his hands and was working on it.

Hemingway was a worker too. In the late twenties, according to Allen Tate, he rose at six in the morning to start work and went to bed at nine at night. This left him little time for cafés, despite his reputation as a frequenter of these social centers gained after he had used them as settings for some chapters of *The Sun Also Rises*. Often quoted is a passage from his preface to the model Kiki's memoirs, where he draws a line between the workers of Montparnasse and the idlers:

> Montparnasse means the cafés and the restaurants where people are seen in public. It does not mean the apartments, studios and hotel rooms where they work in private. In the old days the difference between the workers and those that didn't work was that the bums could be seen at the cafés in the forenoon. This of course was not entirely true as the greatest bums, using the word in the American rather than in the English connotation, did not rise until about 5 o'clock when, on entering the cafés, they would drink in friendly competition with the workers who had just knocked off work for the day. . . . The era is over, it passed along with the kidneys of the workers who drank too long with the bums. The bums were fine people and proved to have the strongest kidneys finally. But then they rested during the day.

As I rested neither during the day nor during the night, I had little time to make acquaintance with either workers or bums. Still, it occurs to me that perhaps I knew more Montparnassians than I realized: I knew them but I didn't know I knew them. Manners were informal. You arrived at a café terrace, saw half a dozen people sitting around a table, of whom you knew only one, so you joined him and entered the general conversation. Nobody was ever introduced to anybody else, and unless you were persistent in attendance, you might never learn with whom you had been talking.

The groups about the tables swelled in function of the hour. As it grew later, more people joined each group, like swarming bees clustering around their queen; two or three or four tables were pushed together and individualization became more and more difficult. Montparnasse was, besides, an interlocking society: If everybody didn't know everybody else, everybody at least knew about everybody else. It was difficult to disentangle those you knew at firsthand because you had talked to them, knowingly, face to face, from those you knew at secondhand, because somebody else had talked to you about them. When you knew everything about somebody else, or thought you did, the question of whether you had actually met him became insignificant.

Perhaps, after all, I had known, personally, more Montparnassians than I remember. But I am sure I am making no mistake about Hemingway. If I had met him, I would not have forgotten it. He was already a legend when I reached Paris in 1927 if only because of his lusty language. "Mr. Hemingway writes like an Angel," Ford Madox Ford had said, "like an Archangel; but his talk—his manner—is that of a bayonet instructor."

No doubt Hemingway's reputation for rough talk was true, but I never personally heard him use any language that would shock your grandmother, though on a number of occasions I was near enough to overhear his conversation. Newspapermen credited Hemingway with a wire that was admired as a perfect example of the now-extinct idiom of cablese, the abridged language we used to circumvent the high cost of cables from Europe to newspapers in the United States. As I heard the story, Hemingway had been caught off base when some hot news developed suddenly in a spot the *Toronto Star* thought was being covered by Hemingway, who had permitted himself a little leave without thinking it necessary to mention his absence to his editors. The *Star* wired a reprimand and he answered: ADVISE YOU UPSTICK JOB ARSEWARDS. The orthodox story is that he gave up journalism because Gertrude Stein told him he would have to do so if he wanted to write seriously.

Another sample of Hemingway's irreverent handling of language was also current in Montparnasse at that time, in the form of a poem attributed to him, which was taboo because it contained a word that was still considered unprintable when *For Whom the Bell Tolls* was published in 1940. So Hemingway replaced it wherever it occurred (and it occurred rather often) by "[obscenity]," which may have been his way of expressing contempt for a timorous publisher or a prudish public.

I seem to remember dimly that Hemingway eventually recognized the paternity of this poem, and even that it was published, perhaps by the *Little Review*, which was anything but timid. But if not, here it is, as nearly as I can remember it:

> The age demanded that we sing
> And tore away our tongues;
> The age demanded that we laugh
> And threw dust in our lungs;
> The age demanded that we dance
> And crammed our souls in leaden pants,
> And in the end the age was handed
> The kind of shit the age demanded.

I saw Hemingway most often, I think, in 1927, the year when everybody seemed to be trying to fly the Atlantic to Paris in emulation of Lindbergh's flight and none of them made it. Among Parisians, it became chic to traipse out to Le Bourget airfield to await the arrival of fliers who never turned up to join the party, but this seemed to dampen no spirits and the bar at Le Bourget profited enormously. Hemingway always seemed to be there, easy to pick out from the crowd not only because of his broad shoulders but also because he was always accompanied by a girl whose trademark was a scarlet beret—the Brett of *The Sun Also Rises*.

By 1927, Hemingway was already in only intermittent residence in Paris; the chief reason I never met him was probably because our calendars did not coincide. His most continuous Paris period was 1921 to 1926; mine was 1927 to 1940. After the success of *The Sun Also Rises* (his best book, it seems to me, but that may be only because I know everybody in it), he moved about more. The fact that he no longer considered Paris his base was symbolized by his abandonment there in 1927 of two trunks filled with notebooks and other papers, about whose contents he seemed surprisingly unconcerned when it is considered that he bewailed a number of times the theft of another trunk that contained some of his early manuscripts. He recovered the forgotten trunks only thirty years later, when a patient baggageman finally asked to be relieved of their custody. Reading his description of his early poverty-stricken days in Paris in *A Moveable Feast* I could not restrain a chuckle when I remembered where he had abandoned those trunks—in the Hotel Ritz, even in those days little frequented by the poor.

The last time I saw Hemingway is hardly worth recounting. It might have been about 1955, when, on a quiet afternoon, I stepped into Harry's Bar for a beer, and sat down at the bar stool nearest the door. There were only two other persons at the bar, Harry and Hemingway, talking about big-game hunting, in irreproachably proper language. Harry had his back to me and did not see me; if Hemingway did, he would not have recognized me anyway. A few minutes later Hemingway led Harry away to show him some films he had made about lion shooting and Harry passed without noticing me. If I had been a big-game hunter myself I could have spoken to him and would then, I suppose, have been introduced to Hemingway. But I am not a hunter by nature, either of animals or celebrities, so I passed the opportunity.

My last link with Hemingway resulted from the fact that after 1967, when I retired as correspondent of the *Washington Post* and was no longer under any obligation to represent that paper with becoming dignity, I let my beard grow. I began to notice, in public places, people staring at me, and occasionally I overheard a whispered: "Isn't that Ernest Hemingway?" This has not happened lately, not, I think since 1971, when I was attending services at a bar in St. Germain des Prés called the Village. Two men sitting at the far end from me beckoned to Jean, the bartender, and put the usual question. Jean, who knew me well, assured them solemnly that I was indeed Ernest Hemingway, and I was afraid they might ask for an autograph. Mercifully, they refrained. It was not particularly flattering to be mistaken for Hemingway, for I can safely maintain that at that time I was handsomer than he was. He had been dead for ten years.

Now that I have explained at length that I didn't know Hemingway, it becomes necessary to explain how it happened that my first permanent address in Paris was given to me by Hemingway. The way of it was this: A mutual friend in New York wrote Hemingway that I was due to turn up in Paris and asked if he could suggest a good place for me to live. I called on Sylvia Beach at the bookstore Shakespeare and Company and found a letter waiting for me from Hemingway. He was not in Paris (he had gone to Spain, I think; this would have been about the opening of the bullfight season), but he had left a note for me, with his recommendation.

Hemingway's idea was that the best introduction to France was to throw oneself into a completely French atmosphere from the start. It was a good way to develop command of idiomatic French, which is not always identical with the French that is taught in the textbooks. (I would be offered an example of the difference myself some time later when a French girl with whom I was talking suddenly burst into laughter. "Did I make a mistake?" I asked. "Not at all," she said. "It was very good French—except that no one has used it that way since Corneille.") I seem to remember that Hemingway added that he had stayed himself at the place he proposed to me, a *pension de famille* at the corner of the rue St. Jacques and the rue Soufflot on the Left Bank. Its pleasant, roomy house sat in the middle of a garden where we took our after-lunch coffee on pleasant days, sheltered by a low wall over which we could see the dome of the Panthéon. I had a spacious, comfortable room on the ground floor, with large windows opening directly onto the garden.

I quickly learned the idiosyncrasies of pensions—for instance, the economy of the table. It was customary to start the meal with one or two introductory courses, low-priced ones, to take the edge off the boarders' appetites before the expensive meat dish came on. One of the favorite entrées was spinach with hard-boiled eggs.

What I admired about this dish was the art with which its most expensive component, the egg (I was a little hasty in using the plural above) was handled. The steaming dome of spinach was studded here and there with wedge-shaped sections of egg and an unobservant diner would have thought there were at least half a dozen of them. Actually there was one. I have no idea by what technique the lone egg could have been divided into so many almost paper-thin slices without crumbling into bits. I do not mean this as a criticism of the food of this very pleasant pension. Although a decent respect for economy was evident, we had plenty to eat and its quality was excellent.

One object of living in a pension was admirably served: practice in French. We all sat around one large, round table and talked nothing but French. Indeed the only boarder except myself who knew any English was a Cuban law student with whom I quickly became friendly. I forget how many boarders there were, six to eight at a guess, presided over by the woman who ran the place, a dignified, somewhat formal, and obviously cultivated widow whose husband had left her the house, but not much else. She had divided it into individually habitable rooms to enable her to take in boarders and make a living.

I remember only two of my tablemates besides the Cuban, of whom one was very agreeable to look at and hence very easy to remember—our hostess's daughter. She was a tall, possibly athletic, brunette whose good looks suggested character rather than prettiness. She appeared to have been made of porcelain—not Danish porcelain baked in tender colors, but something nearer to rock china, which looked as if it could be dropped without breaking. She must have been about twenty, an enticing age (I was twenty-three). It was an enticing age for the Cuban, too, but neither of us ever had an opportunity to talk with the young lady alone. Mother kept a sharp eye on us and a tight rein on her daughter; it was not her intention to allow any accidents.

¶

Beggaring the Chicago Tribune

¶

Toward the middle of May, awaking lazily and gradually in my comfortable bed in Ernest Hemingway's *pension de famille*, I rang for breakfast. When the maid brought the tray it carried not only the customary café au lait, croissant, and brioche, but also a small sheet of discreetly folded paper. I opened it and read: "Payable May 31, half-pension, 450 francs." It was nice of them, I thought, to give me this much notice. The sum of 450 francs, $18 at the time, did not seem unreasonable for nearly a month's bed and board, less lunches, but I was down to 200 francs. It seemed advisable to earn some money before May 31.

Armed with a letter of reference from Herbert Bayard Swope, the editor of the *New York Morning World* and the friend of a friend, I called on that newspaper's Paris correspondent, Arno Dosch-Fleurot, a man who concealed behind ferocious eyebrows the kindliest of characters. He apologized for being unable to offer me a job himself since the *World* was already adequately represented in Paris by himself and his assistant Pierre van Paasen, who would later become known as a novelist. He gave me, however, three of his business cards, each bearing a message to a friend at one of the three American dailies of Paris, describing me inaccurately as a *New York World* reporter personally recommended by Swope, then held in awe by American journalists as being responsible for what most of them considered to be the best-written newspaper in the country.

"Go to the *Paris Herald* first," Dosch-Fleurot told me. "They pay best. If you don't make it there, try the *Paris Times*. They're second best. If worse comes to worst, you can always fall back on the *Chicago Tribune*. Bad pay, but some people manage to live on it."

It was about ten in the morning, but I headed straight for the *Paris Herald*, too green to know that morning newspapers are produced at night and that their editorial offices are often deserted until noon. Dosch had given me a card to the publisher, Larry Hills, who was of course not in. I was advised to come back in the afternoon, so I went on to the *Paris Times*, an evening paper, where I discovered that evening papers are in the throes of creation at the end of the morning, so no one has time to talk to a job-seeker. For the second time I was told to come back in the afternoon.

In view of Dosch's advice, I should logically have knocked off for the time being, to make another stab at the better-paying papers before I sounded out the last resort. But I was afraid that my zeal for finding a job would wear off if I paused, so I went on to the *Chicago Tribune*, a paper that—from the isolation of New England—I had never heard of. It was a morning paper too and I half hoped, perhaps, that it would be deserted also. It wasn't—exceptionally, as I learned later.

Dosch-Fleurot had addressed the *Tribune* card to Hank Wales (his name was Henry, but I never heard anyone call him that). Theoretically Wales had nothing to do with the Paris edition of the *Chicago Tribune*; actually, he carried a great deal of weight there. He was chief Paris correspondent for the *Chicago Tribune* of Chicago, the parent paper of the Paris Edition, with direct access to Colonel Robert McCormick, its publisher, before whom everybody quailed. They quailed before Wales too, as the colonel's ambassador, so his word came close to being law for the Paris Edition. I interrupted him in the act of performing one-finger exercises on the typewriter, an instrument he had never managed to domesticate. He did not look like a foreign correspondent, whatever a foreign correspondent ought to look like, but like a police reporter, which was exactly what he had been before coming to Europe in 1915 to cover the world war. He read Dosch-Fleurot's card and said in the rasp that served him for a voice, emitted through the hole worn into the righthand corner of his mouth by the cigar that, lighted or unlighted, usually occupied it, "*New York World*, huh? Comwa me!"

I came with him and was led into the city room of the *Tribune*, inhabited, despite the unseemly hour, by Bernhard Ragner, the paper's managing editor. Ragner stumbled to his feet, oozing servility. Wales stabbed the card at him, said, "Feller from the *New York World*. Canyer givem a job?" "Yessir, Mr. Wales," Ragner said to Hank's retreating back, and to me: "Can you start tomorrow?" I had steeled myself to going back to work but this was a little sudden. "Could we make it Monday?" I asked. "All right," said Ragner, relieved that I had consented to work for him. "Monday. Report here at eleven o'clock and ask for Mr. Kospoth. He's the city editor." He hesitated. "We can't pay very much, you know. Starting salary is 1,500 francs a month." He sensed that I was struggling with the mysteries of foreign exchange. "Don't bother to work it out," he said hurriedly. "Everything's cheaper here, you know. It's enough to live on in Paris."

It turned out that I would be beggaring the *Chicago Tribune* at the rate of $60 a month, a little less than $15 a week. But that *was* enough to live on in Paris, provided you were a fresh arrival with enough clothes to last until you could manage a raise.

I had signed on with the poorest-paying paper in Paris—one of the luckiest things that ever happened to me.

At eleven o'clock on Monday I arrived at 5, rue Lamartine, headquarters of the European edition of the *Chicago Tribune* (its official name, but everybody called it the Paris Edition), fearing that my spurious claim to newspaper experience would be swiftly demolished. I felt a trifle reassured by a familiar odor escaping from the basement windows beside the iron door, a perfume compounded of printer's ink, damp proof paper, and acrid fumes from the stereotyping department, known to me since my college days, when I edited the Tufts paper. I pulled open the heavy door and jumped quickly back into its shelter just in time to escape an unidentified flying object hurtling down. When it, and my heart, had settled down to a controllable rhythm of oscillation, the object became identifiable: It was a wicker wastebasket, dangling from a long cord. This was a laborsaving device invented by the employees of *Paris-Midi*, a French newspaper situated one floor above the *Chicago Tribune*. To save themselves the effort of walking down six flights of stairs to pick up mail, newspapers, or other deliveries and then toiling up again, *Paris-Midi* had improvised a dumbwaiter from a wastebasket on a long rope, which was tossed into the void of the stairway and hauled up again from time to time with the catch.

The city editor eventually turned up, faithful to his theory that he should try to reach the office in time to go out for lunch. B. J. Kospoth was

22

the *Tribune*'s mystery man, the first mystery being what the "B. J." stood for. Nobody knew.

Kospoth was fiftyish, lean, wore a small moustache, and gave the impression of being sand-colored. He was a meticulous dresser. His laugh was mirthless and dry, an expressionless paroxysm, like a soprano horse whinnying, that burst from him without warning. On my first day at the office Kospoth took me to lunch at an excellent Touraine restaurant, Au Petit Riche, where I have been eating ever since. It has not changed much since 1927, and I have been assured that it was the same two generations before my time. Kospoth's figure was spare, but his appetite was good and discriminating; he was at his most amiable while eating. He never invited me for a meal again, and it may be that his motive this time was reconnaissance. The appearance of someone he believed to be a big-city newspaperman on his staff may have struck him as a potential threat to his own privileged position in the hierarchy. After looking me over he must have decided that I was not likely to endanger anybody.

One of his sinecures was the editorship of what the *Tribune* called, somewhat pretentiously, its Riviera edition. The Paris edition of the *Tribune* reached the Riviera with its general news one day late but, as this part of France, during its high season, accounted for the largest segment of the paper's circulation after Paris, a single page devoted to up-to-date news of Americans' activities on the Riviera was printed in Nice and folded into the Paris paper when the leisurely trains of those days got it to the Mediterranean. Producing this single sheet involved a minimum of effort, for most of its news was phoned in by social climbers who hoped to see their names in the paper. Editing the Riviera edition thus meant a paid vacation in a pleasant part of the world.

I will not assert flatly that Kospoth was one of the triumvirate of Riviera reporters who made a good thing out of being the only English-language newspapermen in the neighborhood, but I know that there were three. One of them was the stringer for the *London Daily Mail* (a stringer is an unsalaried correspondent paid, in those days, only on space rates when he managed to get something printed by his paper). The second was a free-lancer (in other words, a journalist who sells his gleanings to anybody and, he hopes, everybody) who later joined the *New York Times*. If the third was not Kospoth my memory is out of whack and Kospoth, out of character, missed a trick. The three cronies would get together over an apéritif every few days and manufacture out of whole cloth some story so extravagant that their respective papers could hardly fail to buy it, and as its details appeared in three unrelated publications, each of them "confirmed" the others. Journalism was easy in those days.

Kospoth's sinecure in Paris consisted of writing a weekly article about art. Its quality was high and it did credit to the paper. His regular duties were not onerous, which was the way he liked it. A considerable proportion of his work consisted simply of finding and delivering to the stereotyping room the papier-mâché mats, mailed by the Chicago paper, from which the Paris Edition produced many of its features—pictures so little afflicted by timeliness that their printability had survived the slow passage from Chicago, the bridge article, the crossword puzzle, and, most important of all, the comic strips. Kospoth was not a man of order. His method of filing the mats was to chuck them into a closet when they arrived and paw through them daily to find the right ones for that particular date. The characteristic image of the city editor that remains in the memories of *Tribune* alumni today is the view of his rear protruding from the closet to the accompaniment of the anguished wail: "Where's 'The Gumps'? Who's taken 'The Gumps'?" (It was the most popular of the *Chicago Tribune* comics, followed closely by "Little Orphan Annie" and "Gasoline Alley.")

Kospoth was also entrusted with selecting timely photographs illustrating current news from the envelopes sent us daily by various agencies. Since they expected to be paid if we used any of their offerings, he gave preference to those supplied free by Atlantic and Pacific photos, owned by the *Chicago Tribune*. Its Paris quarters were installed in what looked like a squatter's shanty on the other side of the corridor from the city room, which it infested from time to time with the thick stench of developer chemicals. Another chore was the application of scissors to what appeared to be several miles of proof supplied by Chicago, to chop from it what he deemed a sufficient chunk of copy for the morrow's installment of our running romantic serial, which it is probable nobody read. A certain amount of attention was required in keeping up to date the listing of arrivals and departures of the principal Atlantic liners, which in those days meant a score or so within a week or ten days. Kospoth was charged too with reading the French evening papers and clipping for the attention of the night staff any stories that might seem worthy of its attention. As often as he could, Kospoth worked these chores off on his underlings.

The most delicate task entrusted to the day staff, to which I was attached at first, was selecting the next day's editorials. These were reprinted from the home paper, which meant that they were seldom fresh, since they arrived by mail, a week or more after they had been printed in Chicago. The alternative, however, would have been to cable the editorials (too costly) or to let the Paris staff write them (too risky). The colonel did not trust his Paris minions to write editorials. Their opinions might run counter to his own; indeed, they frequently did. So the colonel personally clipped from the home edition such editorials as he considered suitable for publication in Paris, marking each with a large blue A or B. Others bore a large red NO. An editorial marked A had to be run, outdated or not. An editorial marked NO was not to be used in any circumstances. When the A's were exhausted, a modicum of initiative was permitted: Paris could pick and choose among the B's. If we ran out of B's, we could reprint from the Chicago paper any editorial on which the colonel had not deigned to express an opinion.

A single linotype operator arrived in the afternoon to set this routine material, plus what we called resort copy, since the term "tourism" had not yet been invented. A respectable proportion of the paper's revenue came under this heading, obliging us to create appropriate reading matter to place beside the ads. The raw material was usually provided by publicity men whose opinions of the places for which they worked were so unrelievedly dithyrambic that they had to be rewritten to become even barely credible.

As my duties were explained to me, my fear of being unequal to the task faded away. The two day staff men unoccupied with resort copy divided between them the embassy beat and the hotel beat. The first meant checking daily, weekly, or occasionally with official or semiofficial sources of news—the American Embassy, the American Chamber of Commerce, the American Club, the American Legion, the American Hospital, the American Library. The hotel and boat-train beat was more interesting and it produced most of our interviews. The publicity men of the steamship companies sent us lists of the important personages they were delivering to our shores and we tried to intercept them when the boat trains came in. A dozen hotels frequented by Americans were visited daily and the reporter picked up at each desk a slip thoughtfully providing the names of guests the hotel thought newsworthy. If the reporter agreed, he nipped upstairs to interview his subject or, in his absence, tried to make an appointment.

Our own work was supplemented by that of voluntary reporters who phoned us accounts of their activities, which might not seem as interesting to us as they seemed to them. Some of these unpaid informants were motivated by professional interest, like the two American undertakers of Paris, who kept us informed on the noteworthy dead, asking that we include the name of the officiating mortician (another term, I think, that had not yet been invented). One of the two was always referred to by us as "the laughing undertaker," for his obituary information was frequently interrupted by gales of merriment. "You should *see* the *state* of the *cadaver*," he would exclaim. (Whoops of laughter.) "Can't imagine what they could have been *doing* with it."

Into our cut-and-dried routine, real news stories would break unpredictably from time to time—accidents, embezzlements, crimes, scandals—but the best of them were off bounds for us. If they were important enough to interest Chicago as well as Paris, the *Chicago Tribune* Foreign News Service would cover them and give us their carbon, to be printed in the Paris Edition credited to the FNS. French politics was almost automatically beyond our jurisdiction. Any diplomatic development worth a call on the press services of the Foreign Ministry, for example, would be handled by our betters of the Foreign News Service. What few news stories the day staff did turn out were not processed by it. They were transfixed on a large spike placed in the center of the copydesk for the inspection of the night staff, which would decide whether to use the story and what prominence to give it, or even to have it rewritten by more competent journalists. The night staff had a low opinion of the ability of the day staff and, after a few days on it, so had I. I need not have feared that I would be out of my depth; the waters were shallow.

During those first few days I went home each night having seen the development of no news more important than the names of the prominent people taking the cure at Vichy and wondering what in the world could be found to fill the paper the next day. Yet each morning there was delivered to me a *Tribune* bursting with news of the city, the country, the continent, America, and the world. It seemed a miracle and indeed the Paris Edition would one day be described as just that—the daily miracle.

¶

The Flying Fool

¶

During my first days on the Paris Edition, I was still isolated from the matter-of-fact world by the euphoria of finding myself in Paris, above which I seemed to be floating without touching the ground. Oblivious to mundane matters I entered the office one morning in the first or second week of my employment by the *Chicago Tribune* to be met by unusual behavior on the part of Kospoth.

"The crazy fool," he said. "He'll never make it!"

"*Who'll* never make it?" I asked.

"Lindbergh," Kospoth answered.

"Who's Lindbergh?" I inquired.

By not knowing who Lindbergh was at 11:00 A.M. on May 21, 1927, I betrayed the fact that as a newspaperman I was being grossly overpaid at $15 a week. Nobody in the city room winced at my question, and Kospoth answered as if my ignorance were the most normal thing in the world: "Crazy young feller thinks he can fly the Atlantic. He'll never make it."

This exchange disposed of Lindbergh for the day, and we went about our routine with no consciousness that drama was occurring somewhere over the North Atlantic. I don't remember what I did that evening. It seems incredible that I would have stayed home during this period of exploring Paris, but quite as incredible that I could have roamed the streets without noticing that they had been more or less emptied. Subsequent reports put the number of Parisians who flocked out to Le Bourget to wait for Lindbergh as high as a million, which was a third of the total population of Paris at that time. Half a million would probably have been closer to the truth, but even that should have created a noticeable void in the streets and cafés. All Montparnasse seems to have moved to Le Bourget, but I had not yet found Montparnasse. It was therefore in complete ignorance that I strolled into the office at eleven the next morning.

"Where the hell you been?" Kospoth snarled. "Get over to the embassy as quick as you can for the press conference."

"What press conference?" I asked.

"Lindbergh's," said Kospoth. "He made it."

An absentee witness, I have to depend on what other journalists told me to reconstruct what happened on that historic night at the airfield of Le Bourget. They were not all in agreement with one another nor with the accounts that have been printed since, even including Lindbergh's. His book *The Spirit of St. Louis* is perhaps not to be accepted as gospel since it appeared twenty-six years after the event, time enough to play tricks with the memory. And, though Lindbergh signed it, I am inclined to wonder in what proportion he wrote it. Having done a good deal of ghostwriting myself, I think I can sense the telltale perfume of the ghostwriter, particularly during a passage in which Lindbergh described his sensations as he was being tossed perilously about by the crowd that was carrying him in triumph from his plane. As far as I can find out, this never happened.

The wild night at Le Bourget was a comedy of errors whose unifying characteristic was that nobody, including Lindbergh, had understood in advance the full amplitude of the event—except the public. The professionals—the diplomats, the airport authorities, the police, the journalists—were taken by surprise. Only the amateurs were sensitive enough to be kindled by the romance of Lindbergh's one-man exploit. It was the *people* who began flooding toward Le Bourget in a first wave when radio broadcasts announced that Lindbergh had been sighted over Ireland at 4:00 P.M., and when he was reported over England at 6:00 P.M., a second surge swelled the crowd and was still going strong even after Lindbergh had landed and left.

The great rush toward Le Bourget produced what was perhaps the first great traffic jam in history. We are accustomed to this sort of thing nowadays, but fifty years ago there were barely enough automobiles anywhere in the world to create such a phenomenon. Certainly no one would have believed that there were enough cars in Paris to fill the whole four miles of road from the city limits to Le Bourget. The French police—who apparently never even tried to do anything about the traffic jam, a hopeless task in any case—were not prepared to control the crowd at the airfield. They seem to have sent only one busload of officers to Le Bourget.

I have forgotten the size of the police buses of those times, but this may have been somewhere between twenty and forty men to deal with half a million. When reinforcements turned up—a handful of policemen on bicycles—those who saw them arrive laughed. But bicycle police were not a bad idea; only bicycles could thread their way through the stalled cars on the road.

The American Embassy had been no more imaginative about what might happen if Lindbergh landed. Two weeks earlier a pair of French fliers, Charles Nungesser and François Coli, had taken off from Paris for, they hoped, New York, crossing the North Atlantic the hard way (its prevailing winds blow west to east), and were never heard from again. Ambassador Myron T. Herrick had cabled to Washington that under the circumstances the American aviators who were preparing to fly from New York to Paris should postpone their projects, for fear that an American triumph in the midst of French mourning would cause resentment in France. Perhaps he thought that this had put an end, for the moment, to transatlantic flying.

But it was too late for an ambassadorial admonition to check the momentum of the race that was getting under way for the $25,000 Raymond Orteig prize for the first direct nonstop flight between New York and Paris. Four planes that had been preparing for months to make the attempt were reaching the takeoff point at New York. Of the four, Lindbergh, the only one who planned to risk the crossing solo, seemed about the unlikeliest to get away first.

The news of his takeoff left the embassy as unperturbed as it had left the day staff of the Paris Edition. No plans were made for any reception. No doubt the diplomats, like Kospoth, believed he would never make it. If anyone gave a thought to the unlikely possibility that he might, he perhaps considered that the occasion might be marked sufficiently with a hastily organized cocktail party for a few French officials and prominent members of the American colony of Paris—visiting senator's treatment. While Lindbergh was pushing his way across the Atlantic, Ambassador Herrick was attending what he considered the most important event of the day: the doubles finals of the French international tennis championships at St. Cloud, between Tilden and Hunter for the United States and Borotra and Brugnon for France. He did not see its end (the French won, but it

30

is probable that few Frenchmen noticed it, for the following day's papers had room for nothing but Lindbergh). It was in the middle of the match that a messenger brought to the ambassador the news that Lindbergh had been sighted over Ireland. The ambassadorial party left the stadium in considerable disarray. But if Herrick had been slow to anticipate the event, from the moment that it occurred he reacted with all the skill of a practiced diplomat to turn Lindbergh's personal exploit into a national triumph for the greater glory of the United States.

At Le Bourget, the airfield administration had been caught off balance like everybody else. I have purposely used the term airfield rather than airport for to have called the Le Bourget of 1927 an airport would have been a considerable exaggeration. This was before the days of regularly scheduled passenger services. Le Bourget was used mainly by military planes, whose hangars occupied one end of the field, while the civilian facilities, mostly for mail planes, were at the other. There were no runways—planes took off and landed on grass. The airfield had never been called on to deal with any such situation as it met with now, and reports vary on its unreadiness when the test came. Many witnesses insist that though the beacon on Mont Valérien, on the outskirts of Paris, had been lighted to guide Lindbergh to Paris, the landing lights at Le Bourget itself were not turned on until Lindbergh's motor was heard overhead. There could have been considerable confusion on this point, for military planes landing at the far end of the field had caused several false alarms.

All versions agree on one point: As Lindbergh touched down, an uncontrollable mob rushed toward his plane and he was barely able to cut his engine in time to avoid mowing a swathe through his well-wishers.

At this moment the only people who had correctly estimated what was likely to happen at Lindbergh's arrival played their largely unnoticed role. They were members of a small group of French pilots—three to my knowledge, but there may have been more—who had organized an unofficial reception committee. Fliers themselves, they had a practical appreciation of what a man who had spent thirty-three-and-a-half sleepless hours at the controls of a plane would need most—and it wasn't official ceremonies. They felt his most immediate need would be rest, and they had prepared a cot for him in the office of Major Pierre Weiss, commander of the bombers of the forty-third aviation regiment, based at Le

Bourget. Two of the French fliers, Michel Détroyat, a military pilot, and "Toto" Delage (I do not know his real name), a civilian one, had placed themselves near the point where the plane came to a halt. When it did they were aided by a misunderstanding that everybody since has reported— Lindbergh's helmet, torn from his head or thrown into the crowd, was snatched by a young American who bore a slight resemblance to the flier and was accordingly borne off triumphantly by the crowd to Ambassador Herrick, waiting in the airfield's administrative building. One version of this story has either Delage or Détroyat clapping the helmet on the false Lindbergh's head, but this sounds almost too quick-witted to be true.

However it happened, the error gave the two French fliers time to hustle Lindbergh off to the haven they had prepared for him; the stories that say he was carried off on the shoulders of the crowd, including the account in his own book, seem not to have been true. Lindbergh was delivered to the cot in Major Weiss' office, too excited to sleep. He asked anxiously if he would have any difficulties because he had entered France without a visa, an idea that for a few moments rendered the French fliers speechless with laughter. Delage asked where he wanted to go and Lindbergh answered with a single word, "Ambassadeurs," the name of the hotel where the *New York Times* had reserved a room for him, underestimating the impact of the event to the extent of believing it could have an exclusive story by signing Lindbergh up to write his account of the flight. Delage understood him to mean the American Embassy and drove him there, getting through the traffic I don't know how. At the embassy an attempt was made to put him to bed for a second time, and the journalists who came pouring into the embassy were told that he was sleeping, exhausted, and could see no one until the next day. But Lindbergh was still too excited to sleep. About two in the morning he sent down word that he would see the press, and it was then that he gave his first brief interview, sitting on the edge of his bed, dressed in a pair of pajamas lent him by Herrick. It was no secret that the ambassador was portly, but the press was for once too respectful to expatiate on the elephantine effect his pajamas produced on a young man with the nickname of Slim.

When a big news story breaks, competition among correspondents of individual papers is frequently fierce and among correspondents of news agencies it is ferocious. I was thus able to believe a story about that night at Le Bourget, told me at the time, which I was unable to confirm later. I pass it on without guaranteeing its authenticity but it is not at all improbable. According to this account, the chief correspondents of the Associated Press and the International News Service arrived at Le Bourget to discover that their opposite number of the United Press had preceded them, distributing legal tender in the right places to such good effect that all the airfield's phone booths (there were only six, which until then had proved sufficient) were occupied by burly citizens instructed to keep the lines busy and to yield their places to no one not employed by the United Press. The representatives of the Associated Press and the International News Service decided on concerted action. Addressing themselves to taxi drivers who had brought customers to the field and were waiting to take them back again, they hired twelve bruisers who outweighed the United Press's men and assigned them to battle stations, with instructions not to act until the signal was given. There was no point in giving the enemy warning in time to permit a counteroffensive.

When the United Press bureau chief came pelting into the room and seized the telephone from one of his hirelings, the charge was sounded and the infantry gave assault. For a few hectic moments, a royal battle waged around the telephone booths. The one that contained the United Press correspondent was thrown to the floor, wires ripped from the wall, doorside down, with two men sitting on it. Inside its prisoner raged, shouted, swore, kicked, and threatened dire retribution but nobody paid any attention. In the struggle, all the telephone wires were torn out, and nobody was able to use the public phones that night.

In the offices of the *Chicago Tribune*, the Foreign News Service and the Paris Edition did not see eye to eye about the importance of the Lindbergh flight. Hank Wales knew he was faced with a big story, Bernhard Ragner did not. Like Ambassador Herrick, the editor of the Paris Edition felt that the important event of the day was the tennis match; unlike Herrick, he proved unable to shift gears when it became apparent that it was not. He assigned only one man to Le Bourget, Jules Frantz. William Shirer asked if he could go along to help. "If you want," Ragner said, "after you finish the tennis story. Whichever of you gets back first can write the story." This turned out to be Shirer. He beat the traffic jam by running three of the four miles from Le Bourget, until he was lucky enough to come upon a taxi driver who had been trying to get to the airfield and, discouraged, had decided to turn back. "OK," said Ragner. "You write the story. Keep it short."

Frantz arrived, breathing hard, forty minutes later. He had run the whole four miles to the first subway station at the city limits. He tore down to the composing room, where Ragner was just finishing the makeup of the first page. Shirer's story, or as much of it as Ragner had considered necessary to use, gleamed from the page in freshly composed metal, not yet touched by ink. There was a three-column headline on it.

"Three columns?" said Frantz. "Every paper in the world will put a banner on this story!"

"What for?" Ragner replied testily. "He landed. We've got the story. That's all there is to it."

Frantz offered to write a color story on the spectacle of the crowd at Le Bourget to supplement Shirer's story of the landing.

"It's too late to pull the paper apart and remake it now," Ragner said. "I have to catch my bus."

In desperation, Frantz proposed that he run over to Commercial Cables, where he knew Wales was writing his story, to bring back a carbon. For once even the dreaded name of the Foreign News Service boss failed to impress Ragner. "Go if you want," he said, "but we won't be able to use it."

Frantz went all the same. When he returned, Ragner had left and the table on which pages are made up in composing rooms was empty, with the last pages already trundled off to the stereotyping room. For a wild moment Frantz was tempted to mutiny: There was time to call the front page and an inside page back and remake the paper with, on the Lindbergh story, the eight-column headline it deserved. But Ragner, foresighted for once and obstinate as always, had left orders with the printers that under no circumstances was the paper to be remade.

Wales, meanwhile, had cabled his story to Chicago. He had cast it in the form of an exclusive interview with Lindbergh, undaunted by the handicap of never having set eyes on him nor heard his voice. Jay Allen, his assistant, had telephoned from the embassy a report of the brief 2:00 A.M. bedroom press conference, but everybody had that—only Wales dared promote it into a private interview. I heard envious correspondents say later that Wales had written most of it during the afternoon before Lindbergh arrived, which would not have been impossible. It was not difficult to imagine in advance some of the phrases that were bound to be uttered on such an occasion, including the sentiments the embassy would prompt Lindbergh to utter in the interests of French-American amity. Wales was on excellent terms with Herrick and it wouldn't have been beyond him to acquaint Herrick with what he intended to write and make sure there would be no denial of it. Indeed he might even, as a friend of the ambassador, have served as a sort of unofficial adviser on what angles it would be politic to persuade Lindbergh to stress, in which case he could interview Lindbergh in absentia with a minimum of risk, for he would in essence be interviewing himself.

Whatever the mechanics of the affair, there arrived for Wales the next day a cable from Chicago: CONGRATULATIONS YOUR LINDBERGH EXCLUSIVE STOP MAILING FIVE HUNDRED BONUS. MCCORMICK.

Five hundred dollars was a lot of money in those days.

I had missed the historic arrival but for the rest of the time Lindbergh stayed in Paris, a week or two, I felt as though I were living in his pocket. I hardly let him out of my sight, unless he were in bed or the bathroom, about the only places where he could enjoy a little privacy. The adulation must have been more of an ordeal than the flight.

When I arrived at the embassy for Lindbergh's first formal press conference, I found the street outside the building besieged by hero-worshipers hoping to catch a glimpse of their idol as he passed in or out. The crowd would thin out as the days passed, but a hard core remained there as long as Lindbergh stayed in Paris.

As I entered the embassy, Lindbergh was descending the stairs between Herrick, who had imprisoned the flier's right arm under his own, and the representative of the Ryan airplane company, which had built the *Spirit of St. Louis*, in similar possession of his left arm. Lindbergh looked as if he were being led to the electric chair between two husky guards. He was, indeed, about to be thrown to the hounds—the pack of reporters who jammed the entrance hall. The first question came, idiotic but inevitable:

"What do you think of Parisian women?"

"I haven't seen any yet," Lindbergh said, which was his last contribution to the conversation except for the syllable "Uh." This I took to be in the nature of a clearing of the throat, preparatory to developing the theme further, but he was never given a chance to do so. If a question opened an opportunity to make political capital, Herrick answered for Lindbergh before he could get his mouth open. If it were technical, the Ryan man pounced on it. Between these answers, Lindbergh was helpless. Only once did a question stymie both of Lindbergh's custodians. It was his one chance to speak but he let it pass. The question had been put in the rasping voice of Hank Wales: "Say, Lindy, did you have a crapper on that plane?"

It was on that first day, I think, that I attended a lunch in Lindbergh's honor at the Clos Normand, a now-vanished restaurant on the edge of the Bois de Boulogne. Lindbergh was led to the place of honor, where he regarded with puzzled disbelief the forest of glasses rising behind his plate. I seem to remember that there were seven, for an apéritif, four wines, cognac, and even, the largest one, for mineral water. As Lindbergh sat down, the sommelier, all attention, sprang to his elbow, bottle cocked and ready to fire. Lindbergh pushed all the glasses back except the big one and requested water. It would have been polite for the rest of us to follow his example, but I do not recall that anyone did.

The days that followed were carbon copies of the first. There were two press conferences a day at the embassy because the reading public was mercilessly hungry for information and had to be fed. We followed Lindbergh through a succession of presentations of awards, official receptions, banquets, and laudatory speeches, reporting word after banal word. Never in human history had the name of Lafayette been so frequently brandished. Lindbergh was moved through this labyrinth of ceremony like a puppet, wearing a perpetual expression of bewilderment. He seemed to be wondering why everybody was making such a fuss about him; all he had done was what he had been accustomed to doing daily as a mail pilot—taking off from his point of departure and landing as planned at his point of destination. The press, which had started out by calling him the Flying Fool, had now shifted to Lucky Lindy. It was wrong both times, but as we watched him receive the accolades like a wide-eyed adolescent, we found it difficult to believe that he had achieved his exploit on purpose.

That was the impression, and it was completely wrong. He may have seemed helpless as he was guided through the unfamiliar political and social world, manipulated, apparently, by men more sophisticated, and more self-seeking, than himself, but in his own milieu he was complete master of his profession. His exploit was not the result of luck, it was the result of shrewd analysis of the factors making for failure or success, of unerring judgments in finding the best answers to the problems presented him, of courage in accepting the risk of applying those solutions, and of minute preparation for his flight.

Eight or ten of us found that out when we sat down with him at a lunch of the Anglo-American Press Association of Paris. It was a different Lindbergh who had come to eat with us, no longer the bewildered boy who had been promenaded helplessly through meaningless ceremonies, but a technician who knew precisely what he had done and why he had done it. Herrick was not with him. The Ryan representative was, but he hardly opened his mouth. This time Lindbergh did the talking. Why hadn't he taken a radio? Because, given the limited range and the cumbersome dimensions of the apparatus of those times, he had judged the added element of security insufficient to justify the expenditure of fuel required to transport its weight. Why did he alone dare fly solo? In a way, for the same reason: a copilot wasn't worth the gasoline it would take to carry him. What, after all, were the functions of a second man? First, to spell the first pilot when he became tired; second, by his presence to bolster the other's morale. Lindbergh judged he could keep awake long enough and maintain his morale without help from anyone else. Why, most important of all, had he taken off over the Atlantic on only one motor when all his rivals planned to use two? "Because," he said, "two engines meant twice as much chance of engine failure."

In case of trouble, a second engine might have saved his life, but it could not have carried him to Paris. His preoccupation was not with safety, but with success. And so he succeeded. During the next three years other pilots (with more men and more motors) would try to duplicate his feat but all of them failed. The first flight had been the perfect flight, and it has not been bettered since.

¶

It Is All Simple

¶

I was still in my haze on first being in Paris when a young man who was working as a proofreader on the *Tribune* took me to a cocktail party. If he told me who was giving it, the information did not register.

Caught in the usual dense, slowly milling crowd with a glass in my hand, I noticed vaguely, sitting in a large armchair as if it were a throne, a solidly built woman who might very well have been the hostess, but nobody introduced me to her, or if someone did, that didn't register either.

I was too much enthralled by the paintings on the walls to notice anything else; they surpassed everything of their period that I had yet seen, except for the recently discovered collection of Impressionists in the Luxembourg Museum. I spent the rest of my time wondering at them and have no recollection of leaving; I must have slipped away impolitely without saying good-bye to anybody.

It was two or three months later that I realized for the first time that I had been the guest of Gertrude Stein at 27, rue de Fleurus.

The inspection of her pictures was the only personal contact, if it can be called that, that I ever had with Gertrude Stein, but I was of course constantly aware of her existence as a large luminary located in the same galaxy that I was using. Insignificant as I was, I have reason to believe that she was aware of me, if only as a public nuisance. This was because for five years I wrote most of the book page of the Paris Edition, where it seems, I learn from Hugh Ford's book *Published in Paris*, I once remarked that she had ceased to amuse even the "ephemerally clever persons who at first liked to talk about her because her particular brand of nonsense was at least a change from the sort of nonsense to which they had previously listened."

I do not suppose that this pleased her, and some of my subsequent criticisms may have pleased her even less, but as I reread them now, almost half a century later, I do not think I was particularly unfair to Gertrude Stein.

I would not maintain today that "nonsense" is a complete summing up of the work of Gertrude Stein, nor was that my attitude in the 1930s either. I certainly did not approach it with any preconceived attitude of hostility. I had read both *Three Lives* and *The Making of Americans* (the latter all the way through, a task that Edmund Wilson, who did not manage it, thought might be impossible) before I came to Paris, so I must have gotten hold of the second almost at the time of its publication: It came out in 1925 and I reached Paris in the spring of 1927. I find by digging into my files that I wrote, when *The Autobiography of Alice B. Toklas* was published: "It appears to me that after *Three Lives* and *The Making of Americans* Gertrude Stein dived into a tunnel, emerging briefly with *Composition as Explanation*, and then disappearing again until she popped out with the present book."

I remarked also that "Miss Stein has all but eliminated punctuation, but her sentences are so perfectly phrased that no punctuation is necessary. They can only be read one way." This does not sound particularly malevolent to me, though I am perhaps a prejudiced observer.

Gertrude Stein did indeed have a gift for putting together sentences so concise and so spare that they fall from the page with the thump of the inevitable. She possessed a recognizably true style, by which I mean one that is distinguished not merely by a pattern of writing, which is ornamental, but by a pattern of thinking, which is structure. You feel the same beat in the universally accessible *Autobiography* as in her less-intelligible pieces, in which I fear it serves no good purpose.

It was another writer who picked up this tool and used it most effectively—Ernest Hemingway. His style improved when it developed to a point where it owed less to Gertrude Stein; but it was then so close to hers that she was virtually praising herself when she sent an unsolicited review of *Three Stories and Ten Poems* (vintage 1923) to the Paris Edition, which printed it but did not deem it necessary, under the circumstances, to pay for it.

"*Three Stories and Ten Poems* is very pleasantly said [Miss Stein opined]. So far so good, further than that, and as far as that, I may say of Ernest Hemingway that as he sticks to poetry and intelligence it is both

39

poetry and intelligence. Roosevelt is genuinely felt as young as Hemingway and as old as Roosevelt. I should say that Hemingway should stick to poetry and intelligence and eschew the hotter emotions and the more turgid vision. Intelligence and a great deal of it is a good thing to use when you have it, it's all for the best."

Gertrude Stein not only gave advice about writing to Hemingway in public, she also did it in private, and he profited by it. In addition, he picked up echoes of her style by induction, when he helped type the manuscript of *The Making of Americans* and read proof on it. Eventually he outgrew her, and her greatest contribution to his future work may have been models she provided for him of the well-turned sentence. I admire perfect sentences myself, but they are necessarily achievements on the small scale. That Gertrude Stein had the force to create on the large scale may be doubted: *The Making of Americans* is long, but length and breadth are different dimensions. Some analyzers regard with admiration her employment of what she called "the continuous present." Perhaps this is only another way of saying that development through time was out of her reach. Her music was unmodulated, played from beginning to end in the same key.

The review of mine that was the most likely to have caught the attention of Gertrude Stein was of her *Lucy Church Amiably*; one might dare deduce that she noticed it from the fact that she never sent me a book to review again. It took the form of a parody of her style, a device employed by others, including Hemingway, even before he broke with her. I fear it is far from being a masterpiece of the genre, but it may still possess some slight documentary interest:

A REVIEW AND WHICH SMELLS LIKE A NOVEL

Lucy Church Amiably: a Novel of Romantic beauty and nature and which Looks like an Engraving, by Gertrude Stein, published by "the plain Edition an Edition of first Editions of all work not yet printed of Gertrude Stein," Paris.

You can read sometimes Three Lives. Sometimes you can you can read sometimes Conversation as Explanation. You can read even you can read sometimes you can read if you have time sometimes you can read The Making of Americans.

You cannot read Lucy Church Amiably. Not even sometimes.

As an authoress writes a book a punk story.

Can you read much of this. She said can you read much of this. Can you read much. Of this on page nineteen. Nineteen and two is twenty-one. Twentyone twentyone twentythree. Read much:

"To leave on the thirtieth and to arrive on the second and to be on the way on the fourth and to be settled by the fourteenth and to be having word of their decision on the sixteenth and to be forgiven on the seventeenth not twice but once. This makes it as noiseless as ever."

But not noiseless enough.

We can continue. We can continue as if we liked it.

We can continue as if as if we continued. We continue:

"She said. It is a great pleasure to put it there. She said it is a great pleasure when it is there. She said. It is not only necessary but needful and for many reasons and because of not having any present plan. She said that it was not very well said."

She said it herself. She not only said it she said it. It was not very well said. She said it, I said it, we all said it. It was not very well said.

Lamartine was not a queen. William James did not know dames.

Some parts of Lucy Church Amiably are more difficult than others. Some parts of Lucy Church Amiably are less difficult than others. Some parts of Lucy Church Amiably are more simple than others.

"She said. And with a nod she turned her head toward the falling water. Amiably."

This is less difficult than than than. Others. And with a nod she turned her head toward the falling water. Poulaphouca.

There is an explanation. When a wife has a cow a love story there should be an explanation. With Lucy Church Amiably there is an explanation explanation is is called Advertisement. It is less difficult than the other other parts of Lucy Church Amiably:

"ADVERTISEMENT

"Lucy Church Amiably. There is a church and it is in Lucey and it has a steeple and the steeple is a pagoda and there is no reason for it and it looks like something else. Beside this there is amiably and this comes from the paragraph.

"Select your song she said and it was done and then she said and it was with a nod and then she bent her head in the direction of the falling water. Amiably.

"This altogether makes a return to romantic nature that is it makes a landscape look like an engraving in which there are some people, after all if they are to be seen there they feel as pretty as they look and this makes it have a river a gorge an inundation and a remarkable meadowed mass which is whatever they use not to feed but to bed cows. Lucy Church Amiably is a novel of romantic beauty and nature and of Lucy Church and John Mary and Simon Therese."

This is less difficult than other parts. This is more simple. But then it is all simple.

She said by repeating you can change the meaning you can actually change the meaning.

Repeat.

But then it it it is all simple.

It is all simple. It is all simple. It is all.

Simple.

Rereading this review and some others that I wrote in the early 1930s, it does not seem to me that I would revise today to any great extent the opinions I expressed about her prose.

I did not side with those who, irritated by a sort of writing too foreign from the familiar norms to which they were accustomed, dismissed it automatically and arbitrarily as valueless. I would not have said that she contributed nothing to the development of modern literature, but I did not see her contribution as a major one, certainly not comparable with that of James Joyce—although at that time these two names were often coupled, as if they were of equal value, and even as if they were headed in the same direction, though it seemed evident to me that they constituted antipodes.

I would certainly not have subscribed to the opinion expressed in 1932 by an anonymous writer, "It is an undisputed fact that the influence of Gertrude Stein upon the generation of young writers of today has been the most vital force in American letters," even before I learned that the unnamed authority who had produced this estimate was Miss Stein herself.

It would have been my opinion that if Gertrude Stein was leading young writers anywhere, it was up a blind alley. What leadership she provided for young writers (and she did provide some—Hemingway acknowledged his debt to her before they fell out) was given to very young authors. As soon as they matured, they followed Hemingway's example and cast off the apron strings. Possibly she was a better teacher than a doer, a phenomenon not infrequent in a number of domains. Hemingway, who learned much both from Ezra Pound and from Gertrude Stein, said once, "Ezra was right half the time, and when he was wrong, he was so wrong you were never in doubt about it. Gertrude was always right."

¶

"Ask Him What He Thinks About Elmer Gantry*"*

¶

There could no longer be any doubt about it: I had shown my mettle as a big-city journalist. The Paris Edition might be congratulated for its acumen in hiring me. I had barely started on the paper, and my byline was already appearing daily on the front page. Of course, if the Paris Edition had assigned an office boy to cover Lindbergh, he would have been on the front page every day too.

Within a week I consolidated my position as the paper's star reporter by a feat that resulted from the fact that I was new to the game and didn't know its rules. Memorial Day arrived, and with it an annual chore imposed on Ambassador Myron T. Herrick—the delivery at the American Cemetery of Suresnes, where the American dead of World War I were buried, of a commemorative tribute to them. The experienced American reporters in Paris covered the event in normal fashion: They called at the embassy to pick up a mimeographed copy of the ambassador's prepared address and returned to their offices to select a few quotable passages and write a one-paragraph lead to introduce them. I took a copy of the speech too, but, knowing no better, went all the way out to suburban Suresnes and actually listened to the ambassador as he pronounced it. I read it along with him and was suddenly surprised to find him diverging from it. He was interpolating an unorthodox passage whose implications seemed destined to open a disturbing diplomatic incident with France.

Making this passage the lead of my story, I pointed out that the ambassador had deliberately upset a previously prepared text to make an important point. Nobody else had the story, for nobody else had listened to the speech. I had a scoop, which made the front page (with byline) not only in the Paris Edition, but also in Chicago. Once again, I had demonstrated my talent as an experienced metropolitan journalist, immediately alert to all the angles. True, the sharp reaction from the French government that I had expected did not manifest itself, but I could imagine mighty rumblings in the secret subterranean channels of international diplomacy, where, as everyone knew, the real business of politics was conducted.

I ran into Dosch-Fleurot a few days later.

"Quite a story you had the other day, youngster," he said.

I summoned up what modesty I could to prepare to receive praise with dignity.

"Listen, kid," he said. "Let me tip you off to something. The ambassador is a good eater and a good drinker. When he has to make one of these ceremonial speeches, he likes to fortify himself beforehand with a good meal, and with a good meal he likes good wine. This provokes a certain freedom of spirit, which inspires him to improvise from time to time—in fact, I would guess that in such circumstances he improvises more often than not. What you heard was not the voice of the United States government, it was the voice of Château Latour 1921. We all know it, and we pay no attention to it. The French know it too, and they pay no attention to it either."

Another place that paid no attention to my private diplomatic incident was the American Embassy. The measure of the irrelevance of my story was that the embassy was not even annoyed by it. It would in any case have taken bigger guns than mine to shake in the slightest Herrick's popularity with a French public that viewed him as the greatest ambassador since Benjamin Franklin. He had won this esteem largely because of a grandstand play in the early days of World War I, when it looked as if the Germans were about to reach Paris. Herrick announced, after a good dinner, perhaps, that if this happened he would hoist the American flag over the Louvre and other important public buildings and take them under the protection of the American government. It was fortunate for him that he was not put to the test. Any such action would have embarrassed mightily a State Department making at that time every endeavor to remain neutral. Herrick appealed to the French also because he had the right kind of vices. This was not the word the French would have applied to the lifestyle of a bon vivant who loved good food, good wine, and good-looking women. He bore no grudges. He never mentioned my story to me, but perhaps that was because he had never noticed it.

It was something of a mystery that he was ever given a chance to notice it. Why did the Paris Edition print it, and even play it up? Someone on the staff should have been acquainted with the ambassador's foibles, but a possible explanation occurs to me. Memorial Day used to fall on the last day but one of its month: It may have been payday. Payday nights were the least likely times for finding sober editorial judgment in full possession of the Paris Edition.

No matter. In Paris my reputation was now assured. Its bases were largely spurious, but nobody knew it. The paper had gotten into the habit of putting a byline on my stories, the readers had gotten into the habit of seeing it, and I had become an Authority. As a result, I was automatically given the best assignments, which meant the most important stories, the best positions, more bylines, and enhanced reputation. In short, nothing succeeds like success—which was a French proverb before it became an English one.

Even the best day-staff assignments, it must be admitted, were not precisely passionate, particularly in the lull following the Lindbergh saga. They consisted chiefly of interviews with passing American celebrities, and for all of them Ragner primed me with the same question: "Ask him what he thinks about *Elmer Gantry*." A native of McKeesport, Pennsylvania, and a pillar of the American Church of Paris, Ragner had imported the standards of McKeesport into Paris and the blasphemy of *Elmer Gantry* had shaken him. I was so accustomed to this invariable admonition that on one occasion I waited for it with a slight touch of malice, as I prepared to set out for an interview. This time it did not come since Ragner had remembered that the person I was about to interview was Sinclair Lewis.

I cannot say whether I brought back a good interview or not. All my memory retains is a vague physical impression of a lanky loose-jointed man who seemed to flap about like a rag doll. There must have been something about his personality, or mine, that prevented him from registering on me. A year or two later I was present at his marriage to Dorothy Thompson in London's crowded, dark, dusty Savoy Chapel, and I can call up no image at all of his presence, though I presume he must have been there. Even worse, I cannot remember Dorothy Thompson, who was harder to ignore. Fifteen years later, when I was a member of the Association of Radio News Analysts in New York, the question of taking in women members would be raised from time to time at our weekly lunches in the Algonquin Hotel. "We think we're liberal and up-to-date," somebody would say. "We ought to think about admitting women." The response was always the same: "Of course we should. But the first woman we would have to admit would be Dorothy Thompson." Silence would fall and after a moment someone would introduce a different subject of conversation.

Neither Sinclair Lewis nor Dorothy Thompson enjoyed a good press in the Paris Edition, nor was Lewis a popular figure in Montparnasse on the rare occasions when he appeared there. True, he had not courted popularity in those circles. He had opened hostilities himself by writing in the *American Mercury* an article that scarified the Montparnassians in the idiom of George Follansbee Babbitt. He launched a special shaft in the direction of Harold Stearns, an easy target, who was recognizable as Lewis' "king of kings, Osimandias of Osimandiases, supremest of Yankee critics, *ex cathedra* authority on literature, painting, music, economics, and living without laboring."

It was my impression that Lewis' attacks on the Americans of Montparnasse betrayed the fact that he envied them. He would have liked to lead their life, but he couldn't adapt to it or even approve of it; the author of *Elmer Gantry* was a Puritan and of *Main Street* a small-town bourgeois. It is true that there were a good many loafers in Montparnasse whose conversation dealt largely with the great books they were going to write or the great pictures they were going to paint as soon as they had finished their beer—unfortunately the beer never ran out. These practitioners of the *dolce far niente* were usually pleasant and often picturesque company, and as they exalted the pursuit of art and literature whether they understood much about them or not, they furnished a propitious background for the artists and writers who actually were working and achieving. "It was a useless, silly life," Stearns wrote after he had returned to the United States, "and I have missed it every day since." Lewis was unable to regard it in this fashion. "Europe spoils Americans," he wrote to the French writer Paul Morand. "It unsettles them." He left America for Europe during the last years of his life, and it unsettled him. He died in Rome, from alcoholism.

Among the people I interviewed during this period, the one who made the most vivid impression on me was perhaps Roger Baldwin, director of the Civil Liberties Union. He was one of those rare people with whom you feel yourself in tune at the first meeting, as though you had known them all your life. He sparkled with energy, talked brilliantly, and presented lucidly ideas that I considered incontrovertible, no doubt because I held them myself. Instead of writing a standard interview with him, I used our conversations as a basis for a "Who's Who," which was a daily feature of our editorial page, a column-length biography of someone in the news. It could easily have been described as a eulogy.

For some reason William Shirer, though he was by then in the Foreign News Service and in principle little interested in the Paris Edition, descended to the composing room the day I had written the Baldwin biography and found Ragner reading it in proof. He read it too.

"You aren't going to print *that*, are you?" Shirer exclaimed.

"Why not?" Ragner asked. "What's the matter with it?"

"The matter with it," Shirer returned, "is that Roger Baldwin is the colonel's bête noire. He prints an anti-Baldwin story about once a week."

"Oh, dear," said Ragner. "What am I going to do? I don't have another ready."

"You could bring out the paper for one day without a 'Who's Who,'" Shirer said. "Put something else in its place."

The idea of deviating from routine terrified Ragner almost as much as the colonel terrified him (the colonel terrified a good many people more intrepid than Ragner too).

"Look," he said. "Why should *I* take responsibility for it! After all, it was Root who wrote it. If he signs it, that lets me off the hook."

"If he signs that," Shirer said, "he's a damned fool."

I was upstairs in the city room. The intercom phone tinkled.

"Uh—Root," Ragner said. "That Roger Baldwin story—it's very good. Wouldn't you like to sign it?"

"Of course," I said. I knew so little about the colonel's private hatreds

47

that I even thanked Ragner. The paper was delivered to me with breakfast at my pension the next morning. I regarded my byline with pride; ordinarily the "Who's Who" was not signed.

When I arrived at the office a couple of hours later, Kospoth deigned to notice my entrance.

"Got your new job lined up yet?" he asked. "You've got about ten days until the paper reaches Chicago." And he explained to me the enormity of my crime.

For the next ten days, and a little more, I lived in apprehension of the arrival of the message from Chicago ordering that I be thrown to the wolves. It never arrived, and I finally decided that the colonel had not noticed the article. He had, though, but he may have missed the byline. It was only later that I learned through a visitor from the Chicago paper what his reaction had been. He remarked simply: "Roger Baldwin has played the Paris Edition for a boob."

¶
The Daily Miracle

¶

It was Whit Burnett, the magazine editor, who nicknamed the Paris edition of the *Chicago Tribune* the "Daily Miracle." This appeared in an article he wrote for the *American Mercury* of January 1931, in which he added that it was one day a work of genius and the next a ghastly mistake. His story, "Your Hometown Newspaper: Paris," was actually about the Paris *New York Herald*, for which he had worked, but he had a good deal to say also about the *Tribune*, where he had not worked, a fact he seemed to regret.

Both the *Tribune* and the *Herald* owed their presence in Paris to the idiosyncrasies of the publishers of their parent newspapers in the United States. The epoch of the domination of great newspapers by sometimes spectacularly individualistic editors was drawing to a close, but James Gordon Bennett, Jr., who founded the Paris edition of the *New York Herald*, and Colonel Robert Rutherford McCormick, who founded the Paris edition of the *Chicago Tribune*, were members of a species not yet quite extinct. Journalism has lost something with the disappearance of the giants, not to say monsters, of earlier times. Boards of directors lack the color of the often eccentric, frequently tyrannical editors of the old school. The papers they produced were no doubt less expert than those of today, but their personalities produced publications more picturesque than have developed under the inspiration of managers obsessed with the intricacies of cost accounting.

James Gordon Bennett, founder (on a capital of $500, a sum a good deal smaller than the $75,000 Adolph Ochs paid for the *New York Times*) and owner of the *New York Herald*, was one of American journalism's great eccentrics, who held that the function of a newspaper was "not to instruct but to startle." His successor and son, James Gordon Bennett, Jr., followed worthily in his father's footsteps. A good many incredible

49

anecdotes have been told about him, some of them true—for instance, that he once happened to enter the press room just after a printer who was so drunk that he fell into a barrel of ink had been fished drippingly out. "There is a man really immersed in his work," Bennett said, and promoted him to editor-in-chief on the spot. (The staff, of course, reversed this decision as soon as the boss had forgotten about it.)

Bennett's eccentricity eventually reached such heights that he found himself in deep trouble with the law and decided that it would be advisable for him to leave the United States. If my memory is exact, the trouble was involved with dueling, which would account for his choice of France, where dueling was then considered normal, as a land of exile, in which he lived for the rest of his life. It annoyed him not to be able to read his own paper at breakfast, so he created in 1887 the Paris edition of the *New York Herald*.

When Colonel McCormick, publisher of the *Chicago Tribune*, established its Paris edition thirty years later, his motives were more complicated. One theory was that he thought a newspaper in the country where the war was being fought would enable him to explain to an army that had not been intelligent enough to name him commander-in-chief how to conduct its operations. Cynics suggested that the colonel thought he would have a better chance of becoming a general if his voice were present so close to the theater of war. That hope was dashed during a battle when the artillery unit he commanded aimed its barrage too short and slaughtered its own infantry. The colonel met criticism with bravado and named his country estate Cantigny in memory of this command.

The colonel's own explanation for the founding of what was then called the army edition of the *Chicago Tribune* was that he felt it his duty to provide for American soldiers the news they wanted from home, which showed a rather cavalier disregard for the presence of the *New York Herald*, not to mention the army's own paper, *Stars and Stripes*, of which he should have been aware for, if my memory is correct, *Stars and Stripes* was printed on *Tribune* presses. This may have contributed to a confusion between the *Tribune* and *Stars and Stripes* that gave birth to the frequently repeated assertion that in its early years the *Tribune* was distinguished by the presence on its staff of a number of writers and journalists who later became famous. I have undoubtedly forgotten some of them, but I remember that they included Alexander Woollcott, Franklin P. Adams, Heywood Broun (and even his wife, Ruth Hale), and James Thurber. I have found no trace of any of them among *Tribune* reporters except Thurber, but Alexander Woollcott at least was on *Stars and Stripes*, and some of the others may have been as well.

With or without their illustrious presence, the first issue of the Paris edition of the *Tribune* managed to struggle onto the streets on the symbolic date of the Fourth of July 1917, also chosen by the American army for its first parade down the avenue des Champs-Elysées—a token detachment, for there were not enough American soldiers in all France at that time to put any in the field.

The colonel had pledged that the army edition would not be published for profit (possibly he had not expected it to make any) and he was as good as his word. When the army edition ended its existence with the sailing of the *St. Mihiel*, carrying the last soldiers of the American Expeditionary Force home, Floyd Gibbons, then the most famous of *Chicago Tribune* correspondents, handed to General Pershing, in a well-publicized ceremony in January 1919, the profits of the *Tribune*'s year and a half of operations—112,000 francs, or $2,240. Without missing a day, the army edition of the *Chicago Tribune* was followed by the European edition of the *Chicago Tribune*.

Why did the colonel decide to keep his Paris paper alive? To spit in the *Herald*'s eye? One might have suspected as much from the editorial the colonel wrote to explain his decision:

> Almost on Armistice Day, a further need for an American paper in France arose. [The colonel was perhaps able to ignore the existence of the *Herald* because he did not consider New York American (too many foreigners) nor the *New York Herald* a genuinely American paper.] The departure of the American forces from Germany rings a chime of tender memories and marks a milestone in our history. It also dedicates us to a new role, *as the remaining link of communications, in both directions, between the old world and the new.*

The emphasis was the colonel's. It seemed to constitute a body blow to the long-established *Herald* and a sideswipe at certain other links of communication, apparently, in the colonel's view, negligible—such as diplomatic relations, trade exchanges, and movements between the continents of actors, musicians, students, and artists. Presumably Europe would have been abandoned to an obscure fate if the colonel had not chosen to stand like a colossus, feet planted firmly on either side of the Atlantic, "the remaining link of communications . . . between the old world and the new."

Others have suggested different motives for the colonel's decision to maintain his outpost in Europe—that a paper there would be usefully placed to support his campaign against the League of Nations. Its presence produced at least what the *Chicago Tribune* called "the scoop of the century," and though the paper was given to superlatives (for instance, when it called itself "The World's Greatest Newspaper"), its description this time was justified. It was a representative of the *Chicago Tribune* who was able to hand to the United States, coincidentally with its publication in the paper, the text of the Versailles Treaty, which its drafters had until then kept secret. *Tribune* accounts of the way in which this document was obtained are vague, but permitted the conclusion to be drawn that this exploit was the result of the excellence of the paper's Foreign News Service. As I heard the story, from the inside, it was an accident.

According to this version, a disgruntled representative of one of the smaller nations, feeling that his country was being slighted by the big powers, decided to make the text public in the hope of forcing a change. He walked into the *Tribune* office in Paris and simply handed it to a surprised representative of the paper. It had been the donor's intention to give this document to a New York publication, for in his eyes, if not in the colonel's, New York represented the United States; logically, therefore, he should have taken it to the *New York Herald*. He was not well versed in the ramifications of the American press, however, and did not know that there were two American dailies in Paris. So he made a present of this remarkable news break to the first American daily whose address he happened to find, which turned out to be the *Chicago Tribune*. The acquisition of the text was not an exploit, it was a mistake. I do not vouch for this story, but that is what was told me when I joined the Paris Edition.

When the army edition of the *Chicago Tribune* became the European edition, there was no reason to suspect that it was going to acquire a prestigious reputation, first among newspapermen and then with the general public as, dare we say, a cultural phenomenon.

The army edition had not exactly been obsessed by cultural matters; no newspaper is in time of war, and in time of war cultural manifestations themselves are few and pallid. But even in time of peace, the men who had produced the army edition would not necessarily have thrown themselves with abandon into the stream of culture. They had not come to France deliberately. The accidental by-currents of war had washed them up on the shores of the Seine, where they might otherwise never have set foot. Few of them had put down any roots, and with the end of the war they started to go home. Their vacated places were filled by young men who had come to Paris on purpose, some because it was the capital of the intellectual world, some because it was the capital of gaiety and nightlife, most for both reasons, and all because you could get fifty francs for a dollar. This became twenty-five a little later, but even this was enough to make Paris accessible to a type of American who had never been able to afford Paris before, even when he managed free passage by working his way across the Atlantic on a cattle boat as some of them continued to do. This postwar American invasion was of the young and eager. Many of them possessed creative talent, and those who had none admired those who had.

Before their arrival, the artistic quarter of Paris had been Montmartre. The newcomers established themselves, I have no idea why, in Montparnasse, where, after a while, they were joined by the last holdouts from the Butte Montmartre and a sprinkling of artists, writers, musicians, and intellectuals from various parts of the world. The Montparnassians created a minisociety, a society that needed a newspaper to reflect its ideas and its way of life. This the *Herald* could not do but the *Tribune* could.

Looking back on it from the remoteness of half a century, I have often wondered whether the paper's prestige was deserved, whether its glamour had not been overrated by those of us who viewed it through the rosy haze of softened memories. I was inclined to think so when Hugh Ford, a student of this period, located the bound volumes of the *Paris Tribune*. In 1976 he printed samplings from them under the title *The Left Bank Revisited*. I read them first eagerly, and then with disappointment. The writing struck me as run-of-the-mill, not to say mediocre.

On second thought, I am not so sure that the nature of the material reprinted in Ford's book indicates that the *Tribune*'s reputation was inflated. A newspaper cannot be judged on the basis of selected isolated articles. It is the spirit that animates it day after day that counts and it is perhaps impossible ever to recapture that spirit fully once the time and the setting in which it was manifested have become irrevocably a part of the past. For that matter, Ford was not trying to recapture the spirit of the *Tribune*; he was trying to recapture the spirit of the Left Bank in the 1920s and 1930s by reprinting what had been written about it in its heyday by the publication that had given the most attention to it.

This was an achievable objective, but I doubt if it would have been possible to revive the flavor of the *Tribune* itself by reprinting excerpts from it. The simple physical work involved was redoubtable—the manipulation of heavy bound volumes, each with the length and breadth of a full-sized newspaper page, covering the seventeen and a half years of the paper's existence—which would run to something like sixty-five thousand pages. From this it was evidently possible, since Ford succeeded in doing it, to extract pertinent articles on a given subject, in this case Left Bank life, for they could be identified simply by reading headlines. But if he had tried to choose material to illustrate the intrinsic quality of the paper, he would have had to read, at least in part, all the important articles of those sixty-five thousand pages. To make it worse, Ford had to go it blind. He had spent many years studying this period, but he remained, after all, an outsider: He had not served on the paper or lived in the society that fascinated him; he was far too young for that. Even an insider, like myself, who served the *Chicago Tribune* for eight years, would have had trouble, across the gap of half a century, in remembering and locating the salient stories that would have had to be published, though I still remember some that perhaps deserve reprinting and the approximate dates they appeared.

And I recall enough of the background details of the paper's operations that I would hardly have printed, either as a reflection of Left Bank life or of the *Tribune*'s viewpoint about it, this review of what I tend to consider Ernest Hemingway's best book:

> *The Sun Also Rises* is the kind of book that makes this reviewer at least almost plain angry, not for the obvious reason that it is about utterly degraded people, but for the reason that it shows an immense skill. . . . Why then be

angry at it? Because the theme itself is so gestury [*sic*]. Just as it was a per-fectly fair criticism to say that *Main Street* was a picture out of proportion to gain an end, so it is also fair to say that *The Sun Also Rises* is entirely out of focus. The difference between them is that although *Main Street* did gain an end of parts, *The Sun Also Rises* leaves you feeling that an artist has just done something to be smart. . . . Most of the time the picture is so trivial. It isn't just that you mind its being drunken or of a sort of hypercivilized crudity, but you do mind horribly having a man who obviously has the tal-ent that Hemingway has . . . concerned with such utter trivialities that your sensitiveness objects violently to it. The wasting of a genuine gift on some-thing that is exactly what you would expect a mediocre young man from Oak Park, Ill. [Hemingway's birthplace], and not one with real talent, to write about Paris is what makes you unhappy. Every young man from every Oak Park in the United States probably gets just such an angle on the group of rotters that are to be found in any city and place, and he always writes about them. . . . Hemingway can be a distinguished writer if he wishes to be. He is even in this book, but it is a distinction hidden under a bushel of sensationalism and triviality.

These are strange words indeed to find in a newspaper that was not only sympathetic to the Montparnassians but even a participant in their soci-ety. Yet Ford did extract this review from the Paris Edition, under the sig-nature of Fanny Butcher. What he did not know was that Fanny Butcher was the literary critic of the *Chicago Tribune*, not of Paris, but of Chi-cago; her article had simply been reprinted from the parent paper. Even so it surprises me that it got into the Paris Edition at all. It would be my guess, though I don't know, that it appeared in the Paris Edition's Sunday magazine section. This was largely a scissors-and-paste job, and as the review appeared in the paper's hit-or-miss period (1926), I should think it probable that it went down to the composing room without ever having been read by anyone on the Paris paper.

The *Tribune* seems to have benefited by comparison with the relatively colorless *Herald* (the *Herald* gained in interest toward the end of the *Tri-bune*'s life, in an effort to meet its competition). James Thurber wrote that "The Paris edition of the *Chicago Tribune* was a country newspaper pub-lished in a great city," but this was an opinion uttered in the paper's erratic period, for he had already left when I arrived in 1927, and it would take another three years for the paper to develop a really cosmopolitan out-look. According to Janet Flanner (the *New Yorker*'s Paris correspondent, whose articles were signed Genêt), it was the *Herald* that was "a village paper, a hick village paper. It was well read but then came the *Chicago Tribune* which actually harbored . . . more of a nest of writers than the *Herald Tribune* [an anachronism; the *Herald* did not become the *Herald Tribune* until 1935]. . . . The *Herald Tribune* did have some writers but the *Chicago Tribune* was more influential."

Whit Burnett, even if he did think the *Tribune* was, on its off days, a ghastly mistake, added that it was never dull, while the *Paris Herald* was almost always dull. He added that the *Herald* was sloppily edited, but ventured no opinion on the editing of the *Tribune* in his day, the early 1920s. Possibly he would have suggested that we operated on the basis of trial and error, and when, by chance, the error turned out not to be one, we enjoyed our day of genius.

Hugh Ford described the difference between the *Tribune* and the *Herald* by saying that the *Herald* catered to "the 'lobster-palace Americans' [a phrase borrowed from Colonel McCormick himself] on the Right Bank of the Seine while the *Tribune* began reporting the activities of the cultural adventurists from America, as well as of Europe, who were turning the old Latin Quarter of Montparnasse [Montparnasse is not in the Latin Quarter, but never mind] into an artistic and social *pied-à-terre*."

The sincerity of the compliments that were directed at the *Tribune* can hardly be doubted in the case of those that did not come from nostalgic alumni of the paper but from observers who worked for our rival, like Al Laney, first sports editor and then news editor of the *Herald*. Laney, a man of more gusto than the *Herald* usually tolerated, said of this period, "Never in the history of journalism have so many men had such a wonderful time on so little money." In his book about the *Paris Herald*, Laney admitted that the *Tribune* far surpassed the *Herald* in its coverage of the life of the Montparnassians, and he called the death of the *Tribune* "one of the saddest things that could have happened."

Jules Frantz was certainly not immodest when he described the style of the paper he edited as "brash, lusty and breezy." Lawrence Blochman, best known as a mystery story writer, also a *Tribune* alumnus, went a little further when he wrote that the "Paris edition did serve as a school of journalism for the international apprenticeship of many of the top names in American newsdom and letters."

I would not have called it a school, except in the sense that any news-paper that provides the opportunity to learn by doing is a school. In this sense, the *Tribune* constituted a particularly good school. It was, mea-sured by volume, a small paper—eight to twelve pages usually—and any small paper provides better basic training than a big one, for its modest scale permits, or even obliges, every member of its staff to become ac-quainted with all the phases of the production of a newspaper. But as a rule small papers are situated in small towns, and small towns have small-town mentalities. The *Tribune* was situated in a world capital, precisely the one bursting with an artistic and intellectual vitality unmatchable anywhere else. It was read by a cosmopolitan audience that demanded the intellectual level of a sophisticated metropolitan daily. The *Tribune* sup-plied it. Perhaps Thurber intended a compliment when he said that the *Tribune* was a country newspaper published in a great city.

The *Tribune* even achieved, during its last years, a high degree of tech-nical excellence, something I did not then realize, having nothing to mea-sure it against. We attracted from time to time big-city newspapermen—usually because working for the *Tribune* allowed them to savor the plea-sures of Paris—for six months or a year, or even two. All of them told me that we ran a fast desk, with a pace surpassing what they had been used to. I discounted these remarks at the time, assuming that they were not really comparing our performance to that of metropolitan dailies, but only with the low level they expected from so modest an operation: They were surprised because we were less inept than we should have been. It seemed axiomatic to me that large-city newspapers would function more efficiently than we could.

With surprise I discovered, when I returned to New York during World War II, that our temporary staffers from America had simply been telling the truth. I visited city rooms of the *New York Times* and the *New York Herald Tribune*; they looked lethargic. The feverish atmosphere of the Paris Edition would, it seemed, have overwhelmed them. When I went to work for a New York daily myself, I had to admit that in Paris we had handled the news faster and better than New York copydesks could han-dle it.

If many of our alumni did indeed become "top names in American newsdom and letters," it was probably first of all because the kind of young men who were drawn to Paris when it was the center of a lively cultural life were also the kind of young men who were likely to achieve a certain eminence anyway, whether they had passed through the mill of the *Tribune* or not. If we garnered more of them than the *Herald*, that was because we were interested in the same aspects of Parisian life that interested them, and even participated in that life. "*Tribune* columnists mingled with . . . the cultural adventurists from America, as well as Europe," Hugh Ford wrote, ". . . on the terraces of Left Bank cafés like the Dôme and the Select, alert for undiscovered idiosyncrasies, signs of genius or bits of gossip."

One could make a good case for the importance of the *Tribune* in the intellectual life of Paris on the basis of a remark about the avant-garde magazine *transition* by its founder, Eugene Jolas. He said that in many respects *transition* was "an offshoot of the *Tribune*." That might be a slight exaggeration. It would perhaps be more exact to say that a channel of communication existed between Montparnasse and the *Tribune* via *transition* since not only Jolas but also his first two coeditors, Elliot Paul and Robert Sage, were on the copydesk of the *Tribune*. Jolas left to devote himself solely to *transition* shortly before I arrived, but Paul and Sage stayed on.

The *Tribune*'s affinity with Montparnasse accounted for the occasional appearance in its columns of articles signed by some of the important actors on the Left Bank scene. They contributed their thoughts unsolicited and gratuitously when they had something to say to a larger public than that of the little magazines: There was really no way to reach it except through our paper. I do not recall the names of all the notables who thus served us as occasional writers, but I remember that among them were Gertrude Stein, Ford Madox Ford, and George Antheil. As for regular staff members, almost everyone wrote about the doings of the Montparnassians at one time or another, occasionally under running titles that gave them virtually the status of Montparnasse columnists. The only staff member whose reporting appeared regularly enough, and lasted long enough, to really deserve the title of columnist was proofreader Wambly Bald, whose articles ran under the heading of "La Vie de Bohème." Hugh Ford called him "the Boswell of the Lost Generation," but in my opinion "the Walter Winchell of the Lost Generation" would have been more like it. Janet Flanner said he was the only Tribuner whom none of the Montparnassians failed to read. "Obviously," wrote Frantz, "he should have been on the editorial staff, but he repeatedly turned down my invitation to move upstairs." He preferred to stay with the proofreaders, which wasn't a bad choice. One indication of how deep cultural interest penetrated in the *Tribune* was that its proofreaders might have provided a relatively brilliant editorial staff for any other paper.

Three inseparables graced this staff—Bald, who served as the model for Van Norden in Henry Miller's *Tropic of Cancer* and was not happy about it; Alfred Perlès, the original of Carl in *The Tropic of Cancer*, who would become Henry Miller's biographer; and Miller himself. It may seem ironic that the most notorious writer of the period (the word "notorious" is used deliberately, as being synonymous neither with "famous" nor "best") should have been consigned to the *Tribune* proofroom without ever having been permitted to write a line for the paper, and even more so that he should have been fired from the paper, as he said he had been. This claim was not strictly true, but the idea probably appealed to Miller's quiet sense of humor. What actually happened was that Miller, who had worked for the paper only briefly, was invited to make a free trip through Belgium and took off without warning anybody. His place remained vacant for a couple of weeks, while efforts to reach him were unavailing; in the meantime the other proofreaders had to operate one man short. Frantz finally decided that Miller must have quit without giving notice, a phenomenon not unknown on the *Tribune*, and hired somebody to replace him. When Miller returned, he was hardly in a position to ask for his job back, and if my memory is correct, he didn't. Miller was not made for keeping regular office hours and I suspect that he lost the job without regret. Being fired relieved him of boring routine work without offending Perlès, who had gotten him the job, and it permitted Miller to revert to his probably preferred status of having no visible means of support except what he could cadge from others. Perlès must have been speaking only for himself when he wrote in *My Friend Henry Miller* that their proofreading period was the "most highly fertile of our life in Paris."

I wonder if one of the chief reasons the *Tribune* employed such excellent men, from proofreaders to editor, was not that it paid them so badly. This assured the paper of being staffed by men who were willing to accept sacrifices for the sake of performing a fascinating task in a fascinating city. Writers who were interested in money first and their work second gravitated naturally to the better-paying *Herald*; those who put professional ardor first and money second came to the *Tribune*. Some newcomers started on the wrong paper, but there was a constant exchange of personnel between them, and in the long run the writers sorted themselves out and found themselves working for the papers that best suited their temperaments.

Poverty, within reasonable limits, has its privileges, foremost being the possibility of independence. Our masters in Chicago did not pay us enough to be able to dictate to us what sort of paper we should produce. You might say that we took part of our pay in the power to put out our kind of paper, which compensated for the poor return in terms of money. The less we were paid, the less it would have cost us to quit; and once established in Paris and known in the world of Paris-American publications, it was not difficult to find a new job—which, since we were at the bottom of the ladder, could only be a step upward. In short, the ownership of the paper was more vulnerable to the loss of its staff than the staff was vulnerable to the loss of its jobs. So we were left alone to create our own Paris *Chicago Tribune*, a paper decidedly not cast in the image of the Chicago *Chicago Tribune*.

The paper was our own. We had conceived it and we worked on it with love and enthusiasm. I have held a great many jobs of different kinds, but I can remember no other in which there was so much comradeship, such a harmony of ideas, so complete an esprit de corps in the pursuit of a common purpose—to put out the best paper of which we were capable. No wonder that men who had once worked, even briefly, for the Paris Edition returned to the United States to sing its praises. There were a great many of them, since our labor turnover was so rapid. They may have exaggerated somewhat, for their memories were gilded by the enchantment of having been young and in Paris during one of its most exciting periods, but they could hardly have exaggerated the gusto with which they lived and worked.

¶

"What Do I Mean by This?"

¶

Colonel Robert Rutherford McCormick was the absolute monarch who ruled over the wage slaves of the *Chicago Tribune*. Even the staff of the Paris edition of the *Chicago Tribune*, which otherwise feared neither God nor man, cringed before the colonel, who partook of the nature of both. Like other lordly figures, he was never referred to by name but by his title. Everybody called him "the colonel"—as though he were the only holder of that rank in the world—except his mother (and a very few other close relatives). She called him Bertie.

"Bertie's not quite right in the head," his mother used to say. "They'll have to put him away some day."

Mrs. McCormick herself was one of the Paris bureau's recurring problems. She spent a good deal of time in France, though she disliked it ("I fell out of bed in that damn country," she explained), but she was encouraged to stay abroad by a family that felt the farther she was from Chicago the less embarrassment would result for her dear ones.

The colonel was not unaware of the slurs cast upon the mental stability of his family, and indeed he gloried in them. He was fond of announcing in public, "All the McCormicks are crazy except me," and once reduced his Washington bureau chief, Walter Trohan, to complete confusion by adding, "You wouldn't agree with that, would you, Walter?" Trohan may have had his doubts. He had once received from the colonel a clipping from the *Chicago Tribune* of an article that the colonel had written himself, on which he had scrawled a marginal question: "What do I mean by this?"

From the time of the Roger Baldwin episode, the consciousness of the colonel's unpredictable and redoubtable existence weighed on me, as it did on everyone who worked for him, but I met him for the first time only a year or two later, when I was the lowliest of the four correspondents then maintained in the *Chicago Tribune*'s London bureau. The ominous tidings that the colonel was en route to London threw the office into a state of apprehension that persisted for the two weeks that elapsed before the failure of Jon Steele, the bureau chief, to show up at the office informed us that the colonel had landed and Steele was waiting attendance on him. Nobody dared leave the premises; the colonel might appear at any moment, and when he entered one of his outlying bureaus, he expected to find all his minions there to welcome him.

There was no news of the colonel until the middle of the afternoon, when Steele telephoned to say that the colonel had invited the staff to have dinner with him. This touched off a debate on whether we should dress formally; it was finally decided not to do so, which turned out later to have been the correct choice. The hour of the colonel's rendezvous turned up, but the colonel did not. We sat waiting, chatting inconsequentially in an attempt to master the nervous stomachs we were working up to digest the colonel's cheer. Only our English cable editor, Sidney Cave, an imperturbable character who looked like John Bull and thought like him, maintained full composure. Cave, who was something of a gourmet, filled in the time by speculating on where the colonel would take us (Simpson's, probably) and running over an imaginary wine list in his mind, on the assumption that as the office expert on such matters he would be asked to select the vintages.

The colonel, escorted by Steele, arrived an hour and a half late, and we were duly presented. The ceremony had about it the air of a military inspection. The formalities over, the colonel announced, "I passed a little place around the corner that doesn't look bad. Let's eat there." Cave's face fell an Imperial British foot. The colonel led us to the little place around the corner, no treat for any of us since we ate there almost daily, and after we had ordered from its all-too-familiar menu, the colonel demanded, "What would you like to drink?" Cave brightened and cleared his throat in preparation for speech, but Steele beat him to the punch. "What are *you* drinking, Colonel?" he inquired. "Beer," said the colonel. Everybody wanted beer.

I arrived at the office the next morning to find the staff in a state of collective hysteria. The colonel had sent word that he planned to take a walk through London and I was to accompany him. Since I was on my way to the office, it had naturally been impossible to reach me, and nobody dared envisage what might happen if I could not be found. When the colonel ordered a body delivered he wanted the body, not an explanation of why it could not be produced.

It was for me, though not for the colonel, an agitated morning. He measured six feet four inches and walked with a long stride, at military parade cadence. I am not short myself, but I had to shout upward to communicate with him, and to develop a sort of lope to keep up. To add to my difficulties, I had to act as his personal disbursing officer, a role for which I was ill-fitted, for I have always been a fumbler of money and a slow-witted calculator of change. The colonel never carried money. In Chicago he didn't need to: He popped into a shop, rattled off an order, and popped out again. The shop knew where to send the bill. In London the colonel refused to compromise with the possibility that there might be shops where he would not immediately be recognized. The office had armed me with an impressive wad of bills, and as he ducked into one shop after another and out again, strewing orders behind him, I had to sprint to the cashier's desk, pay, and get out on the double in pursuit of the colonel's receding back.

From time to time, the colonel tossed me a word of wisdom: "Best hatter in London, Root. Buy all my hats here. Advise you to do the same." The words sprang to my tongue: "Colonel, do you happen to know how much you are paying me?" I swallowed them.

The approach of lunchtime put an end to the footrace. I piloted the colonel back to his hotel, where Steele was waiting uneasily for the pleasure of eating with the boss. To my dismay the colonel invited me to stay to lunch too. He liked to eat surrounded by underlings.

The conversation consisted of a monologue by the colonel, punctuated at discreet intervals by assorted monosyllabic noises signifying approval from Steele or myself. We were just reaching dessert when the colonel pulled out his watch and consulted it. "Root," he said, "I understand things are pretty bad in the Welsh coal mines." He was right; practically nobody had worked there for two or three years. "There's a train for Cardiff at three o'clock." He must have been studying the timetables. "I want you to hop aboard it and give us seven or eight good stories on the situation there."

"Cable, Colonel?" I asked.

"No, no," he said. "Mail will do."

Those were preplane days. It would take a week or more for my stories to reach Chicago. There seemed to be no great hurry, so I ventured to suggest that if I took a later train, that would at least give me time to warn my wife, who was out for the afternoon and not immediately reachable, that I was off on a trip.

"I think," the colonel said firmly, "that you should take the first train available."

I had about forty-five minutes to get home, pack, and catch my train. I rushed off, leaving Steele and the colonel to their dessert, of which, like a naughty child, I had been deprived. As I tossed clothes into a suitcase, it occurred to me that I could take a later train and nobody would be the wiser. An alert guardian angel intervened and got me onto the colonel's choice by the skin of my teeth. Fifteen minutes after I had checked into my hotel in Cardiff the phone rang. It was the colonel's secretary, with supplementary and superfluous instructions. It was obvious that the real reason for the call was to find out if I had obeyed orders.

After my departure from London, the colonel left too, for Paris, where he gave another staff dinner. I heard that his uneasy employees, about thirty of them, were assembled about a large table whose center was occupied by a single bottle of Sauternes ("None of us drink," Hank Wales had assured the colonel). Jack Hummel, publisher of the Paris Edition, sat at the colonel's right and it would have seemed normal for Wales, bureau chief for the Foreign News Service, to have guarded the other flank, but Wales, a canny character, had somehow avoided this responsibility. There was no notable rush to occupy this place, which was taken by a member of the Paris Edition staff gifted with the unabashable character of innocence, our sports editor, Hérol Egan. Egan felt that military men should stand, or sit, together, and he had arrogated to himself the status of warrior on the basis of a brief and particularly inglorious period of service with the British Royal Air Force.

Egan launched into a discussion of military matters, doing a great deal more talking than was usually considered tactful for a guest of the colonel's, but he was allowed to ramble on, for his theme was one pleasing to his host. Egan was discoursing on the ineptitude of the American High

Command, of which the colonel had no high opinion either, since it had proved itself inexcusably obtuse in its choice of officers to elevate to the rank of general. He listened complacently until the fateful moment when Egan, in a voice audible to everyone present, said earnestly: "And the worst thing, Colonel, the very worst thing that happened in our army was when our artillery shelled its own infantry at Cantigny."

The silence of horror descended over the company. Everybody else in the room knew the colonel had commanded the artillery at Cantigny. He rose from his chair. "That man has spoiled my evening," he said, and he walked out. It was taken for granted that a new sports editor would be found the next day, but Egan had always led a charmed life, and his luck was still with him. "Never fire that man," the colonel ordered, "and never give him a raise."

The first part of the edict held, but the second was in time forgotten. Three or four years later, when Jules Frantz had become managing editor of the Paris Edition and I its news editor, the New York Stock Exchange crash of 1929 caused us to be ordered to cut the editorial payroll by I-have-forgotten-what percentage. How to do it was left to us. We could fire some of the staff, we could reduce wages, or we could do a little of both, but we had to arrive at the arbitrarily fixed limit. We were averse to firing anybody, so we sat down to the painful task of cutting salaries. We began by slashing our own wages unmercifully, for we were the two highest-paid editorial employees (the days of the $15 week had passed). "Now," said Frantz with relish, "we're going to take a big chunk out of that bastard Egan. He's getting twice as much as he is worth already." The word "bastard" should be considered as a term of endearment. Frantz was particularly fond of Egan, as were we all; his likability was the coin by which he compensated for his frequent incompetence. This aside, it was incontrovertible that he was overpaid.

We had barely finished the thankless and harrowing task of downgrading everybody when Egan came in. His eyes were focused on nothing in particular and his face had been invaded by the characteristic vacuous grin that announced at least one glass too many. "Whaddaya think," he announced. "Jus' been rollin' dice with good ol' Jack [Hummel] an' I won a hunder' percent raise." I had heard Frantz swear at Egan before, in moments of stress, but always good-naturedly. This time he really meant it. Egan stood dumbfounded and bewildered under the torrent of abuse, but he didn't suggest renouncing his doubled salary. We took the case to Hummel later, but couldn't get the raise annulled. Hummel was not notorious for keeping his word, but a gambling debt was a special matter, at least when he was losing the paper's money instead of his own. Actually, he had been playing with the staff's money; we had to return to our labors and subtract from the wages of the others the money Egan had won from Hummel.

The role the colonel had played at Cantigny where the American artillery barrage had fallen short and mowed down the charging infantry, has never been cleared up. It is true that he was awarded the Distinguished Service Medal for half-a-year's active duty in 1918, with a citation that mentioned his command at Cantigny, but there were people cynical enough to suggest that this decoration reflected less his merits as an officer than his influential position as the master of the biggest paper in the Middle West. The colonel might have preferred promotion to the rank of general, but the army thought it better to give him a medal.

The colonel's attitude toward the Cantigny story was curiously ambivalent. As the Egan episode showed, he did not relish its invocation by others, but on occasion he insisted on it himself. When he took over his mother's property at Wheaton, he changed its name from Red Oak Farm to Cantigny, and he once sent William Shirer to the battlefield to see if he could find a pair of binoculars that he claimed to have left in a barn there nine years before. Although he was armed with a detailed map drawn by the colonel himself, Shirer failed to find not only the binoculars but also the barn.

According to Hank Wales, whatever happened at Cantigny need not have bothered the colonel one way or the other, for he wasn't there. There are two theories about his whereabouts at the time of the battle, aside from the assumption that he was actually present: one, that he was in Paris, where life was more agreeable than at the front, and the other that he was ill. The colonel himself once explained, though indirectly and with a minimum of clarity, that he had been ordered out of the line by the medical officer of his unit because he had come down with influenza. If the colonel was not in fact at Cantigny at all, and was therefore without responsibility for whatever happened there, his contradictory reactions to the utterance of this name seem all the stranger.

Several years after my London lunch with the colonel, the same scenario was repeated, with variations, in Paris. Once again I arrived at the office to find it in a state of turmoil, as in London and for the same reason: The colonel had expressed a desire for my company, and my colleagues were going mad trying to find me. I was less flattered than flabbergasted by the royal command, for my program for the day had been to work on a special supplement I was preparing for the paper, a job that involved much manipulation of inky proofs and their buttering with large quantities of paste. I had accordingly put on a suit better adapted to serve as a palette for paste than for display in the elegant atmosphere of the Ritz, where I was ordered to meet the colonel before driving out to Versailles to lunch with him. I made a determined attempt to hurry home and change clothes, but I was overruled and outnumbered, stuffed almost by force into a taxi and dispatched to the Ritz. I waited in the luxurious small salon the hotel maintains for such purposes, feeling conspicuous, and it was only a slight relief when the colonel appeared and I discovered that he was wearing a suit that looked as if he had slept in it.

We emerged into the classic setting of the place Vendôme and stood on the sidewalk before the Ritz as the car the colonel had ordered began drawing up before us. The process took a certain amount of time. The door of the juggernaut finally reached us, a gold-braided doorman, cap in hand, opened it, and the colonel waved me courteously in. I entered, he followed and began to scream.

"Get out, Root!" he shouted. "Get out at once! This is an outrage! This is intolerable!" He all but pulled me out of the car, and his roars became unintelligible. All around the place Vendôme pedestrians stopped short and turned toward the Ritz to see what was happening. I had a ringside seat, but I didn't know what was happening myself. Neither did the flunkies who began pouring out of the Ritz and prostrating themselves on the sidewalk. Hoarseness finally restored the colonel to relative coherence, and he was able to reveal what was wrong: A previous occupant of the car had left some ashes in the ashtray. The colonel did not smoke.

The chauffeur plunged into the rear of the car and began scrubbing frantically at the ashtray. The colonel waved him out, dismissed the contaminated vehicle, and called for another limousine. In what seemed a matter of seconds it arrived, longer, if possible, than the first. Its ashtrays were impeccable.

¶

The Population of Patagonia

¶

The colonel's promenades in the company of a Seeing-Eye dog were one of the best known of his eccentricities. He must have been the most conspicuous blind man in Chicago. Since his photograph appeared almost daily in one local publication or another, he could hardly have been disguised adequately by the pair of black spectacles he wore on these occasions. The colonel saw himself during these sorties as a modern Haroun-al-Raschid, eavesdropping incognito on his subjects, which was about the way he regarded the readers of the *Chicago Tribune*. He was certainly in error; anyone in Chicago unable to recognize him would also be unable to participate in any conversation worth listening to.

He seems to have felt a special fondness for dogs, Seeing-Eye or other, since the monogram on his bulletproof car (the only one in Chicago except Al Capone's) was composed not of his initials, but of those of his favorite bulldog. His private plane was called the *'Untin' Bowler*, a term that had amused the colonel when he heard it in England applied to a derby hat. The plane was also monogrammed, so to speak, by the flags of a number of countries that the colonel visited when he made an extensive tour through Europe and Asia. This provoked some embarrassment when he touched down in Madrid to call on Generalissimo Francisco Franco, whom he admired, for airport authorities were distinctly unpleasant—until they found out who he was—about an error made by the flag painter who had adorned the *'Untin' Bowler* with the Spanish Republican banner.

The horse, like the dog, played a considerable part in the colonel's life. When the colonel's first wife died, he honored her with a military funeral: A horse with stirrups crossed and eyes hooded in black followed the coffin. A bugler sounded taps as an American flag was lowered and folded ceremoniously and a detachment of troops fired three rounds in salute over her grave. It is true that she came from a family infested with generals, but many of the colonel's friends and relatives felt he had exaggerated.

One disputed story involving this animal tells how a picnic of *Chicago Tribune* advertising men was invaded by a large horse-carrying van whose tailboard was lowered to form a ramp, down which the colonel rode, booted and spurred, to deliver a pep talk to his salesmen from the saddle. The exhortation finished, he rode back up the ramp into the truck and was driven away. The colonel later insisted that this story was only an exaggeration of a youthful prank when, showing off before Alice Roosevelt, Theodore's daughter, he rode a horse up the steps of a house in Chicago.

It is possible that some of the startling utterances attributed to the colonel were unrecognized jokes. A wheeze that delighted the staff of the Paris Edition at the time of the Versailles Conference was that the colonel remarked there that he had always thought the Ukraine was a musical instrument. He knew very well what and where the Ukraine was, having passed through it before the United States entered World War I when he visited the entire Russian front under the guidance of no less a person than the Grand Duke Nicholas Nicholaievitch, commander-in-chief of the Russian Army. The colonel described that experience in *With the Russian Army*.

The colonel's writings, indeed, offer evidence that his mind was a machine that functioned excellently when permitted to do so. He had to his credit two respectable volumes on the campaigns of the Civil War, *Ulysses S. Grant* and *The War Without Grant*. He had already shown his mettle before he produced those books. He was only twenty-three when he became president of the Chicago Sanitary Commission, which, by its control of the Ship Canal linking the Great Lakes with the Mississippi, constituted a sort of subgovernment of the Chicago area. He handled the job with undisputed competence, even achieving the triumph, for that time and place, of keeping its administration free from graft. Its president, of course, was proof against corruption, for nobody had enough money to bribe him. The colonel was not as rich as most people thought, but he was rich enough; he left about $20,000,000 when he died in 1955, a considerable fortune at the time.

When the colonel first entered the *Chicago Tribune*, where it had been declared that there was "no place for him," he was an unpaid financial manager with no official status. He proceeded to put what had become a vacillating business on its feet again. In 1911 he became the paper's president, still without a salary; he was not even a director of the company. But in a few years, as coeditor, then editor, then publisher, he made the *Tribune* his own. There was no longer any doubt about who was running the paper.

The colonel ruled it like a dictator, and on the whole he dictated well, demonstrating foresight and imagination for the shape of the future. In 1928 he wrote to his mother that the price of stocks was exceeding all reason, and predicted the disaster that occurred a year later. He realized long in advance of actual need that a great newspaper had to control its own source of paper, and set up in Canada a vast company that owned forests, the mills for making paper from its trees, and the boats to ferry their newsprint across the Great Lakes to his presses. He foresaw the possibilities of radio for the transmission of news, and the result was Press Wireless, a worldwide network handling press dispatches only. He was also alert to the development of radio for public news broadcasting and established *Tribune* station WGN (for World's Greatest Newspaper), which gave birth to the Mutual Broadcasting System. When I was working for it, from 1938 to 1940, it was one of the big three, the two others being the National Broadcasting Company and the Columbia Broadcasting System. The importance of these achievements may well offset his eccentricities; any young man who enjoyed the colonel's power, prestige, wealth, and virtual impunity might well have indulged his irrational whims and fantasies more spectacularly than the colonel ever did.

Whenever two or more of the diminishing group of survivors of the *Chicago Tribune*'s Paris Edition encounter each other nowadays, their conversation turns inevitably to the personality of the colonel and to the question: "Was he a genius or a disaster?" My own feelings about the colonel are mellower than they were when I was working for him, and if forced to classify him, I would be inclined to put him down as closer to a genius. He belonged to an epoch of colorful journalism and personal journalism; the careful corporate management of many of our newspapers today produces paler publications than those of earlier times, when great newspapers were the lengthened shadows of the great men who ran them—Horace Greeley, Joseph Pulitzer—or of the families that cherished their ownership like heirlooms—Ochs-Sulzberger for the *New York Times*, Meyer-Graham for the *Washington Post*, the Chandlers for the *Los Angeles Times*, three papers whose greatness has lasted to this day. The *Chicago Tribune* fell into both classes. It was owned by a family clan, the McCormick-Pattersons (as was, later, the *New York Daily News*), but it was also a one-man paper, as much a part of the colonel as his liver.

We had the best of the colonel on the Paris Edition for he was, most of the time, four thousand miles away, which was more tolerable than having him close by, where he was uncomfortable company. He seemed to expect his underlings to be walking encyclopedias and frequently fired at them disconcerting questions on matters that for one reason or another happened to pop into his head: "Root, what was the population of Patagonia when Charles Darwin visited it in the *Beagle*?" The best technique in such circumstances was to come up with any plausible answer, for the colonel would probably never give it another thought.

He was also prone to launch his correspondents on research projects whose importance was not perceptible to them, but their evaluation of his queries was not pertinent. It was advisable to drop whatever else might be in hand, however important, and give absolute priority to the information the colonel demanded. Once, when I was in the London bureau, I received a cable from the colonel informing me that he had to make a speech commemorating the anniversary of the Battle of New Orleans, at which, he had heard, a British regiment participated that had also been at the Battle of Waterloo. I was to identify the regiment and find out exactly what it had done there. I spent the next three days in the British War Museum, which had a series of plans of the shifting dispositions of the troops engaged there at, I seem to remember, something like quarter-hour intervals. This enabled me to send a lengthy cable giving the minute-by-minute movements of the regiment that interested him.

When the appropriate issue of the *Tribune* reached London, containing, inevitably, the full text of the colonel's speech, I hastened to read it to see what my labors had produced. Somewhere in the middle of his long discourse, I came to a remark that one regiment at the Battle of New Orleans "was reported to have participated also in the Battle of Water-loo"—in other words, exactly what the colonel had already known before he cabled me. My only consolation was that for a few weeks I was probably the world's leading authority on the Battle of Waterloo. (My knowledge ebbed quickly and today I hardly know who won, except the Belgian Tourist Office.)

It was the colonel's idea, catered to but not shared by his correspondents, that one function of the Foreign News Service and of the Paris Edition was to provide evidence to support whatever personal theories or prejudices he might be nursing at the time. Sometimes the two organizations got into each other's way. It was no secret that the colonel felt the French government should have recognized, by bestowing on him the medal of the Legion of Honor, the services he had rendered during the war—a theory the French did not seem to agree with. Someone in the Foreign News Service set out to procure this honor for the colonel, with the idea of profiting by his gratitude, and so did someone on the Paris Edition. Neither, of course, communicated his secret to the other, with the result that the Chancellory of the Legion of Honor found itself beset from two sides by a campaign in favor of the colonel, which led it to conclude that it was being abusively pressured into rewarding somebody whose record did not warrant it.

When the colonel learned that the efforts made on his behalf had failed, he came to the opinion that it was un-American to accept decorations from foreign governments, and ordered the Foreign News Service to cable the names of all American holders of the Legion of Honor so that they could be held up to public obloquy. When he received a list of several thousand names he decided to forget about it.

George Seldes has written on several occasions the story of how he ran afoul of the colonel when Seldes was *Chicago Tribune* correspondent in Berlin. At the time the colonel was promoting the theme that American railroads were immeasurably superior to European railroads, which had been ruined by the socialistic practice of government ownership and operation. He sent a round-robin message to all his correspondents calling for reports from their territories testifying to this indisputable fact. Seldes either failed to get the idea, or didn't want to, and filed a message on the great efficiency of German railroads. The colonel, however, was interested only in their inefficiency. Seldes made a second stab at the assignment, but found it impossible to fault German railroading sufficiently to satisfy the colonel, who had someone else do the kind of story he wanted.

I think this was the issue on which Seldes and the *Tribune* parted company, but it may be that my memory is at fault; it could have been something else. Seldes was normally bristly and aggressive and had managed to get himself expelled from so many countries—often, it is true, on the side of virtue—that it became more and more difficult for the paper to find a country to which it could assign him.

It was not necessary to have had a flagrant difference with the colonel to be fired by him, but it *was* necessary to avoid the most heinous crime on his list of reportorial offenses—insubordination. I can recall only one instance in which he forgave a clear-cut example of this sin. It involved Hank Wales, one of the colonel's most durable favorites. It occurred after World War II, when Hank was in the United States, temporarily stationed in San Francisco. The colonel called on him unexpectedly for some service or other, and he was not to be found: He had gone to Hawaii without asking permission or giving notice. The order to fire him had, I believe, already been issued when the colonel learned that Wales had abandoned his post because he had become enamored of a girl and had followed her to Hawaii. This was the sort of thing the colonel could understand since he had always been more vulnerable to women than successful with them. Wales was forgiven.

One point on which the colonel might have been rated as a disaster was his treatment of the Foreign News Service. In the 1920s and 1930s, the *Tribune* had a remarkably good network of correspondents whose reports were syndicated to newspapers all over the United States. It enjoyed, at various times, the services of some of the best-known American journalists—Floyd Gibbons, Edgar Snow, Vincent Sheehan, William Shirer, Edmond Taylor. The difficulty of holding onto men of this caliber was that they had an irrepressible habit of thinking, and it was the colonel's feeling that he was capable of doing all the thinking the *Chicago Tribune* needed. The thinking of these correspondents, to make it worse, had a habit of conducting them to political points of view antithetical to those of the colonel. Sooner or later a clash was bound to occur, as a result of which the colonel would drop the boom on his correspondent or the correspondent would depart of his own volition, slamming the door behind him.

One thing that could be said for the colonel was that when he fired anybody, it was usually with generous severance pay. The colonel was never niggardly, which would have contradicted a character that operated with bravura and on a sweeping scale. When I was in the Foreign News Service, our instructions were to take the top class in boats and trains and to stop at the best hotels. It was the colonel's theory that the *Chicago Tribune* would be forever shamed if one of its representatives were caught using second-class accommodations, and this was one notion on which we saw eye to eye with the colonel.

I have been told that the colonel kept in his office a large map of the world studded with colored pins marking the points where his correspondents were stationed and that he became restless if they remained in the same spots for any great length of time. He itched to deploy his troops from one station to another as the changing fortunes of war demanded. I cannot testify to this personally, for I had the good luck never to have entered the colonel's office nor to have been in Chicago at the same time he was, but I could observe from afar that the colonel had a habit of ordering his correspondents to leave their accustomed headquarters for remote points where he anticipated news developments that as a rule didn't happen.

It was a practice fundamentally unsound, for correspondents are based in permanent offices in national capitals or other important centers because it is there that most routine news develops. Other sorts of news—disasters, for instance—explode unpredictably in unexpected places. In this case the correspondent sitting at the center of a network of communications is best placed to hear about such events and get quickly to the place of action. The colonel's belief that he could sense where a big story was going to break and put a man on the terrain in advance ready to handle it was erroneous, but not unwelcome to his correspondents. It often meant an interesting trip at office expense to some region we would not otherwise have visited, inspecting it without the distraction of any exacting labor when the colonel had guessed wrong.

Sometimes he guessed right, but his timing was erratic. This once worked out very pleasantly for me. In 1929, the colonel rushed David Darrah, chief of the Rome bureau, to Madrid to report the impending Spanish Civil War. The war came all right, but it took seven years to do so. I had been dispatched from the London bureau to Southampton to meet some uninteresting American bigwigs. On reaching Southampton I took the routine precaution of calling the office to tell them where I was. "Forget about that story and get back to London as fast as you can," I was told. "You have to leave for Rome." The Concordat between the Italian government and the Vatican had been signed, and we were caught flat with nobody on the spot to cover it.

I was on the Rome Express that night (it was before the days of planes), but in those times it was close to two days from London to Rome. The Concordat was not much better than a one-day story, so by the time I got to the spot, very little was left to report. Rome was a stagnant news source, but after the fiasco on the Concordat story nobody dared call me back to London, so I spent some very pleasant weeks in Rome, mostly in museums, with touristic side-trips to Naples, Pompeii, and Venice. I trust Darrah was enjoying himself as well in Spain.

Several years later, after the Paris Edition had given up the ghost, bequeathing some of its men to the Foreign News Service, the colonel predicted another development too soon, but this time with less wide a margin—the invasion of Abyssinia by Italy. He cabled Will Barber, then in the London bureau, to head for Addis Ababa to cover the war when it broke out. Barber looked into the inoculations against tropical diseases that it was then thought necessary to have before entering Ethiopia and wired the colonel that it would take two weeks for all of them to be administered. He asked whether he could delay his departure for a fortnight.

The colonel fired back one of the lapidary cables on which he prided himself: ARE YOU A HISTORIAN OR A NEWSPAPERMAN?

Barber left London the next day, and for six months sat idly in Addis Ababa waiting for something to happen. On the day the Italians invaded, he died of blackwater fever.

75

¶

PRINCE OF WALES BASHES BOY'S BRAINS OUT WITH BLUDGEON

¶

One of the first people I met when I moved onto the night staff of the Paris Edition was a man who should not have been there at all. He had been fired long before I came on the paper, yet there he was, padding about the city room, short, potbellied, in vest and shirtsleeves—these embellished by the elastic armbands that, in the days before it occurred to shirt manufacturers to make sleeves of different lengths, enabled short men to keep their cuffs out of the soup. His name was Spencer Bull.

Spencer walked with a slight limp, and I was informed at the same time about his limp and his legend. He had acquired the limp by wrenching open an elevator door, theoretically immovable since the elevator was not at the same floor, a feat he could never have performed sober. He reached the bottom of the shaft without benefit of elevator and got off lightly with only the limp. Drunken men, it appears, fall gently, like flowers.

His legend concerned the story that caused him to be fired, which made his presence when I arrived so difficult to explain. I do not remember that he was there long. Perhaps he had been taken back temporarily in an emergency to fill a gap, inscribed on the payroll under a nom de plume (we were paid in cash, not checks), perhaps even as a proofreader: The image I retain of him from those days always shows him with a clutch of proofs in his hand.

Spencer Bull was a good reporter, but he had one failing. He lost the ability to distinguish between fact and fantasy when he had a snootful, and he had a snootful not infrequently. He had already lost a couple of jobs before he came to us from the *Paris Herald*. He had turned in there one day a story that he represented as being an exclusive interview with the president of the Republic, and exclusivity was indeed one of its qualities, although not the most striking. The city editor of the *Herald*, a relatively sober paper, read the story as far as the passage in which Spencer depicted himself as entering the courtyard of the Elysée Palace, to be hailed from a window with, "Come on up, Spencer," by the president, who received him in his bedroom, dressed in robin's egg blue pajamas. At this point the story went into the wastebasket and Spencer went to the cashier's window.

We hired him all the same, for he was quite an asset when sober, and he did his best to stay that way. He was unhorsed when the Prince of Wales made an official visit to Paris and Spencer was assigned to cover it.

It was an assignment of exquisite boredom—layings of cornerstones, visits to British hospitals, receptions of war veterans, garden parties for women in large floppy hats, and the like. On the first day Spencer trotted dutifully in the footprints of the prince, and discovered at the end that his exertions had been unnecessary. The British Embassy distributed to the press a mimeographed account of every gesture made by His Royal Highness, every word he had uttered, and every word that had been launched at him.

The Prince of Wales was known not to enjoy this sort of performance, but it was his job and he could not get out of it. Spencer did not enjoy it either, but though it was his job to report it, he saw in the embassy handout a means of getting out of most of it. Reconnaissance of the neighborhood disclosed a pleasant café where he might while away the time until the embassy press service had its report ready. On the second day, he abstained from personal duplication of the prince's wanderings, but repaired to his observation post in ample time to collect the official bulletin when it appeared. He had to wait a little longer than he had expected, and the inevitable ensued in his time at the café. Nevertheless he was in sufficiently good condition to collect his official information, return with it to the office, and address himself firmly to his typewriter. He pecked away at the keys slowly and with caution, for he wanted to remain in control of the situation, but when he reached the report of the prince's review of the British Boy Scout troop of Paris, creativity got the better of him. As it was reported to me, his story then ran on something like this:

"Stopping before one manly youth, the prince inquired, 'What is your name, my lad?' 'None of your God-damned business, sir,' the youngster replied. At this, the prince snatched a riding crop from his equerry's hand and beat the boy's brains out."

It was to the credit of the *Chicago Tribune* night staff that this work of art was processed with the utmost efficiency. The copyreader conscientiously corrected the placement of commas, rectified a few misspelled words, revised awkward phraseology, and handed the story to the night editor. Realizing its news value, this worthy marked it for a two-column head on page one. The headline writer found a happy formula: PRINCE OF WALES BASHES BOY'S BRAINS OUT WITH BLUDGEON. The French linotype operators, who understood little English, set it up, and the proofreaders corrected the typographical errors. The makeup editor fitted the story into the prominent position on the front page that it merited. The page was converted in the stereotyping room into papier-mâché and then reconverted into a curved metal plate that was bolted onto the press cylinder. The press began to roll, and the staff went home, content in the consciousness of duty well done. Everything, indeed, *had* been well done. The execution was perfect. The only flaw in the operation was that not one of the half-dozen people who had read the story was sufficiently sober to realize that it couldn't possibly be true.

The British Embassy was on the phone early next morning—*very* early next morning—and shortly thereafter a staff routed from bed scurried about Paris buying up every copy that could be found on the newsstands. They succeeded in rounding up most of the copies in Paris before they could stupefy the public, but nothing could be done about the papers that had been mailed to subscribers, or those sent to other cities in France or to other countries, including the British Isles. The Paris Edition did not appear on English newsstands for the next six months.

Spencer was of course out of a job again, but he lived happily on free booze and meals offered him by admirers who wanted to meet the man who had accused the Prince of Wales of murder.

Although I heard this tale from a good many witnesses, including Spencer himself, the more I thought about it, the more unbelievable it seemed. One day I set out to track it down. By hunting through the files of *Le Temps*, then the best paper in Paris, I was able to determine the time of the prince's visit to Paris and the exact day when he had reviewed the Boy Scouts. Armed with this information, I slipped into the publisher's office at night, when I knew it would be empty, and looked for the paper from the fatal date among the bound volumes containing every issue of the Paris Edition since its founding. The paper was missing from the file.

Stanley Grammar, the Cockney office boy of the Paris bureau of the *Chicago Tribune* Foreign News Service, led a hard life. Nobody talked about trauma in those days, but if they had, Stanley would have realized that he was being traumatized by the unseemly behavior of the Americans by whom he was surrounded. Transferred to Paris from the London bureau, Stanley may have suspected beforehand that Paris would be different from London, but he could hardly have imagined that the Yankees there would turn out to be even more barbarous than Britons expected them to be.

Stanley belonged to the generation before mine. He had already left the Paris bureau before I arrived, but I caught up with him later when I was transferred to the London bureau, to which Stanley had returned. The chief Paris correspondent when he took over his job was Vincent Sheehan and it was Sheehan who administered what was probably Stanley's first soul-shaking shock.

Sheehan had hurried breathlessly into the office, thrown himself at his typewriter, and had begun to hammer out a story. The subject turned out to be more obdurate than he had expected. He made a couple of false starts, tore the paper out of the typewriter, started all over again, and finally called Stanley in from the outer office.

"Stanley," he said, "this story is going to take longer than I thought. Run downstairs and tell the Prince of Wales to step across the street and have a drink at the Chope Cadet until I finish it. He's waiting in front of the door in a taxi."

Stanley's universe did a double back flip and left him gasping.

"Hi sye," he said, "you don't mean you left 'Is Ryle 'Ighness wytin' in a taxi!"

Then the only possible explanation washed over him in a reassuring wave and he assumed an appreciative smile.

"Aw," he announced comprehendingly. "You're pullin' my leg."

"Stop wasting time," Sheehan said, "and do what I told you."

Stanley crept down the stairs quaking, maintaining his courage by repeating to himself that it must be a joke. There was indeed a taxi in front of the door and seated in it was the Prince of Wales. One step short of swooning, Stanley managed to babble his awful message. "Quite," said the Prince of Wales, "thank you." And he headed across the street for the Chope Cadet.

Stanley staggered up five flights of stairs that seemed to be swaying in the wind and collapsed into his chair. It may have been at this moment that he initiated the maneuvers that eventually returned him to the London bureau and the safety of a country in which such horrors could not happen. He lasted, nevertheless, a while longer and suffered what was probably the second greatest shock of his Paris career.

The colonel's mother was in Paris, as she was only too frequently, in the opinion of the Paris staff, and her companion telephoned the office to ask that a cable be sent to the colonel. "Companion" was a euphemism. She was more of a guardian or nurse, with a smattering of psychiatric knowledge, strength enough to use force if necessary, and sufficient discretion not to do so. Mrs. McCormick was, to put it kindly, eccentric, and if her son and my master was in her opinion not quite right in the head, he might well have derived his oddities from Mrs. McCormick. She had been disappointed at his birth when her child turned out to be a boy since she had hoped for a girl to replace her daughter Katrina, who had died in infancy. If she was dissuaded with difficulty from naming him Katrina II, she could not be prevented from dressing him in girl's clothing until, at the age of seven, his tantrums became so violent that she had to resign herself to the fact that he was male.

The argument about his name may account for the fact that his official birth certificate gives none. It records the fact that a male infant had been born, but the space left for filling in its name remained blank. After the attempt to make him Katrina II was foiled, the child was called Robert Sanderson McCormick, for his father, whom Mrs. McCormick hated so wholeheartedly that she attempted to obliterate every reminder of him, including his name. When the future colonel was ten, she changed his name to Robert Rutherford McCormick, but even "Robert" was too reminiscent, so for years she obliged her son to sign his letters "Rutherford," especially those to her. Not until he became a grown man did the colonel venture to change his signature to "Robert R. McCormick." His mother shifted to "Bertie"; he had expressed a preference for "Bert," but she paid no attention to it.

The message the guardian wanted sent to the colonel was that his mother had just bought $50,000 worth of jewels: Should she send them back? Relaying this question must have given Stanley food for thought. This was the period when reporters were making $15 a week. I do not know what office boys were getting, but it would be a fair supposition that they earned less than reporters. Stanley may well have reflected bitterly that Mrs. McCormick, in a single shopping foray, had just spent at least a hundred times his yearly salary.

A little later in the afternoon the "companion" called again. Mrs. McCormick was lonely and wanted somebody to come over to keep her company. Hank Wales, then head of the Foreign News Service, was alone in the office. "Hell," he said, "I'm not going to spend the afternoon holding her hand. Stanley, you run over to the Ritz and jolly her along. Look out she doesn't bite you."

Stanley was delighted. The Ritz, no less! And a chance to win favor with the McCormick family! He sallied forth in higher spirits than would have been felt by any *Tribune* employees who had already been called upon to perform this chore. One of them was William Shirer, who told in *Twentieth-Century Journey* how he had on occasion been so afflicted, once taking down at Mrs. McCormick's dictation a long cable for the president of the United States—Abraham Lincoln. Shirer was less lucky in the quality of the refreshment provided for him than was Stanley. "The 'whisky' she offered me," he wrote, "turned out to be a concoction invented by her doctors which obviously looked and tasted to her like whisky but which had no alcohol and to me tasted like dishwater."

Stanley seems to have gotten the real thing. He was not used to much drinking, and as the afternoon wore on he grew happier and happier, and so did Mrs. McCormick. She seemed to be enjoying his company immensely, and Stanley allowed his mind to revel in rose-tinted fantasies about the heights to which he might rise in the *Chicago Tribune* thanks to the influence of its master's mother.

Came the moment when Mrs. McCormick's custodian appeared and made it plain that it was time to go. Stanley rose, a little unsteadily, and so did Mrs. McCormick. She insisted flatteringly on accompanying him to the head of the stairs that led to her second-story apartment. And there, after stepping back a pace or two for momentum, she plunged forward and dropkicked him neatly into the lobby.

Stanley regained the office with a swimming head and an aching back. The answer to the guardian's cable was lying on the desk. It read: LET HER KEEP THEM STOP FIFTY THOUSAND ISNT BIG MONEY.

¶

Send Over Some Fliers

¶

The Paris edition of the *Chicago Tribune* had no editor—or, rather, it had an editor, but he wasn't there. According to the masthead the editor of the paper was Colonel Robert Rutherford McCormick, a busy man who could hardly exercise daily supervision over us from the distance of Chicago. The Paris *New York Herald* did have a resident editor (who was also its publisher), Laurence Hills. There were people who did not look upon Larry Hills' capacities as outstanding, including Frank Munsey, who bought the *New York Herald* during Hills' incumbency, but left him in charge. "The Paris paper doesn't need a good editor," Munsey explained.

The hierarchy of the Paris *Chicago Tribune* started with a managing editor, Bernhard Ragner when I arrived. Number Two was the news editor, or night editor, Ralph Jules Frantz. Number Three was the city editor, or day editor, B. J. Kosposth. There were a few specialists, like the sports editor, Hérol Egan, and the finance editor, Virgil Geddes, soon to be supplanted by Dick King.

How did it happen that I was performing functions (I certainly did not have the title) of the news editor of the staff on August 23, 1927, only four months after I had joined the paper, and of the managing editor on the night of October 11, a month and a half later? I don't remember, but I can fix these dates because of the events that marked them: On the first, Sacco and Vanzetti were executed; on the second Ruth Elder fell into the sea in an unsuccessful attempt to be the first woman to fly the Atlantic.

I must in any case have been promoted from day staff to night staff very quickly, for I was already working at night two months after my debut, on June 29, another date identifiable by what happened on it—the transatlantic flight of Commander Richard Evelyn Byrd, an event not only in the history of aviation but also in the history of the ruthless competition between the *Paris Herald* and the Paris *Chicago Tribune*.

We were tense in the office that night. Byrd was somewhere over the ocean, but he had not been sighted. Press time was approaching and so was the time when his plane would run out of fuel, and there was no news of him at all. A rumor reached us that he had landed at the military airfield in the suburb of Issy-les-Moulineaux and I hopped into a taxi to investigate. The airfield was dark and deserted, and so was Issy. I had to phone the office to report that the rumor was false and went to a café. I got a male operator—this was long before the days of dialing—and when I gave the office number, he snarled at me.

"You're a German," he said.

"No, I'm not," I said. "I'm an American."

"You can't fool me," he said. "I know a German accent when I hear one. You're a German, and this is the anniversary of the day my brother was killed in the war. I'm not giving any numbers to Germans tonight."

And that was that.

(Thirty-five years later, talking over old times with William Shirer, I learned that he had an almost-identical experience the same night. The Foreign News Service had also heard a false rumor and Bill had sailed forth, in a different direction from mine, to run it down, with the same result. He was, however, luckier than I. His operator was a girl, who also balked at putting his call through, although I have forgotten why—it could hardly have been the same reason unless we assume that the entire French army had been wiped out a decade earlier. But Bill got both his number and a date with the girl.)

When I returned from Issy that night, the paper had gone to bed with no news from Byrd. The *Herald* had some. BYRD LANDS IN PARIS, a banner screamed from its front page, above a detailed account of the landing at Le Bourget. From it the reader could learn that the first person to reach the plane as it slowed to a stop was a reporter from the *Paris Herald*. The story told what he had asked Byrd and what Byrd had replied. It was expertly handled and there was only one thing wrong with it: At almost the same moment that the *Herald*'s presses were spewing out its copies, Byrd and his crew were struggling through the waves to the beach of Ver-sur-Mer in Normandy, off which they had ditched their plane.

In the *Herald* city room most of the staff had not yet had time to start home when a boy brought up a few mint copies, still damp with printer's ink, from the press room. Immediately someone rushed to the intercom and bawled, "Stop the presses!" and the staff clattered down the stairs to prevent any papers from leaving the building. They were too late: The trucks carrying papers for the Paris newspaper kiosks had disappeared. For the next five hours, everyone even remotely in the employ of the *Herald* was in the streets buying back all copies of the paper. The news dealers may have been baffled by the windfall, but it didn't displease them, especially as they received a little later a more conservative edition of the paper for their regular customers.

I heard about this monumental blooper early the next day and did a little sleuthing around the newsstands myself, but couldn't find a single copy carrying the *Herald*'s exclusive story. Our English rival, the *Continental Daily Mail*, did secure one, for at that time the *Herald* and the *Mail* were printed in the same building. The following day, the *Mail*, introducing its poisonous contribution to journalistic history with a single deadpan sentence, "The following story was printed yesterday by an American daily of Paris," reproduced the *Herald*'s story. And the day after that, we announced, "The following story was printed yesterday by the *Continental Daily Mail*," and republished the whole, including the *Mail*'s laconic introduction. We added one more line at the end: "The American daily of Paris which printed the above story was *not* the *Chicago Tribune*."

Well, all's fair in love, war, and newspaper competition, but it was somewhat unjust for the *Mail* and the *Tribune* to call the *Herald*'s mishap to public attention. To the newspaper reader, the *Herald* story must have seemed complete irresponsibility but it was actually the result of foresight and good technique, baffled at the last minute by an accident against which it had occurred to no one to take precautions. In the interests of speed, the *Herald* had prepared *two* front pages. The banner of one read, NO NEWS FROM BYRD; of the other, BYRD LANDS IN PARIS. When the deadline arrived, the French printers trundled the wrong page off to the presses.

There remained the detail of that imaginary interview with Byrd. If he *had* landed, was this fiction what the *Herald* intended to put before its readers?

It was not and had been written with no intention of seeing print. Its sole purpose was to serve as a measuring rod. The man who wrote the story could turn out the greater part of it in advance—he had at his disposal background information on the plane and its crew, the cable from New York describing the takeoff, and the telephoned report of his own man at Le Bourget, where Byrd was awaited. The only thing he could not prepare in advance was the story of the actual arrival. This would have to be written at the last moment, if the landing occurred, and it had to be the lead—the first few paragraphs of the story. Space would have to be left so that this information could be inserted when it became available, but how much space? The writer estimated this by writing an imaginary lead, inventing the sort of detail that might happen. This was composed and placed in the page form to allow the printers to complete the time-consuming process of justifying the page—wedging the type tight so that when the page was locked and lifted from the form it could not drop out. If Byrd had landed, this lead would have been removed from the page and replaced by the same number of lines, giving the actual facts. The writer saw no harm in allowing his imaginary reporter a scoop, for he knew his flight of fancy would never be printed. Unfortunately, it was.

At the *Chicago Tribune* our chief souvenir of the Byrd flight was a masterpiece of the news photographer's art, brought back from Ver-sur-Mer by the *Tribune*-owned Atlantic and Pacific Photo Service and never published. It showed, in the foreground, a sturdy Norman peasant woman, the traditional local bonnet on her head, striding along the sidewalk, complete indifference frozen into her strong features. Beyond her, Byrd and his three companions, backs to the camera, were lined up at what was hardly more than a token urinal, a simple groove in the pavement along a building wall. I doubt if any other photographer ever caught the commander in a mood so literally unbuttoned.

Our photographers seemed to have gotten along very well with the aviators. The photographers staggered into the office late in the evening, and one of them exclaimed feelingly, "I hope to God they send over some *sober* fliers next time."

Surely Lindbergh had been sober enough to meet anybody's standards, and I think it safe to suggest that transatlantic flying as a rule is not compatible with addiction to the bottle. There was, it is true, a lack of sobriety associated with this sport in 1927, but it was not the fliers who were guilty, it was the volunteer reception committees that flocked out to Le Bourget time and again to wait for aviators who never arrived. The waiting was a cheerful process. There seemed to be false alarms at Le Bourget about once a week, and the bar there had never been so prosperous. It had to increase its staff to handle the crowds, which seemed always to include the broad shoulders of Hemingway and the scarlet beret of "Brett." Airplane-watching had become a fashionable activity even though none of the heralded fliers turned up. One pair overshot the mark—Charles Levine and Clarence Chamberlin, who landed in a field in Germany—and others undershot it, as was the case for George Haldeman and Ruth Elder, who was trying to be the first woman to fly the Atlantic.

Ruth Elder, whose plane was appropriately named the *American Girl*, came down safely in the sea more than two hundred miles off the Azores on October 11, 1927, or fifty years to the day before her death was reported in the papers of October 11, 1977. I do not know how it happened that I was in the composing room making up the paper on the night when she failed in her attempt to become the female Lindbergh. It was Frantz' night off, which accounted for one of the two persons who outranked me, but normally when Frantz was not there, Ragner should have been; perhaps he had gone off early to catch his bus, leaving a cub of six months' experience to run the paper.

I don't know why Paris continued to be the goal of transatlantic fliers unless it was that Lindbergh had established a fashion, but in any case I deserted the plane watchers of Le Bourget in the spring of 1928, when I entered the Foreign News Service and was transferred to the London bureau of the *Chicago Tribune*, in a country that did not attract the ocean crossers, except Amelia Earhart, who came down at Burry Port, Wales, but not on purpose. When I returned to Paris two years later, the recurrent treks to Le Bourget had ended, but there was still one exploit to be achieved, Paris-New York uphill—in other words, east-west, against the prevailing winds.

Charles Nungesser and François Coli had died in the attempt to make this crossing in 1927, but two other Frenchmen, Dieudonné Costes and Maurice Bellonte, were preparing to risk it in 1930. I would not ordinarily have gone to Le Bourget to see them off, for a dawn departure was too late to get into the Paris Edition, but Shirer was covering it for the Foreign News Service, so I went along to keep him company. The field was dark and deserted, except for a cluster of busy people around the plane, which had been named, in a spirit of bravado, the *Question Mark*.

Most of them were mechanics and the others had some official connection with the flight, except for a few journalists like ourselves. We were talking to the two fliers when we became aware of another small group approaching. When it got near enough to be inspected in the morning light it turned out to be composed of a woman in deep mourning, surrounded by an escort that seemed to constitute a guard of honor. It was Madame Nungesser, widow of the pilot who had taken off from this same field on this same mission three years earlier and had never been heard from again.

She was led to the pilots and formally introduced to them. I do not know who had conceived the lugubrious idea of bringing her to the field to encourage the pilots, but if they were sensitive to evil omens, they had one in Madame Nungesser. French mourning was thorough in those days, and Madame Nungesser was a weeping willow of black crepe, which enshrouded her head and fell to a level that swept the ground. Her presence alone would have daunted most men, and the atmosphere was not lightened by a series of small mishaps.

The first occurred when the two pilots tried to insert themselves into the cockpit. The plane was open to the air, with no door. Perhaps the idea was to make it possible to get out quickly in case the plane was forced down at sea but, if so, this purpose had not been furthered by barring the doorway with two taut crossed wires in the form of the letter X. Bellonte, a thin man, managed to squeeze through the open side of the X without too much difficulty, but Costes, who was huskily built, made it only at the cost of a struggle that took long enough to allow a plane ample time to sink if he had been trying to perform this feat in reverse.

The realization that he couldn't get out in a hurry must have alarmed him a minute later when a tongue of flame suddenly licked into the air from the upper surface of the wing. We all gasped since everyone knew that the plane was a flying gas tank, for it needed all the fuel it could lift off the ground to be able to reach New York. A mechanic was still standing on the wing and he slapped out the fire with his cloth cap: A little gasoline had been spilled in refueling. I don't know if this small reminder of danger had shaken the pilots' nerves, but it shook mine.

Costes began testing the controls. He pulled back a lever that should have been answered by the turning of a section of the rudder. Nothing budged. Mechanics threw themselves at the defective control and discovered that the wire between the lever and the rudder had snapped. While they busied themselves installing a new wire, I saw Henri Farman, builder of the plane, talking through the wire-crossed door to the two pilots. I could catch only snatches of their conversation, but I gathered that Costes was complaining that the complete check of the plane that had just been finished could not have been very efficient if so grave a defect had escaped notice, and suggesting that the flight should be postponed until the plane could be gone over again, thoroughly, in the pilots' presence. A puff of wind blew in my direction, and I thought I heard Farman say, "But you *can't* put it off now!" Whatever the gist of the argument, the departure was not put off. The mechanics backed away, Costes tried the lever again, and the rudder moved obediently.

The propeller was yanked into motion and the engine burst into a spluttering roar. As soon as it had settled to a steady beat, the plane began moving slowly down the field. It seemed to me a perilously short warm-up, but I supposed the fliers wanted to save every drop of gasoline for the Atlantic.

We held our breaths and watched. We knew the plane was carrying a load of fuel so heavy that even with everything working perfectly it was a gamble whether it could get off the ground. We knew too that if the plane once lifted from the ground and had to touch down again, its landing gear would buckle under the weight of its fuel. We knew finally that a brook or ditch—I have forgotten which—ran across the end of the field and if the plane wasn't off the ground by the time it reached it, the plane would crash. Visibility was slight, and it was difficult, through the dim light, to see whether the plane, diminishing in the distance, was lifting or not. When it reached the point where we judged the brook to be, we had still not seen it leave the ground. It had, though, by a matter of inches.

It turned, in the widest possible sweep, to hold itself as close as possible to the horizontal, and struggled back toward us, only a few feet off the ground. We could feel the fight of the engine trying to take it higher.

89

There was a windbreak of low trees at this end of the field and once again we watched in anguish as it approached them. From where we stood it did not look as though it would clear them. The plane must have brushed their tops as it crossed the barrier and faded from sight, wallowing rather than flying, as it gained altitude inch by inch.

The tenseness of the scene had given Shirer good material for a color story, and I accompanied him to the Western Union office while he wrote it. It was on its way before eight o'clock in the morning—one o'clock at night in Chicago—time to catch the last city edition, and Shirer went off to bed content. He was less so when he awoke, turned on the radio, and learned that the *Question Mark* had landed—at Le Bourget. Costes and Bellonte had turned back.

The official explanation was that they had reached the latitude of the Azores when they ran into headwinds so strong that they judged it would be impossible to reach New York. I suspected that Farman had lost the argument at Le Bourget that he thought he had won, and that Costes and Bellonte had decided not to risk the crossing in a plane they thought unready. They may very well have simply flown in circles over the sea, not too far from shore, until they had used up enough gas to land safely, and then come wisely home. If they had done otherwise, they might have joined Nungesser and Coli in posthumous glory. As it was, they were still alive on September 2, 1930, to set their plane down in New York, the first to have flown the Atlantic from east to west.

¶
C'est Fini

¶

A France that in May 1927 had loved all Americans because of Charles Lindbergh, in August 1927 hated all Americans because of Judge Webster Thayer of Massachusetts.

Any regular reader of the Paris edition of the *Chicago Tribune* during the last few months before the execution of Sacco and Vanzetti would have been forced to conclude that the editorial page and the news columns offered ample evidence of a split personality. Our editorials and our news reports both gave bad marks to the state of Massachusetts, but for exactly opposite reasons. The colonel fulminated against the courts of Massachusetts for being so dilatory about dispatching from this world two men who, guilty or not, could easily be spared. The news printed in the same paper suggested that Massachusetts had not presented a convincing case for punishing them at all for the murder of two payroll deliverers in Braintree seven years earlier.

The colonel's point of view was expressed on our editorial page about once a week, through editorials that had already been printed in Chicago and were then mailed to us with a broad blue A scrawled on them personally by the colonel, which meant that they had to be printed at the earliest opportunity. They suggested that whether Sacco and Vanzetti were guilty of murder was now beside the point (but the colonel had, of course, no doubt that they were guilty; they were anarchists, weren't they?). They were in any case guilty of wasting the time of the courts and consequently the money of the taxpayers by their obstinate resistance to letting themselves be executed like conscientious citizens. The colonel's editorials were reinforced by Alex Small's column, which also ran on the editorial page. Alex agreed with the colonel on Sacco and Vanzetti as, indeed, he agreed with him on everything—not out of servility, but because his thinking ran in the same ruts.

The news columns did not present the opposite opinion from the editorial page since it is not the business of news reports to present opinions, but to present facts. But opinions are, or so one hopes, based on facts, and the facts we were printing, almost daily as the denouement of the Sacco-Vanzetti affair drew near, seemed to me to be capable of leading to only one opinion, and it was not that of the colonel. They had led, indeed, to the almost unanimous belief of the staff that in all probability two innocent men were being railroaded to cover up the inability of the Massachusetts police to solve the Braintree murders, but that even if they were guilty, the trial had been so manifestly unfair that in common decency the state should have abandoned what had become more of a persecution than a prosecution.

Though this was our opinion, based, it may be pertinent to point out, on the facts cabled to us by the colonel's own news-gathering organization, I am in a position to attest that our news stories were not written with the objective of supporting any preconceived point of view, for I was writing them myself, and my conscience is clear.

It was something of a mystery to me at the time why the colonel permitted his Paris Edition to continue to print, day after day, news stories that knocked the ground from under his own violently expressed opinions. I suppose either that he didn't read our news stories or that he considered the juridical misdeeds reported in them to be quite normal. The colonel had never permitted facts to get in the way of his opinions, and no doubt he didn't realize that anyone else might.

As the date fixed for the execution drew closer, the temperature rose in France, as it did all over the world. Ambassador Herrick advised the president to intervene in the interests of French-American relations and leading statesmen in other European countries made similar appeals for clemency.

The *Paris Herald*, fearing violence if Sacco and Vanzetti were executed, asked for and received police protection. We didn't, not necessarily because we were any braver, but either because it occurred to nobody or because we thought an avenging party would never find us. For outsiders, the Paris Edition was at night a fortress of inaccessibility. The *Herald*, then situated in the rue du Louvre, fronted on the street and had a ground-floor office. But for the *Chicago Tribune*, even in daytime, its front door was a back door, a narrow opening on the rue Lamartine, easy to miss; when you did get inside there were five flights to climb. At night even this door was locked. To reach the city room, it was necessary to enter, on the rue Lafayette, where no sign betrayed our presence, the building of the *Petit Journal*, our landlord and printer. It was then necessary to thread a labyrinth leading through the *Petit Journal*'s complicated print shop and mount to our level.

The value of this protection became dubious when the Communist daily, *l'Humanité*, asked if it might send a reporter to our office on the night of the execution to listen to our cabled reports as they came in and telephone their gist to *l'Humanité*. The paper, apparently no recipient of Moscow's gold, couldn't afford to pay for cable service. Getting the confirmation of the execution direct from us would enable it to get to work on the story half an hour or even an hour earlier than if the staff waited for its own news agency bulletins, which were delivered by bicycle.

A series of last-minute stays caused the Communist reporter to become a frequent visitor so that by the time of the actual execution he had mastered the route so thoroughly that he might easily have led an avenging party straight to us, if he had so desired. He did not look as if he harbored any bloodthirsty designs. He was a small diffident man, of cordial manners, named Schwarz, chosen for this task no doubt because he spoke good English.

On the night when the execution seemed finally inevitable, Schwarz phoned to ask if he might bring along a few members of the Communist Sacco-Vanzetti Defense Committee to wait for the news. We agreed, but when the delegation arrived, we wondered if we had not been imprudent. Nowadays a French Communist party meeting could easily be mistaken for a convention of certified public accountants, but in 1927 it was different. We had been misled by the disarming appearance of Schwarz, who was probably the party's emissary to the bourgeoisie. He looked and dressed like anybody else, but his comrades were thoroughly committed to the principle that they were revolutionaries, honor-bound to act the part. It was clear that the items the well-dressed Communist would wear did not include ties. These bourgeois adornments had been replaced by rags, appropriately grimy, knotted scarflike around the neck. Hats were bourgeois too. Our guests wore shapeless cloth caps, dirty also, and one or two sizes too large. None of them actually held a bomb in the hand or clenched a dagger between the teeth, but their clothes were loose enough to conceal these accessories, in case they felt a massacre in our office would be an appropriate reaction to the execution.

We placed a row of chairs along the wall for them, and they sat down, keeping their caps on, as though they wanted to be ready at any moment to make their escape from hostile territory. They may not have been afraid of us, but we were certainly afraid of them.

Perhaps I was sitting in the slot that night because I had been writing the Sacco-Vanzetti stories from the beginning and would be writing the last one. The slot was the most convenient place from which to answer the telephone and take down the cables that informed us, step by step, of the progress of the grisly performance that was unwinding on the other side of the Atlantic. As each dispatch arrived, I translated it for the benefit of the Communists, who sat against the wall, silent and motionless. We were silent too. Typing had stopped. No news seemed of any importance any longer, except the one piece of information we were all waiting for. And at last it came.

"Messieurs, c'est fini," I announced. The Communists rose silently, expressionless still, Schwarz thanked us, and they filed quietly out.

L'Humanité appeared next day with an electric chair superimposed on an American flag covering most of the front page. A demonstration of protest was called for that evening, not by the Communists alone, but by almost all parties except the extreme right. Its organizers announced a march up the avenue des Champs-Elysées, for maximum visibility, after which it was the intention to turn down the avenue d'Iéna to the American Embassy at its foot.

I stationed myself on the Champs-Elysées almost at its end at the Arch of Triumph, to witness for the first time the French police outnumbered by a hostile crowd that might at any moment explode into violence. The operation was a masterpiece of technique. A military field telephone had been set up in the shadow of the Arch of Triumph and from its switchboard the prefect of police directed his troops from listening posts at every street corner.

Tens of thousands of marchers were moving up the incline towards us, filling the broad avenue from one sidewalk to the other. When the first

94

cross street was reached, the police threw a barrier across the avenue, diverting the protesters into the side street, at whose far end another squad of police closed it off. As the street filled, part of the police on the Champs-Elysées sealed off the avenue end of the street, while the rest drew back to let the marchers continue. At each crossing the operation was repeated, and the sea of protesters grew smaller at each intersection. Bit by bit, the main body was broken up into isolated units, each of them surrounded by police. There was no violence and nobody reached the embassy.

¶

3, rue de l' Ancienne Comédie

¶

The weather was pleasant so, as we often did when the temperature permitted, we were taking after-lunch coffee in the garden of Hemingway's *pension de famille*, under the benevolent protection of the Panthéon, whose dome towered majestically beyond our wall. I had chosen to sit under a tree, a presumption resented by its occupants, one of whom proceeded to bomb me—a pigeon, judging from the caliber. Young, sensitive, and conscious of the presence of the landlady's beautiful daughter, I blushed to the roots of my mistreated hair. In a desperate effort at diversion, spying a turtle crawling along the garden path, I picked it up. It promptly discharged a powerful stream over my trousers.

"Why, Monsieur Root," said the landlady's beautiful daughter, "what a curious effect you have on animals!"

It was evident that any chance I might have had for becoming a romantic figure in her eyes had been forever ruined, so I moved.

Of course, this wasn't the real reason for changing addresses. I had by then been promoted to the night staff, and the hours of a worker for morning papers are not compatible with the schedule of a *pension de famille*. I did not move far, about a block and a half, into a small hotel on the rue Monsieur-le-Prince, where I immediately acquired the status of leading client by having a rented piano installed in my room: This was the Latin Quarter, where the arts were held in high esteem in 1927. My arrival leading the way for two burly individuals packing the piano on their backs up a flight of stairs earned me the same consideration as if I had registered at the Ritz, requesting accommodations also for my chauffeur, maid, and manservant.

The hotel on the rue Monsieur-le-Prince was no Ritz, but it was a friendly place in a pleasant neighborhood half a block from the Luxembourg Gardens, a neighborhood well provided with food available to those with $60-a-month incomes. Across the square created by the encounter of the boulevard St. Michel with the Luxembourg Gardens a small Polish restaurant supplied quite decent food in spite of its being the cheapest I then knew in Paris—five and a half francs, prix fixe, for a full meal, including a quarter carafe of the house wine and all the bread you wanted to eat. (That was a detail worth noting in those days, when in any establishment that did not display the sign *Pain à discretion* the waitress would inscribe on the bill an amount equivalent to the number of slices of bread you had eaten.) Five and a half francs was twenty-two cents, but big spenders might splurge as much as a franc for the tip. The same square also harbored a comparatively aristocratic restaurant that served one of the best onion soups in Paris, but it was expensive—as much as sixty cents a meal, or even a dollar if you went in for château-bottled wines.

I do not remember why I did not move half a block farther in the same direction into the Hôtel de Lisbonne, at the corner of the rue Monsieur-le-Prince and the rue de Vaugirard, a picturesque if squalid place that was one of the two gathering points for the staff of the Paris Edition. (It is still there, but has since undergone sandblasting and other hygienic and face-lifting operations.) About half of us lived there, a convenience for borrowing clothes, money, and, on occasion, girls. A sort of buttress of thick masonry protruded from one edge of the building to keep it from falling down, but this seemed to me a superfluous precaution: Its thick coating of grime should have sufficed to hold it together and upright. I had assumed that so much dirt must have been an accumulation dating from the Middle Ages, but this could not have been the case, for Jacques Hillairet's exhaustive *Dictionnaire historique des rues de Paris* alleges that it was built only in the eighteenth century; it must have made a determined effort to acquire so much dirt in a mere two centuries.

William Shirer, one of the staff members who lived there, wrote in his *Twentieth Century Journey* that it bore a plaque recording the fact that both Baudelaire and Verlaine had lived there, which I do not remember, and neither does Monsieur Hillairet, who does record that in 1900 the building harbored a restaurant where the waitresses were "easily conquered Venuses dressed in tight-fitted jerseys." In 1927 the hotel no

97

longer boasted a restaurant and consequently provided no Venuses, so the clients were obliged to import their own. Many of them did, either on a short-term or long-term basis.

The Hôtel de Lisbonne was built around a central court inhabited only by garbage cans. When crossing the court, it was advisable to keep to its center: Lodgers had a habit of disposing of waste, of whatever kind, by tossing it out the window, with cheerful disregard for the possibility that somebody might be underneath. The hotel's interior was laid out in long dank corridors with rows of doors opening into the cells on either side, as in a prison. Each corridor was lighted by a single bare bulb, suspended from the middle of the ceiling, of fractional candlepower. The bulbs burned out frequently.

The plumbing was primitive. Any request for a room with bath would have been received by the management with incredulity. If you wanted to bathe, you could go across the street to a handy establishment dedicated to that purpose, where for five and a half francs you would be provided with soap, towels, and a bathtub containing as much hot water as the employee could be persuaded to measure out into the tub. The charge was per person and several of the bathrooms were provided with two tubs, for conviviality. A considerable proportion of the population of Paris did its bathing in such premises at this period since private bathrooms were rare except for the well-to-do.

The Hôtel de Lisbonne had no bathroom, except for the one in which the proprietor stored coal, but every room had a washbowl with running water, under which was tucked that indispensable article of French hygiene, the bidet. Each floor was provided, for community use, with what was called a Turkish toilet, a sort of sink with its open end set level with the floor. No doubt a civil engineer had been employed to determine the optimum distances between the hole in the bottom and the two islands on either side of it designed to provide standing room for the feet, but it was obvious that no hydraulic engineer had been called into consultation, for he would have been capable of adjusting the inrush of water when the chain was pulled to permit getting off the islands onto the mainland before the tide reached the ankle-tops. These primitive toilets had been fitted, in the interests of economy, with a device that turned on the light only after you shot the bolt, and switched it off again when you pushed it back to leave.

Once, as I shoved the bolt home, I felt a slight electric shock, whose dire potentialities did not occur to me immediately. I registered the fact that the lock had developed a short circuit and went about my business. When I tried to get out, however, I found it impossible to open the door; each time I touched the bolt it delivered a shock that prevented me from taking hold of it. I tried to fool it by using momentum, punching at it from a distance, but electricity reacts faster than I do, and the shock stopped me in full flight every time. Failures of current were not infrequent in Paris in those days, but I felt unwilling to remain in my prison until the next time a power station had difficulties, so I had recourse to my own engineering knowledge, which was slight but included a chapter on insulation. In desperation I wrapped my handkerchief as thickly as possible around my fingers, and it worked.

A place of period plumbing should not have been expected to offer what came close to being a luxury in Paris in those days, central heating, but it did. It had other advantages too. Being an old building, its ceilings were high, so once you escaped from the corridor into your room, you were gratified by a feeling of spaciousness. The wallpaper was hideous but was partly covered by bookcases fixed to the walls, a convenience rare even in luxury hotels. This was the Latin Quarter, whose main street was the nearby boulevard St. Michel, so many of its clients were students, who needed room for books, and were not short-term lodgers, but tenants for the entire school year. The Tribuners were all-year lodgers and many of them had lived at the Lisbonne for several years.

The fidelity of our staff to the Lisbonne may have resulted first of all from the most convincing of its advantages—it was cheap, ten dollars a month. This could not have been its whole charm, however. Perhaps for the *Tribune* staff one of its attractions was what nobody had yet thought of giving the name of "togetherness." Shirer had lived there when he was working on the Paris Edition, but when his entry into the Foreign News Service made him richer he continued to live there. Indeed, he even kept his room when he was not in Paris. The Foreign News Service job frequently sent him on distant assignments, sometimes fairly long ones, but he paid the rent in his absence, to be sure of having his room ready and waiting when he came back. This was quixotic behavior even for Americans who, as every Frenchman knew, were all millionaires. It must have lain heavily on the conscience of the hotel, a sinful waste that violated every rule of good sense by leaving rentable space unoccupied. The management resorted to improvisation to rectify an immoral situation and as a result, Shirer, returning late one night from an assignment that had ended more quickly than he anticipated, found a stranger sleeping in his bed.

Soon I moved again, to an apartment more primitive even than the Hôtel de Lisbonne—and the rent was higher. I have never been happier with a home. While my new address was short on creature comforts, it was long on everything needed to nourish the soul.

I shared the place for a few months during the early part of my occupancy with a Mexican painter, José Pavon, who had been a friend of mine in New York and had turned up in France shortly after I did. Sharing the apartment permitted me to meet the ruinous rent, $16 a month. By the time José decided to spend his year in France painting in the light of the south, I had had a raise and was able to support the staggering burden on my own.

Sixteen dollars a month was sixty percent more than the rate at the Hôtel de Lisbonne in terms of money, but my new place must have been at least one hundred percent dearer if you took into account its liabilities. Like the Lisbonne it had Turkish toilets, but on the floor below. The Lisbonne had central heating but I had a potbellied iron stove in one of my two rooms, which I could feed at my own expense and tend with my own muscles, and no means of heating the bedroom at all.

The Lisbonne had electric light but I had a gas lamp, which on inspection turned out to be broken, suspended from the ceiling in one room; I could always buy candles for the bedroom. The Lisbonne had running hot water but I had what was alternatively the kitchen sink and the washbasin, with one cold-water faucet emptying into it. While the inhabitants of the Lisbonne had to resort to a bathhouse across the street, I could bathe on my own premises on days when I was agile enough. My sink stood in a small alcove opening off one side of the bedroom; under it was the inevitable portable bidet. Beside that was a shelf-table attached to the wall, with two gas burners on top—my kitchen—and, underneath that, my bath—a round tin tub, which, pulled out into the bedroom, could be half-filled with water brought to a lukewarm state over the gas burners. I then stepped in and soaped myself standing, since the tub was not big enough to sit in. The rest of my bathing equipment consisted of an oversize tin funnel whose lower end was stoppered by a cork pierced with several holes. Naked, soaped, and shivering, I now bent over quickly, scooped up a funnel-full of water and, working fast, tried to get it in a useful position over my head before the water could escape. The shower's output was feeble, but in half a dozen tries, rinsing could usually be achieved. This experience taught me that at heart I valued cleanliness: Anyone who takes this much trouble to bathe must really want to.

There was another disadvantage about my new quarters to which, being young and vigorous, I paid no attention at the time: There were six flights to climb, the last of them somewhat rickety, more like a stepladder than a flight of stairs. My apartment must have been an afterthought—tacked onto the roof a century or two after the rest of the building was finished—entered, via the steps, through a hole chopped in the ceiling. There were a few elevators on the Right Bank in those days, but it was an invention that had certainly not reached the Left.

Such was the equipment of my new apartment, which in the cold calculating eyes of real estate men would have been seen as making it less valuable than a room at the Hôtel de Lisbonne. But how do you fix the rate for a view? How do you put a figure on romance and history? And what price picturesqueness?

Picturesqueness! The place was steeped in it. It was not an ordinary apartment, but an artist's studio, with one wall almost all glass, an authentic artist's skylight even though it faced west, not north. From it I looked over the rooftops of Paris with, in the foreground, the perfectly proportioned old stone tower of St. Germain des Prés and, in the background, the Eiffel Tower. The view from the bedroom window was even better. It commanded one of the oldest parts of Paris, whose roofs in 1927 still looked like those of a village, covered with red tiles and bristling with chimneys, each enclosing a tight bundle of pale red tubes, one for each fireplace. The houses were clustered around narrow winding medieval streets. The backdrop was the cathedral of Notre Dame.

Even the address sounded picturesque—3, rue de l'Ancienne Comé-die. The Comédie Française had been situated here, on the other side of the street, for about a century, starting in 1689. In earlier times the rue de l'Ancienne Comédie, not yet under that name, and perhaps with no name at all, had been nothing but a path beaten out by the wooden shoes of peasants rounding the wall built there in 1209 by Philip Augustus; today it runs toward the Seine from the boulevard St. Michel. Five doors down on my side of the street, at no. 13, was its most famous establishment after the Comédie, or even including it, for it was older—the Café Procope, where, in 1670, a Sicilian named Francesco Procopio del Cotillo opened a café and introduced the Parisian public to coffee, an exotic import from Italy. It was perhaps also the first place in Paris to serve sherbet. The café is operating still, with plaques on some of its chairs indicating the spots that the management is willing you should think were regularly occupied by Voltaire, Diderot, Danton, Balzac, and other notables during its three-hundred-year history.

I had rented the studio from a young painter who wanted to glean some income from it while he spent a year or two in South America. He left be-hind a studio full of fascinating objects, of which the least strange re-minded me of my childhood days in New England—a hemisphere glass paperweight with a toy village inside it, which, when I picked the ball up, was suddenly engulfed in a snowstorm. It was the Surrealists who had rediscovered, and made a fad of, *boules de neige*. The Surrealists were also enthusiastic about African art. It was perhaps their influence again that accounted for two of the most striking objects in a studio strewn with unpredictable artifacts—a pair of wooden African statuettes, aggres-sively male and female. Another ornament abandoned to my care pleased me mightily—a life-size, articulated wooden artist's mannequin. A raised platform against the wall opposite the window was occupied by a divan, which served as a bed for José, who was good enough to leave the bed-room to me.

Once settled in my new home, I led a life of unbroken enchantment, whose every day began well and ended well. The beginning came late in the morning, when I arose, pulled up a flap that hung hinged under the great studio window for a table, and had my breakfast of fluffy croissants, or brioches yellow with egg, café au lait, a piece of cheese, and often, for

I had not yet renounced the heresy of my first day in Paris, a glass of white wine (I had still not graduated from the sweet Barsac), enjoying with ineffable pleasure the view spread out below of my most precious possession, Paris. The end started at 2:30 A.M., after the paper had been put to bed, when I set out, as I did every night, whatever the weather, on the walk of a mile or a mile and a half from my place of work on the Right Bank to my place of abode on the Left.

The streets around the *Petit Journal*, when I emerged from the office, were dark and deserted, except occasionally when a newspaper delivery truck rounded the corner carrying our words to the waiting millions (a figurative term since our circulation was eight thousand). This did not last long. One block down the rue Cadet and I was spilled into the rue du Faubourg Montmartre, all glitter and bright lights, where all the buildings seemed to house cafés except the Casino de Paris, which was trying to be the Folies-Bergère, and all the cafés were full. The streets were full too, vibrant with girls, girls, and more girls.

The abrupt change from the subdued darkness of the rue Cadet to the garish brilliance of the rue du Faubourg Montmartre was repeated with equal abruptness in the opposite direction when I crossed the Grands Boulevards into the rue Montmartre proper (the change in name preserved the memory of the time when the walls of Paris stood where the boulevards are now, and what lay beyond them were suburbs—*faubourgs*). This was the least-interesting part of the walk, through a street uninteresting even in daylight. Lined by low, dingy, unkempt buildings, it was improved by the dark. For a few blocks I would see no one and hear nothing except my own footsteps plodding through a deadened city. Then, on the left, the first light would appear. It burned breezily behind a counter at a shop front open to the air, where I stopped and ordered *un cornet de frites*. The stout red-faced woman behind the counter (stouter in winter when she padded herself with several layers of clothing) snatched a half-page of newspaper from a pile prepared in advance, rolled it deftly into a cone with one hand, while with the other she scooped up a liberal portion of fried potatoes (*French* fried potatoes if you are not in France) from the pot of bubbling oil beside her, poured them into the cone, agitated a huge tin saltshaker over them, passed the cone to me, and accepted payment (one franc), all in a single sweeping motion. I proceeded on my way, burning my mouth every few steps with a piece of potato. My speed was so uniform that the potatoes always lasted precisely to the middle of the first bridge across the Seine, where I confided to the river the task of delivering my *cornet* to the Atlantic.

The potato vendor was the prelude to the highlight of my nightly promenade, the crossing of Les Halles. The Central Markets are there no longer, having been moved out of the city to provide staler and more expensive food for Paris, but long before they moved they had lost most of the glamour they possessed in the 1920s and 1930s. It seemed to me that the tourists who in the 1950s and 1960s made the ritual visit to Les Halles at four or five in the morning, to savor its bustle and eat the traditional onion soup in one of the restaurants on their outskirts, were only continuing from force of habit a pilgrimage that had lost its objective, for the spectacle of Les Halles had dulled, like a play that has been running for too long but, because of its reputation, continues to be performed nightly to an undiscriminating audience by listless actors who are bored to death with it. The last time I made the predawn visit to Les Halles with visitors from America must have been in the 1950s and the experience saddened me.

I could see nothing particularly inspiring about piles of crates whose contents were mostly invisible. In 1927 it had occurred to nobody to hide fruit and vegetables, objects that had inspired artists for centuries, behind wooden slats. Unpackaged vegetables and fruit covered the sidewalks, formed by skillful and loving hands into colorful masterpieces of edible architecture—red pyramids (radishes), green cubes (cabbages), purple parallelepipeds (eggplants). The strong men of the markets *(les forts des Halles)* did not propel their loads across the streets on mechanized scooters but built them up into mountains piled on shelves strapped to their backs. In the 1950s the streets were blocked by phalanxes of trucks, but in the 1920s most of the vehicles were horse-drawn farm carts, driven by the same men who had raised the produce and picked it that very morning before daylight so that Paris could have fresh food from the market gardens that encircled it—white beans from Noyon, asparagus from Argenteuil, peas from Clamart, string beans from Bagnolet, cauliflowers from Arpajon, carrots from Crécy. The fields where they grew are buried now under the dormitory suburbs of Paris.

What the farmers did not bring to market themselves was picked up on a circular route and delivered to the heart of the Halles by what the marketmen called "the Argenteuil Express," a ridiculous little huffing and puffing steam-powered train that added to the bedlam of shouting, neighing, and backfiring truck motors a frantic clanging of its bell and blowing of its whistle in a usually futile attempt to clear a few inches of track before it.

The track belonged in the daytime to the Paris tramway system, which abandoned it at night. Paris still had trams then, also operated by bell-clanging maniacs, called, in idiomatic French, *les wattmans*, even when they were women, as they frequently were. By dint of enormous efforts, the train did manage to inch its way forward, puff by puff, through what seemed the fissureless seething of farm carts, farm trucks, and heavily laden porters, who, being unequipped with bells or whistles, gave no warning except abuse as they thrust their way through the crowd with brutal force, denting backs and crushing feet on their way. It was all chaotic, and exciting, and it continued until, under a lightening sky, a bell tolled for the end of trading, as it had tolled in this same place and at this same hour for centuries. At its voice the tramps rushed in to make off with the unsold and unsalable remainders of the day's plenty, which had become their property at the sounding of the bell. The word for bell in French is *cloche*, and it is because of this old custom that the bums of Paris are called *clochards* today.

My exit from Les Halles was less silent than my approach to it, for between the market and the Seine, at the hour when I passed, belated farm carts were still rumbling toward their goal. Once I had crossed the Seine-side street and moved onto the bridge, silence returned, majestic silence, the silence of emptied time. The centuries had dropped away and I stood in the Paris of the Middle Ages. I was alone on the bridge, sole occupant of the calm of bygone ages, the ancient pointed twin towers of the Conciergerie regarding me from the other side of the river, silhouetted against the brightening sky if it were summer, barely discernible in winter.

I passed onto the Ile de la Cité, the Palace of Justice on my right and in a moment, on my left, rising beyond the open place before it, appeared the rich facade and the strong truncated towers of Notre Dame. In the silence and the dusk before dawn nothing was visible of the modern city, only the ancient towers of the Palace of Justice and of Notre Dame, and it was possible for a moment to believe that you had arrived in the Middle Ages.

Only for a moment, though. Across the second bridge, and I was again plunged into light and gaiety, that of the place St. Michel and its boulevard, where students seemed never to go to sleep. If I felt like joining the fun, I continued up the boulevard St. Michel to its junction with the boulevard St. Germain, usually stopping on the way for a beer at a sidewalk café. More often, still under the spell of the serenity of the first bridge and the calm of the Ile de la Cité, I struck off diagonally across the small square of St. André des Arts, behind the place St. Michel, and followed the silent, narrow, ancient rue St. André des Arts.

On this last stage, almost every building I passed was rooted deep in history. At this hour, I had the old streets all to myself and they led me finally to the equally old street on which I lived. I mounted the six flights to my studio and, if I were lucky, saw, through the great window, Venus, the last star to pale before the rising sun.

¶

Gillotte's

¶

As an encourager of esprit de corps, the Hôtel de Lisbonne has to be ranked only second among the Paris Edition's rendezvous, with Gillotte's, our common eating place, first. The two were twins in at least one respect: Neither was afraid of an overlay of good healthy dirt. Gillotte's had the advantage that we frequented it mostly at night, and since the lighting was dim, the dirt didn't show much.

Gillotte's was a small place directly across the street from the offices of the *Chicago Tribune*; its clientele, apart from us, was composed chiefly of the *Petit Journal* printers and, at lunchtime, taxi drivers. This was a good sign. Taxi drivers, comparatively free to roam in search of fodder, tend to nose out the best values in different parts of the city and head for the nearest one available when hunger strikes. The taxi drivers ate in the front room, relaxing before returning to labor by playing *belotte*, a French card game. We also used to play French checkers at Gillotte's among ourselves, with forty pieces on a board of one hundred squares.

It did not look like a temple of gastronomy and was not, but we ate quite well there even though the place's appearance suggested that this was an accident. It was an epoch when one ate well at all levels, even the humblest. If you had your mouth made up for truffles and foie gras the workmen's restaurants could do nothing for you, but if you were willing to put up with foods in their price range, you would get good substantial nourishment, prepared and seasoned with skill. It might be suggested that we were overimpressed, as refugees from American restaurant cooking, but there was the evidence of the choice of Gillotte's by the taxi drivers, who were French—except for some White Russians, who in those days drove a considerable proportion of Paris taxis. They all admitted to being members of the Russian nobility, a class that had some experience in eating well. What Gillotte's gave us, the French taxi drivers, and the former cronies of the czar was hearty French home cooking, *la cuisine bourgeoise*.

Gillotte's space was limited. The building was just wide enough to permit placing one small round table and two chairs at either side of the door on the sidewalk, a token terrace that obliged passersby to step down into the street to pass. Inside Gillotte's began with a front room occupied on the left side by the *zinc*, or bar, with a standing, or leaning, capacity of about a dozen average-sized drinkers. After a brief interval to allow for squeezing out from behind the bar, the rest of the left wall was occupied by a series of shelves. A display of hors d'oeuvres and pastry sat on the shelves and the cat sat on the pastry. The right half of the room contained four or five stone-topped tables set at right angles to the wall, available to the lower classes—printers, taxi drivers, and strays.

The partition that guarded the privacy of the back room was more of a symbol than a barrier, with a wide opening that had no door. It sufficed, however, to separate the riffraff from the aristocracy—in the evening, us. Three tables parallel to the wall stood on either side, and next to the wall not chairs but benches upholstered in the unidentifiable material referred to by the French as "moleskin."

The third part of this domain was the cubbyhole kitchen in the rear whose door was always open, permitting samples of the evening's menu to be wafted into the back room in the form of vapor. Nothing ever smelled unappetizing while cooking.

We often filled the whole back room, but when we did not we had a tendency to seek the kitchen end of the room, leaving unoccupied a table or two nearest the entrance that might be occupied by unknowns. The Gillottes exercised a certain censorship over those who might thus be privileged to dine in our presence. Unworthy characters were informed that the room was private, for the house did not intend to allow its day-in day-out customers to be displeased by the invasion of their quarters by citizens of dubious status. They had noted that we were not dismayed by the presence of comely young women, so table seekers who fell into this category usually got by the barrier. These customers also had the advantage for the house that their dinner checks were almost invariably paid, if not by the girls themselves, at least by somebody, though perhaps not until the end of the month.

Our financial arrangements with Gillotte's, as well as its nearness and its good cooking, accounted largely for the fact that the night staff in toto usually dined there before crossing the street and climbing the stairs to start work at 8:00 P.M. Like the Hôtel de Lisbonne it was cheap, and it gave credit. When I described the Polish restaurant near the Luxembourg Gardens as the cheapest I knew, I forgot Gillotte's, whose prices could not have been much different. But I really don't know, for I cannot recall ever having paid a bill for a single meal there. I ate on the cuff like everybody else. We were paid on the fifteenth and on the last day of the month, and on those days, each of us, as he arrived, stopped at the *zinc* and settled for his half-month's accumulation of bills, preserved by the house, to which we preferred to leave the dull chore of mathematics since we were convinced of the Gillottes' scrupulous honesty.

Only one editor, Egbert Swenson, checked the bills, one by one, against his own memoranda of his consumption, set down meticulously in microscopic script in a small black notebook. This, I think, was not because he was suspicious but because he was orderly. Or perhaps he found it hard to believe the amount of his bills, for he ate twice as much as anybody else. I had seen him plow all the way through a complete meal—hors d'oeuvre, fish, meat, salad, cheese, and dessert—pause a few seconds for reflection, and then eat the same menu from beginning to end all over again. Maybe he knew how much a single meal cost at Gillotte's, but nobody else did.

The paying of the fortnightly bill was completed by an invariable ritual. Papa Gillotte reached under the counter and produced, with a certain formality, an unlabeled bottle containing a pale yellowish-brown liquid, from which he poured, for the customer and for himself, a thimbleful each of *prunelle*, on the house. *Prunelle* was an eau de vie distilled from plums by one of his country relatives. Thus fortified, we were ready for one other half-monthly rite, paying the rent, after which we could spend what remained of our $30 on riotous living. On the sixteenth or the first we were back on the cuff again.

Papa Gillotte was one-fourth of the staff of Gillotte's, if you refrain from counting Toto the dog and Minette the cat. Toto belonged to a nameless category of dog of which a replica existed at that period in every cheap bistro—about Airedale-sized, though there was nothing else about them to suggest so distinguished an animal as an Airedale, rusty black in color and smooth-haired. They had long thrashing tails, excellent for knocking glasses off tables. I have seen none of them for years.

Toto's color seemed good camouflage against all backgrounds, and since he never barked, whined, or growled, you were usually unaware of his presence until a restive muzzle was suddenly thrust into your groin in guise of welcome. This was the only contribution Toto knew how to make to the quality of life, a disconcerting one if you were not braced for it.

Most bistro dogs in France at that period were called Toto and the cats were known as Minette, the generic name in France for cats of all kinds, best translated as "pussy." Minette had a basket behind the bar but preferred to lie on the pastry, except when she was giving birth, as she seemed to do every few weeks. The kittens gradually disappeared, a phenomenon sometimes connected by us, in purposely loud voices, with the appearance of rabbit stew on the menu. The object of this slander was to provoke the wrath of the ordinarily good-natured Mama Gillotte and provoke the display of a vocabulary unmatchable even by the taxi-driving customers. Newcomers to the staff would sometimes try to get a rise out of her by suggesting that Gillotte's beef was really horse, and were surprised at her calm indifference to this theory, until one of the veterans explained that horse meat at the time was more expensive than beef. (Nowadays it costs about the same.)

Papa and Mama Gillotte were from the Auvergne, as were almost all Paris bistro keepers. The classic story of the Paris bistro keeper was that of a peasant who arrived from the mountains of his native Auvergne and set himself up as a *bougnat* (all Parisian *bougnats* were Auvergnats too). A *bougnat* is, or was, for mighty few of them are left today, a small-scale dealer in coal and wood—small-scale enough that he would personally deliver your order, at the frequent intervals and in the small amounts dictated by the limited storage space of most apartments. This was a profitable business when a large proportion of the Paris population heated itself with fireplaces and hardly were aware of the existence of gas ranges, much less electric ones. It also made for frequent contacts with customers who might ultimately be induced to support another type of business. Once the *bougnat* had saved enough money (Auvergnats are a thrifty lot), he would sweep out the wood shavings and scrub away the coal dust from part or all of his premises, install a bar and bottles, and notify his wood and coal customers that he was now prepared to supply internal, as well as external, heat. He thus became a *limonadier*.

The Gillottes were excellent hosts, and I think they felt a certain affection for us. Indeed, they sometimes went so far as to lend us money, which was not a Parisian habit. They allowed us to convert their back room into our private club, and a very pleasant club it was. We not only dined there, we descended in full force at 10:00 P.M. for a half-hour break, and sometimes we returned after the paper had gone to press about 2:30 A.M., though at this hour we were more apt to disperse to foreign parts, sometimes even going home. I do not know if I ever enjoyed any other restaurant more thoroughly than Gillotte's. I suppose it was chiefly the company; we were a close-knit family on the Paris Edition.

Gillotte's was open twenty-three hours out of twenty-four, closing from four to five in the morning, and probably would never have closed at all if the license fee for round-the-clock cafés had not been something like double that for places that took at least an hour off. This timetable regulated the Gillotte life-style, or lack of one. They had no home except the bistro cellar, which was entered through a trapdoor behind the bar. It is probable that they had in reserve a retirement property somewhere in the Auvergne (perhaps where the *prunelle* came from) for this was the rule among the Auvergnat bistro owners of Paris, but in the capital they slept on their business premises. Papa and Mama Gillotte were both above ground at meal times and other busy moments, but in between they took turns descending to the cellar for a little sleep. They had no children.

Under this regime, Mama Gillotte looked as if she never fully wakened, except at moments of anger or laughter. A large, blowsy, friendly, tolerant woman, when she laughed she laughed all over. Papa Gillotte, who weighed in at about half the heft of his spouse, looked relatively awake, if not alert, except that his eyes were set deep into narrow slits that served to protect them from light. He was always a little outnumbered by his large blue apron, and I never saw him without a dirty oversized cloth cap on his head. Mama Gillotte's sartorial aspect I am unable to describe because there was nothing about it on which attention could be focused. All I can say is that she wore a dress, and if it was not always the same dress, it at least was always equally colorless and shapeless. If she were true to her class, she must have accumulated before marriage a plentiful trousseau that had been carefully folded and stored away in a series of bureau drawers, where it would remain until her death, lest it should deteriorate from being worn.

One of the assets of Auvergnats, for expanding their businesses as *bougnats* or *limonadiers*, is an unlimited supply of labor in the form of cousins. The rest of Gillotte's staff fell into this category. Food was transported from kitchen to tables by Raymond, who must have been about fourteen when I first became a guest of Gillotte's, a pasty-faced boy whose complexion suggested that he slept in the cellar too and had never come into contact with open air. (Papa and Mama Gillotte had in their youth in their native province acquired complexions sufficiently ruddy to last them the rest of their lives.) Raymond was full of goodwill, but easily bewildered. On the not infrequent occasions when someone tried to point out to him that the sole meunière he had brought to the table was not the roast lamb that had been ordered, his timid grin was so disarming and so uncomprehending that the diner usually ate what he had been given. Perhaps Raymond was smarter than we thought.

The keystone of the culinary department of Gillotte's was Madame Charlotte, also a member of the family, direction and distance from Mama and Papa Gillotte unknown. She presided over the kitchen, visible through its open door, her sparse gray hair escaping in unmanageable wisps from what might have been referred to charitably as her coiffure, busying herself around the heavy iron range of the type known in Parisian restaurants as "the piano," under its permanent canopy of drying female underwear. "Madame" was a courtesy title awarded in honor of her age, which was indeterminable, anywhere from sixty to eighty, for legally Madame Charlotte was still a mademoiselle.

Madame Charlotte could be peppery and sometimes enlivened the bistro's atmosphere with minor eruptions. These were usually intrafamily, but among us it was Hérol Egan who seemed fated to provoke Madame Charlotte most often, as a result of a communications gap. Egan's French was more fluent than accurate.

The most widely repeated example of Egan's struggles with the French language occurred at a dinner given by sports reporters in honor of the retiring head of I-have-forgotten-which sports association, who happened to bear the title of count. Nobody had asked Egan to make a speech, but he was never one to stand on ceremony, so he got up and made one anyway. He knew vaguely that final consonants are often left unpronounced in French, and though the *t* in *comte* is not quite final, Egan elected to omit it anyway, just for safety's sake. The other diners managed to keep straight faces through a series of references to *"Monsieur le*

Con," but when Egan described the guest of honor as "*ce vieux con usagé par le travail*," the phrase "this old cunt worn out by work" brought down the house.

One communications failure between Egan and Madame Charlotte was pure comedy. One day Egan ordered dinner only to have Madame Charlotte emerge from her lair as soon as Raymond relayed the order. "*Monsieur voulait dire* deux *oeufs, n'est-ce pas?*" she asked. Egan responded that he wanted *douze*, and Madame Charlotte executed the shrug of the shoulders that meant, "All Americans are crazy," returned to her piano, and in a trice Raymond plunked down before Egan a tremendous platter laden with twelve fried eggs.

"What the hell is this?" Egan exploded. "I ordered two eggs, and look what they've given me."

"You horse's ass," said Frantz, from across the room, "you didn't ask for two eggs, you asked for twelve eggs, and that's what you've got. You should have said *deux*; you said *douze*."

"I did not say *douze*," Egan protested. "I said *douze*."

I forget what happened to the surplus eggs. Perhaps Swenson ate them.

This was a minor incident, but on another occasion Egan nearly lost us our excellent cook with a single remark. She had been having trouble with her stove one evening, so the next day Egan, friendly though unintelligible, poked his head through the kitchen door to ask how her *poêle* was behaving. *Poêle is* a justifiable word for stove, though a Frenchman would be more likely to use it to mean a heating stove than a cooking stove, and most likely to use it to mean a frying pan. But it is a good word for a foreigner to avoid entirely, for its combination of vowels can be played only on a French larynx.

What Madame Charlotte heard was *pöils*, and she exploded from her quarters, half screaming and half crying, tore off her apron, and announced that she was quitting on the spot rather than cook for barbarians who insulted respectable women in public by discussing their pubic hair. It took all of us and both the Gillottes to unravel the misunderstanding, after which Madame Charlotte resumed her apron and returned to the kitchen, grumbling. She put off quitting for several years, when she eloped with Raymond, who was about half a century younger than she was.

¶

Really *Harold Stearns*

¶

"I walked past the sad tables of the Rotonde, to the Select," reads a paragraph near the beginning of Ernest Hemingway's *The Sun Also Rises*. "There were a few people inside at the bar, and outside, alone, sat Harvey Stone. He had a pile of saucers in front of him and he needed a shave."

Harvey Stone never turns up in the book again, and readers might well wonder, if their attention is caught by this brief mention, why he is there at all. My guess is that he was there in the book because he was always there in reality, and Hemingway could not leave him out because he would then have felt that he had falsified his scene and thus risked falsifying everything. Harvey Stone had to be there because for everyone who knew Montparnasse in the early 1920s, these few words stamped Hemingway's book with the seal of truth. For those who did not know Montparnasse then it may not seem that Hemingway gave his readers much to go on: a pile of saucers and a stubble. But that was enough. When I reached that paragraph in my first reading of *The Sun Also Rises* I knew at once who Harvey Stone was, and so did every other Montparnassian of that time. His initials were confirmation of his identity: Harvey Stone was Harold Stearns.

In Paris cafés before World War II, cashiers, waiters, and customers kept track of the bills by a method so simple and efficient that one wonders why it was ever abandoned. Perhaps it was because of inflation. Prices were rising so fast that saucers were too quickly outdated—for it was on the saucer that the price of the *consommation*, food or drink, was stamped.

A diligent drinker never lost track of what he owed since he had only to tot up the amounts marked on the saucers in front of him. (I recall a rumpus in the Rotonde one night when the waiters were drawn to the toilet by sounds of breakage. They found two young men attempting to reduce their bill by shying saucers into the urinal. They had acquired so many of them that they had passed the point at which they were capable of realizing that crashing crockery makes noise.)

I have my own memory of Harold Stearns and his stockade of saucers to parallel that of *The Sun Also Rises*. I had arrived at the Select to find Harold sitting there. He had apparently been sitting there for some time, judging by the height of the saucers and his rather comatose condition, but the second indication was deceptive, for it was often difficult to tell whether he was asleep or awake. A Bright Young Thing from the States, engaged in seeing the sights of Montparnasse, entered. The somnolent Stearns was pointed out to her as one of the sights. She became goggle-eyed.

"Harold *Stearns*?" she breathed. "*Really* Harold Stearns? Oh, do you think I could meet him?"

"Nothing easier," she was told. She was led up to his table and her name was pronounced in Harold's direction. He did not acknowledge the introduction, simply raised his head, and asked: "Will you pay for these saucers?"

The girl gasped.

"Why should I?" she asked.

"Because I can't," Harold answered.

She paid.

I did not meet Harold Stearns until after he had reached what Hemingway called "the period of his unreliability," but of course I knew all about him before that, or thought I did, like every other young American with any interest in cultural matters. After graduating from Harvard he had become an editor of the *New Republic* and then of the *Dial*, but what had made him the hope of American literature and of American intellectualism was, somewhat paradoxically, his low opinion of the current content of both. As expressed in his *America and the Young Intellectual* and especially in *Civilization in the United States*, his attacks on the materialistic and puritanical culture of America appealed mightily to nonconformists like myself, of whom there must have been more than I had realized.

Civilization in the United States and Stearns' own example in becoming an expatriate were credited at the time with sending many young

Americans to Europe, especially to Paris, but I suspect that the book was more of a symptom than a cause. It crystallized a disillusionment with America among the intellectual young, which was already exerting a centrifugal pressure on them, impelling them to abandon America, at least temporarily, in order to renew contact with what had been the source of American culture, Europe. The most important single factor that made it possible for them to cede to that pressure was probably the unromantic circumstance that the franc was cheap in terms of the dollar.

Stearns expressed his views on the exodus to Europe in "Apologia of an Expatriate," published in *Scribner's*, one of several intellectual magazines of the time. The article was presented in the form of a letter to Scott Fitzgerald, whose own self-exile had not lasted long. George Wickes summed up the content of this article in *Americans in Paris* thus:

"In giving his reasons [for becoming and remaining an expatriate], Stearns confessed that he knew all 'the bitterness of being an expatriate' living as he did in humiliating circumstances on the edge of poverty; he admitted that America was full of vitality, while Europe was old and disillusioned; yet he had many reasons for staying. He had been driven out of America by the post-war trend toward standardization, philistinism, and intolerance, 'the emergence of articulate mediocrity, armed with self-assurance, a full stomach, and a tenacious determination to destroy anything better than itself.' . . . In Paris Stearns had found the values of an established civilization, not the least of which was tolerance. Here he was left alone to live as he pleased, free to work or make a fool of himself, at ease with himself and society."

This Stearns who had been "driven out" of America does not sound much like the Stearns who in 1921 chose July 4 to leave the United States in a defiant, positive assertion of his desire to seek brighter horizons. A common characteristic of the "Apologia" and of his parting shot at America when he was interviewed by reporters at the dock was self-dramatization—and hence exaggeration. In the first he grieved over his "bitterness"; later he proclaimed that he would stay away "perhaps forever." When he returned, he still described himself in his autobiography, *A Street I Knew*, as "just an uprooted, aimless wanderer on the face of the earth." He seemed to take pleasure in regarding himself as lonely, friendless, and abandoned.

Stearns left Greenwich Village in 1921, two years before I arrived myself for the obligatory stage there, so I did not know him before I reached Europe, but I had read *Civilization in the United States*. The reviews, and the articles and polemics about it, centered always on the name of Harold Stearns, so I was surprised to discover when I bought the book that it was not the work of one man, but a symposium, whose many contributors included a number of writers with reputations better established than that of Stearns. Somehow they had been eclipsed, and it was Stearns who reaped all the credit for a book that was a considerable sensation in its time. It was only fair that he should receive most of it, for he was its editor, but I think he contributed to it only the preface and a single chapter, or at the most two. Stearns was a protégé of H. L. Mencken, and there were rumors that Stearns' chapters had been written largely by Mencken. This I did not believe, not only because Stearns had already demonstrated that he could write without anybody's help, but also because I cannot imagine that Mencken could disguise his distinctive style. No matter: The book won for Stearns a considerable reputation, which had not diminished for me when I reached Paris six years after he did, and discovered that in the interval it had seeped away.

What had happened to Stearns between 1921 and 1927 and when precisely did it happen? As late as July 2, 1926, Alex Small wrote in the Paris Edition about "Harold Stearns, who, if one is lucky enough to get a few moments of conversation with him, will demonstrate that the spark of wit and intelligence still flickers in Montparnasse." This was only a year before I met Stearns and found the spark no longer operating. A year seemed too short a time to account for such a change. I have a theory about this difference between Small's judgment and my own: Alex, like most people who like to hear themselves talk, remembered as most brilliant those conversations in which nobody had interrupted him, and consequently listed as brilliant conversationalists those who had been content to listen. Stearns by the time I knew him had become a master of the art of silence.

It could have been as late as 1925 when Samuel Putnam, who was working on a new translation of Rabelais, was greatly impressed by the knowledge displayed on this subject by Stearns, who seems to have once considered doing the same thing himself. Two years does not seem long enough to have brought about Stearns' degeneration either, since 1925 was the year when Sinclair Lewis' attack on Stearns was published in the *American Mercury*, founded by Mencken. If Lewis' spiteful article was not the best writing he had ever done, neither was Stearns' rejoinder a model of subtlety. Lewis described Stearns as the "very father and seer of the Dôme . . . that Young Intellectual who, if he ever finishes the assassinatory book of which we have heard these last three years ["Studies in Stupidity," of which Stearns apparently never wrote more than the title], will tear the world up by the roots. He is going to deliver unto scorn all the false idols of the intelligentsia, particularly such false idols as have become tired of lending him—as the phrase is—money."

Stearns' answer to this was published in the Paris Edition on December 10, 1925:

> I will not join Mr. Lewis in a competition of ignominy. Just because Mr. Lewis, by his malicious personal attack, chooses to expose himself at last in public as a cad and a bounder, he cannot expect me, in spite of great admiration for his salesmanship talents, to imitate him.
>
> Discussing the article objectively, it is chaotic, cheap, inaccurate and absurd. He missed both the good points and the bad ones of the American Montparnasse colony. . . . The chief good point, of course, is that remotely, somehow, somewhere, even the dumbest American expatriates have been touched by the spiritual forces of French life. The realization that there is something in France which he has missed was what finally drove Mr. Lewis back to a country where his publications have a dignity which, to Europeans, is simply incomprehensible.
>
> In fairness to the people mentioned, I ought to point out, as one of them, that they are only grouped together by Mr. Lewis' spite. With one or two exceptions, they are not social with one another, and in temperament and intellectual outlook are utterly antipathetic.
>
> However ridiculous may be the people he disparages, they were not so ridiculous as to take Mr. Lewis seriously. He has made the traditionally quaint error of confusing hurt pride with high perspicacity.

We may absolve Stearns for some of the phraseology, for it is presented not as an answer written by him, but as an interview, which reaches us secondhand. It seems to me to do little to demonstrate Small's claim that in the person of Stearns, "the spark of wit and intelligence still flickers in Montparnasse" or perhaps it does, for a flickering light is often one that is about to go out. Malcolm Cowley was referring to this period when he wrote of Stearns in *Exile's Return*: "People used to look down at him sleeping on a café terrace and say, 'There lies civilization in the United States.'" Many years later I wrote myself that "before I arrived in 1927, he had become the Parisian equivalent of a beachcomber."

The degeneration of Stearns may have begun when his wife died in childbirth early in the 1920s. For some time afterward he manifested a morbid obsession with death by sitting on the rue Delambre side of the Dôme, where there was room for only two or three usually deserted tables, because it was along this street that funerals passed on their way to the Montparnasse cemetery. Harold sat there for hours, crossing himself as each hearse went by. It was to see the son who had been born that, late in 1924, he made his only visit to the United States until his final departure from Europe. It convinced him that civilization in the United States had not improved. He wrote in the *Baltimore Sun*:

"I had to go back home to discover that I was an American through and through. Also I had to go back home to discover that it would be impossible ever again to live happily in America. . . . With so much and varied good food in the land, I haven't had worse meals for five years."

Stearns returned from the United States, William Shirer wrote, in *Twentieth Century Journey*, "even more disillusioned with the country than when he had first left it. . . . He had returned to Paris, as he said, 'almost completely broke and without a job or a friend or a woman to keep me. That summer and autumn of 1925 were the summer and autumn of my discontent.' A woman named Belinda, he says, had left him 'with enough money for a few weeks.' But soon it was gone and he had wandered the streets of Paris, 'literally wondering where the next meal was coming from.'"

I do not know who "Belinda" may have been, but he hinted to me on one or two occasions that he had become discouraged by an unfortunate love affair. He never ventured details and his remarks were so very vague that I was sometimes tempted to wonder if his story had not been invented to cover up a natural talent for drinking. Not for getting drunk, mind you, just for drinking. I never saw him drunk and, so far as I know, neither did anyone else. His usual tipple was beer, and he was capable of spending all his waking hours screwed into his chair at the Select or the Rotonde as the saucers rose before him, with no visible change in his state except that it became more and more difficult to be sure that he was awake.

I did not feel, at the period when I knew him, that he was particularly interested in women. I remember once standing side by side with him at the bar of the Chope Cadet (the highest ranking bar-restaurant of the office neighborhood; Harold did not patronize Gillotte's) enveloped in one of his long silences, as we so often were, when he withdrew his gaze from his beer, turned his head toward me, and said, apropos of nothing, "No woman was ever as beautiful as a horse." He then returned to the contemplation of his beer.

It was not women but horses that were the ruination of Stearns—not in the usual sense when we say that a man has been ruined by horses, meaning that he has been financially ruined by betting on them. In Stearns' case, he was mentally ruined by fascination with horse racing.

According to his own account, this fascination began in 1923, when he saw his first Grand Prix de Paris. The problems of predicting which horses could run faster than other horses shouldered everything else out of his head. It was pathetic to witness the metamorphosis of the man with whom Hemingway had reported he talked art at the Dôme into a man no longer capable of talking about anything other than racehorses. (I do not know whether Hemingway was interested in racehorses; one has the impression that Hemingway was interested chiefly in animals destined to be killed, from fighting bulls to fighting fish.)

Stearns' new orientation was reflected in an article he wrote for the Paris Edition of June 2, 1927, about the annual influx of summer tourists, a category of travelers about whom it was of course necessary to adopt a condescending attitude. The point on which Stearns chose to berate them was perhaps ill chosen. "The earnest schoolteachers and flip flappers on a vacation that will not improve their minds," he wrote, "seldom have time to arrive before the very end of the month when the Grand Prix has been run and it is all over." This the man who had once taken a whole civilization for his province.

Stearns' exclusive interest in horse racing led to his becoming the *Chicago Tribune*'s Peter Pickem. This was a name owned by the paper, which bestowed it on whoever had been hired to inform its readers on which horses to bet. Peter Pickems came and went every few months or every few weeks because of the unwillingness of horses to cooperate with prophets, until Stearns took over the job and, better at prediction than the others, stayed on for several years.

His own willingness to remain on a job that was not conspicuously well paid was attributed by scandalmongers to the possibility that he had found ways of making it lucrative that had eluded his predecessors. In those days the only way to place a bet was to go to the track. Horse race fans who couldn't make it would confide their money to Harold to place for them, and after a while some of them thought they discerned a pattern in his operations: When their horses won, Harold would return their money with the explanation that he hadn't gotten out to the track in time to place their bets, and when they lost—well, they lost. I don't think any of his clients ever accused him flatly of never paying off on the money entrusted to him but nobody employed him as a betting commissioner for long.

Stearns' vocation as a picker of horse race winners caused Alex Small to dub him "the Hippic Buddha," which, alas, has been converted by at least one historian of this period into "the Hippo Buddha." This is understandable enough, for Harold always wore, over a rotund figure, a soiled raincoat that swept the ground and made him look like a statue draped for an unveiling, which may well have had a hippopotamus effect.

As I remember Harold he would never have been named to the best-dressed men's list. Above the raincoat, he wore a weather-beaten felt hat. If the raincoat were agape, it exposed a shirt that seemed always to be in its fourth day of service. Even more difficult to account for was his unvarying three days' growth of beard, as noted by Hemingway.

Stearns in my time was unsmiling and taciturn. By saying nothing himself he made you do the talking, with the result that you often wound up making absurd remarks, such as offering to buy him another drink. It is safe to assume that you had bought him whatever he was drinking already; I do not recall that he himself ever offered to buy one. Once, out of sheer curiosity, standing with him at the bar of the Chope Cadet, I made a deliberate effort to beat his technique. I had bought him one drink—he was taking cognac, exceptionally, for I was—and I was determined not to finish my glass at the same time that he did and get stuck with treating him again. He took the merest sip from his glass, to match the larger swig I had drawn from mine, and set it down. I waited a longish time for him to continue, but he showed no further interest. At last, I slugged down the rest of my drink and pushed my glass forward for a refill—and there, lo and behold, was his emptied glass standing beside mine. I hadn't seen him move.

His mastery of the art of cadging included money too, but I had been warned about that when I came on the paper, and I kept my guard up. He only got through it once. We were standing, again, at the Chope Cadet bar, having drinks on me, when he suddenly said, out of a clear sky, "Let me have fifty francs, will you?" and I handed it to him like a man hypnotized. I am convinced that he did not then particularly need fifty francs, but was simply indulging himself in the pleasure of exercising what for him was a fine art. I was the only person on the staff he had not yet touched, and it was a question of honor to do so.

Harold's masterpiece of borrowing lasted for months and involved the entire editorial staff of the *Chicago Tribune* and, I understand, a good many outsiders as well. His story was that a horse trainer, grateful for the money he had won on Harold's tips (he must have placed the bets himself), had made him a present of a colt Harold considered promising although its owner did not.

Harold's friends and colleagues were thereupon entrusted with the responsibility of supporting the animal. He borrowed for stable rent, for trainer's fees, for hay and grain, for harness, for the blacksmith. His needs were desperate, but they had to be dragged out of him. He would stand before his glass at the bar, glowering into space, or sit behind his saucers at a table, unspeaking, until whoever was with him felt obliged to break the tension by bringing up the only available subject of conversation, the horse. He would then be presented with the latest bill.

At first there was more than a little skepticism about the horse's existence, but the story became so involved and the details so voluminous that in the end it acquired an unavoidable reality. Besides, the time was coming for a showdown. The colt was reaching racing age and it would become necessary to produce him. Indeed, Harold finally told us the name of the race in which he would make his debut. We chipped in to pay the entrance fee.

Then, one day, Robert Sage went down to the Chope Cadet for a beer, and there was Harold, standing at the bar and staring into emptiness. Bob's first attempts to draw an explanation out of him failed utterly.

"What's wrong, Harold?" Sage asked. "What's the matter with you?"

"Nothing," Stearns mumbled from the depths. "Nothing at all."

"Bad day at the track?" Sage suggested.

"Won about a hundred," Stearns admitted.

The inevitable question arrived.

"How's the horse shaping up?" Sage asked.

Harold shifted position and looked Bob in the eye.

"Broke his leg," he said. "We had to shoot him."

There was a pause, not too short, not too long.

"Have you any idea," Stearns asked, "how much it costs to bury a horse?"

¶

"If I Were a Lady . . ."

¶

Shortly after my arrival in Paris I acquired a recurrent nightmare. While the details of the dreams were different, the theme was the same: I was back in the United States with too little money to buy a ticket to Paris.

What accounted for this charm of Paris? It was not rejection of the United States. Living abroad—in Paris, on the Riviera, in London, Rome, or the Hague—has never made me feel alien to America. I am American to the core, no fonder of these prestigious places than of others, less celebrated, where I have lived rewardingly—Boston, New York, Rockport, Massachussetts, Chelsea, Vermont, or even the city where I was brought up, Fall River, Massachusetts, which for outsiders is distinguished only for the Lizzie Borden murders. Why then should the thought of being marooned in America have made me, in my dreams at least, so miserable? I was in Paris, where I wanted to be, and the thought of being anyplace else was intolerable.

In the 1920s and 1930s Paris was the capital of nonconformism. I had been brought up in the middle-class bourgeois society of New England, where the only way to dissent with impunity was to become the village eccentric. The pressure to conform was constant, and it made me unhappy. Then I moved to Paris and suddenly the pressure disappeared. Paris was a city in which the expression of all ideas was permissible, at least in the part of its society that I entered. There was no dominant body of public opinion so sure of its own standards that it dared tell everybody else what to think. This nearly complete tolerance and freedom often led to extravagance, but extravagance was more interesting than well-worn ruts. Everything of intellectual importance was happening in Paris and I was privileged to be occupying a ringside seat at its immense cultural circus. Paris was open to all ideas, to all opinions, to every mode of thinking: That is why we were all happy there. And that is why the idea of being exiled from its freedom was translated by me into a series of nightmares.

It was only natural that many of the young men who joined the Paris edition of the *Chicago Tribune*, fresh from the United States and steeped in its thinking, were most impressed by one aspect of Parisian nonconformism and freedom—the theory that one's sexual behavior is one's own business. It took a little time for some of us to get the message.

There was, for example, one young man who worked for the Paris Edition so briefly that I have forgotten his name. He shed his conformism when a young woman he encountered in a café proved so enticing that he invited her to spend the night in his hotel room. The morning after arrived, bringing with it the realization of the enormity of his crime. He could not have been more panic-stricken if he had been a murderer with a body to dispose of. The body in this case awoke and reached for the *poire*, or pear, a wooden object so named for its shape, which encloses a button that summons breakfast. The body in the bed pressed the button.

Discovery was imminent and the young American found himself imagining three possibilities: He would be put out of the hotel, expelled from France for moral turpitude, or he would go to jail. Then a knock sounded at the door. "*Entrez*," the girl in the bed called out cheerfully. The door opened and a maid appeared, carrying a tray laden with coffee and croissants for two, plus a small bouquet, which she handed to the young woman.

Robert Sage, an editor at the Paris Edition and a man of foresight, took the precaution of learning in advance about the mores of French hoteliers. Having become enamored of a young woman, he asked his hotel proprietress diffidently, for he was still green in the ways of Paris, if he might entertain the young woman in his room. "Young man," she told him, "I am running a hotel, not a monastery."

For us, sex was not confined to hotels. In 1927 I found myself, with another member of the Paris Edition staff, talking with an American who had just arrived in Paris, where he had been deposited in one of the half-dozen middle-level hotels frequented chiefly by American tourists. He wanted to move to a hotel more authentically French. I suggested the Louvois, a hotel unknown to most foreigners. Its clients were mostly traveling salesmen from the provinces—a good sign, for traveling sales-men spend a good deal of their lives in hotels and develop a faculty for rooting out the best ones. It was also the hotel where A. J. Liebling, a man who knew hotels too, always stayed in Paris.

"The Louvois?" asked our visitor. "Is that the one on a square across from the Bibliothèque Nationale and around the corner from the Chaban-ais?" The Chabanais was then the most celebrated bordello in Paris.

"It's across the square from the Bibliothèque Nationale," my col-league answered loftily. "I'm not the sort of person who would know about the other place."

"That's the one," I said. "I'm the sort of person who would know about both."

I was boasting. I had never been inside the Chabanais, which was too expensive for me, but I knew where it was and that it was supposed to be the place where Edward VII, when he was still only the Prince of Wales, relaxed from the atmosphere of the court of his mother, Queen Victoria. The Chabanais refrained from adorning its facade with the royal coat of arms but when France abolished—or thought it had abolished—bordel-los after World War II, the Chabanais auctioned off its luxurious furniture and described one item as the bathtub reserved exclusively for His Royal Highness. The house enjoyed great esteem as purveyor to a prince of the blood royal, and charged accordingly.

At the Paris Edition we were not good customers of *les maisons closes*, or bordellos, even those cheaper than the Chabanais. We didn't need to be. There were plenty of warmhearted amateurs about, and it was our opinion that it was as unnecessary to pay for love as to pay for breathing. The few exceptions were arrivals from the States who did not yet know enough French to arrange a liaison with a local young woman.

One such newcomer was responsible for my first look at the inside of a bordello. His failing, on his night off, was to get a snootful and then move on to one of these houses, where he splurged on such extras as champagne until he had spent all his money. He therefore took the precaution of leav-ing most of his money with us in the office, but this proved to be less than a perfect solution. What it led to was a weekly phone call demanding that someone be sent with funds to bail him out. (The fee for amorous services was always collected in advance but most places would trust the customer for champagne until the end of the evening.) One such SOS, received during my first week on the night staff, informed us that our colleague's clothing had been confiscated and would be returned only on payment of his bill. I volunteered to act as the messenger boy out of a spirit of help-fulness and curiosity: Although I knew such houses existed, I had never known so much as the address of one.

When I arrived at the address given me in the rue Navarin I thought that I must have made a mistake. It was an elegant building in a Gothic eccle-siastical style. I learned later that it had been a convent. The empty niche above the door had contained a statue of the Virgin Mary, which had been removed as inappropriate. There was a bigger niche inside, in the wall of the entry, which was provided with a curtain that could be drawn across it. If a customer who did not relish being seen in such surroundings were trapped in the entry as someone started down the stairs, he could step back into the niche, pull the curtain, and wait until he was alone.

I was received in a small, discreet parlor by the courteous mistress of the house, who led me upstairs to the quarters occupied by my penniless colleague. This was the first time I had seen a room that not only had all its walls covered with mirrors but even had one on the ceiling. My friend was in bed with an amiable but, for my taste, too well-upholstered blonde. There was no animosity about the bill, animosity being incom-patible with the house's function. I handed over the money and was taken downstairs by the woman who had received me. She asked whether I would not like to stay on but made no attempt to persuade me when I de-clined.

This was a house of extreme respectability and refinement, as I realized after I expanded my acquaintance of such establishments. New cus-tomers unfamiliar with the resident beauties were received in the parlor and shown photographs of the house's *pensionnaires*—boarders, as they were tactfully called—before being led upstairs to confirm their choices. There was no vulgar trotting downstairs of a girl, or girls, for preliminary inspection. A grade lower in bordellos, girls whose photographs had been found pleasing would be called down to a reception room to help in the final decision, but only when you were well down the ladder did you find yourself ushered straight into a large public room filled with girls. These premises resembled cafés with tables set along the walls for the customers to sit down and order drinks (soft drinks, beer, or champagne but no hard liquor) and the center of the room left open for the circulation of the girls, who might come up to ask if they could share a table but would not be offended if the customer refused. We often visited such places, in small groups, after the paper went to press, with no intention of doing anything other than drinking a beer or two in the agreeable atmosphere and perhaps exchanging a little banter with the girls. The spirit was about the same as that of any social outing.

The rule was that the amount of clothes worn diminished with the class of the place, so our two favorites, one in the rue Blondel and the other in the rue Ste. Apolline, must have been a considerable distance below the average since most of the girls there wore nothing but shoes. Visits like ours, which went no further than ogling and involved no trips upstairs, were common enough and not unremunerative, for the price of the drinks had been calculated to include the floor show. The bordello of those times was sometimes described as the workingman's club, which was apt enough in small towns; it was a pleasant place to go to meet friends for a drink.

It was rare for any of us to go upstairs. I succumbed only once myself, when a girl with whom I was talking proved to be irresistibly seductive, and I fear that in so doing I contributed to misunderstanding between the French and American people. One reason for visiting these temples of Venus was to show them to curious visitors from the United States, and on this occasion I was acting as a guide for Westbrook Pegler, whose sports column was syndicated by the *Chicago Tribune*. When I went upstairs with one of the two girls at our table, I left Pegler with the other. When I came down he had gone. A few days later he produced the first of a series of articles on the immorality of the French.

I thought that the rue Blondel or the rue Ste. Apolline, whichever it was, was wholesomeness itself compared with another place to which I took Pegler on the same visit. This was a party given by the Paris office of the *London Daily Express* for Putzi Hanfstaengl, the Harvard alumnus who had become an insider at Hitler's court and der führer's favorite piano player. Hanfstaengl was accompanied by a handful of people from Berlin and every one of them gave the impression of being morally deformed. There was an example of nudity here too, a dancer who had discarded even shoes, unless you considered as clothing the indolent boa constrictor coiled around her.

Pegler, a bristly character, did nothing to lighten the atmosphere. He was introduced to Hanfstaengl, who asked him to repeat his name. He did so but Hanfstaengl still failed to get it and again asked him to repeat it. "Goddammit," Pegler said, "if I can understand Hanfstaengl, you ought to be able to understand Pegler." A few minutes later Hanfstaengl responded swiftly to the suggestion that he play something appreciated by Hitler. He sat down at the piano, remarked, "This is der führer's favorite piece," and proceeded to thump out a military march with no expression at all. "If I had a five-year-old son who couldn't play better than that with a pair of tack hammers," Pegler observed loudly, "I would drown him." I led him away before he could enter further into the spirit of the party.

I was never able to believe in Pegler's tough-guy attitude, which struck me as superficial. Perhaps he had adopted the attitude as a defense against the constant anguish that beset him when he was away from home, as a journalist often has to be. "My wife's got a bum ticker," he told me often. She was so badly afflicted with heart trouble that Pegler lived in perpetual dread of receiving the telegram that would announce her death. Perhaps too it was this fear that embittered him to such an extent that when he became a political columnist his writings became too reactionary even for the readers of the *Chicago Tribune* and he shifted to the Hearst empire. It was a sad thing to see a man who wrote so well, if often so bitterly, waste his talent on indefensible causes. An ounce of something more here or something less there and he might have become another Ring Lardner.

It was while introducing another visitor to the sights of Paris that I gained an office reputation for being blasé. I had taken our visitor to a small and considerably more subdued establishment than the one that had disgusted Pegler. Situated in the rue Papillon near our office, it boasted a small stage where three or four girls mimicked various acts of erotic behavior, homosexual and hetero. I fell asleep in the middle of their writhings. The performers, whom I remember as matronly in figure, seemed unable to stop giggling, which seemed incompatible with the roles they were attempting to portray. The really remarkable fact about this expedition was that the visiting fireman for whom it was staged had demanded the tour the moment he stepped off the Rome Express, having stepped onto it the day before immediately after a private audience with the pope. Not everybody is favored with private audiences with the pope, but the beneficiary was Arch Ward, sports editor of the *Chicago Tribune* and a nephew of Cardinal Mundelein of Chicago. I think it probable that no one since Lucifer has achieved so wide a leap in the moral sphere so quickly.

Since I had never been upstairs in a bordello except to bail out my free-spending colleague and when I shocked Pegler, I had no firsthand acquaintance with the esoteric installations provided by some of the houses for customers with curious tastes, but others had. Harold Stearns told me that he once passed a closed door in a bordello and heard such weird sounds that he asked the girl with him what was going on. "See for yourself," she answered, opening a peephole in the door. Harold saw a naked man, his hands manacled to two rings set in the wall above his head, being belabored vigorously by a girl with a cat-o'-nine-tails. The man was uttering a varied series of groans and cries, which did not include the word "Stop."

"Do you get many like that?" Stearns asked. "So many that we have two rooms for them," the girl said. She pushed open the door of the next room, showed Harold a similar pair of rings embedded in the wall, and, before he realized what was happening, clamped his wrists into them. Two other girls appeared, pulled his pants down, and began to beat a tattoo on his bare buttocks, laughing uproariously. Harold indicated that he failed to share the joke.

It was often difficult to find an appropriate place to show American tourists what they asked to see at the intensity at which they were willing to see it. If you took them to discreet upper-level houses, there was no public room and consequently no spectacle. At the level of the rue Blondel and the rue Ste. Apolline there was spectacle but for many tastes too much of it. The Chabanais, I have been told, had a public reception room where a number of *pensionnaires* were on view but it proved to be disappointing because it was too demure. The atmosphere was fin de siècle, upper-class Toulouse-Lautrec, where dimly lighted girls, covered down to the knees in frilly costumes, sat on red plush divans against heavy velvet draperies. The problem of where to take American visitors to introduce them to the wickedness of Paris in a tolerable degree was solved when a bordello named the Sphinx opened in 1935. It was in the rue

Edgar-Quinet, just behind the carrefour Montparnasse, by that time nearly abandoned by American expatriates, victims of the 1929 crash of the New York Stock Exchange. The Sphinx was a model of modernity, spotless and blazing with light, teeming with healthy girls.

It replaced the Chabanais almost immediately as the leading and most luxurious bordello in Paris. This rapid success was also the Sphinx's chief drawback, for if you visited it, you risked running into friends. But if you were going to be caught in a bordello, the best one was the Sphinx, where it was almost smart to be seen. I even took my wife along on some excursions to the Sphinx, once with an old friend from the United States and his wife. A man sitting at a table on the other side of the room decided that my wife, although fully dressed, was better looking than the scantily clad women parading in the center of the room. He lurched over to our table and invited her to join him.

My friend jumped to his feet, his right arm cocked. "Can't you tell a lady from a whore?" he roared. My wife tugged at his arm. "Sit down and don't be silly," she said. "If I were a lady would I be here?" By this time the efficient staff of the Sphinx had deposited her admirer on the sidewalk.

Despite my wife's observation, a great many ladies did visit the Sphinx. The girls were well-mannered, happy to sit down at your table and have a drink if invited but not insistent. Reassuring too were the other spectators who shared the room, well-dressed, clearly respectable people assembled in carefree groups at their tables. Most of them had come simply to have a drink and feast their eyes on beauty. In addition to the girls, the Sphinx had been conceived by the most tasteful interior decorators in Paris. An example of their work was the two handsome pharaohs incised on the walls of the men's room.

My acquaintance with the Sphinx, while restricted to the area downstairs, was fairly intimate for, by the time it opened, the Paris edition of the *Chicago Tribune* had folded and I had become the overnight man in the Paris bureau of the United Press. My working hours started at midnight and ended at eight in the morning. Except in such unusual circumstances as election nights, my chief role was to be there in case of emergency. Otherwise there was not a great deal to be done between one or two o'clock in the morning, by which time I had cleared up any loose ends left by the day staff, and six, when the New York wire opened. About once a week I could count on the unannounced arrival of a vacationing employee from another United Press office with a request to be shown around. I did not have to be a clairvoyant to deduce what aspect of Paris a 3:00 A.M. visitor wanted to see, so I would tell the night office boy to phone me at the Sphinx in case of need. My arrival there was marked invariably, following an effusive greeting by the house's mistress, by the setting up of a branch office devised by this woman after the first two or three times the office boy had to call me there. One of the house's three phone booths was blocked off for my exclusive use and a pad of paper and several sharpened pencils were placed in it, ready for action. When a call came for me, I would be summoned by a scantily clad girl.

The treatment immensely impressed my visiting colleagues and their reports to the home office on how efficiently its Paris bureau operated in the wee hours of the night gave me quite a reputation. I was gratefully surprised at the care the Sphinx lavished on me and it did not occur to me until years later why I had been favored: I must have been the only runner the house had who never asked for a commission.

¶

I Did Know Elliot Paul

¶

I was still at Tufts College, so it could have been no later than 1923, when I read in the Sunday Feature section of the *Boston Post* a half-page article about the author of a just-published novel, titled *Indelible*, that seemed to be a work of genius. The article, what is known in the trade as a tearjerker, described the author's life of toil as a waiter in a Boston restaurant. After a hard day's work, he would return home, staggering under the weight of fatigue, climb the stairs to his garret (the word "garret" was unblushingly employed), and write until dawn by the flame of a candle, the only light he could afford. I bought the book. The name of its author was Elliot Paul.

A half-decade later, sitting in the editor's slot of the city desk of the Paris *Chicago Tribune*, I had on my left my best copyreader—Elliot Paul. I told him I had read the *Boston Post* story. "Not a bad piece," he said. "I wrote it myself." Paul had been a reporter on the *Post*, which let him get away with his hoax, a thing then possible since the era of the byline had not yet really begun and most newspaper stories were anonymous. When he received the advance for this first novel—$500, a lot of money in those days—Paul corralled a couple of friends, hailed a taxi, handed the $500 to the driver, and said, "North." They reached Montreal.

The episode was typical of Paul, a man who loved a good joke, particularly if no one else understood it. Paul entered the Paris Edition as a proofreader when he already had three novels to his credit. Left to himself, he might have been content to remain there, for he was not ambitious in the usual sense: He was capable of writing a story about his own book as a joke, but he would not have done so with the sole object of selling more copies.

Paul was anything but acquisitive. "Get rid of things. Don't let yourself be tied down by objects," I remember him saying. An easygoing, well-mannered extrovert, Paul never worried about consistency, and he

133

possessed things and objects aplenty in his apartment on the Champ de Mars, an aristocratic address that was a far cry from the hotel on the rue de la Huchette whose praises he celebrated in *The Last Time I Saw Paris*. I seem to remember that his apartment contained an excellently chosen collection of art works, including African statuettes, surrealistic *objets trouvés*, and a number of paintings by such later-celebrated artists as Joan Miró.

After Paul's abilities had been discovered and he was elevated from the proofreading department to the editorial staff—a promotion never granted Henry Miller when he worked for us as a proofreader—he became an intermittent employee. He would sit for a few weeks or even months on the rim of the copydesk, chuckling from time to time as he edited stories, and then he would be gone, to turn up again after a prolonged absence. I imagine that he worked on the Paris Edition when he needed the money and knocked off when he didn't. His disappearances probably coincided with the arrival of royalty checks; by the time I moved permanently into the slot as news editor, and he sat as permanently as he wanted to at my left hand, he had five novels to his credit.

Despite a carefully trimmed, pointed beard, Paul made an avuncular impression—imperturbable, blessed with a quiet sense of humor, a man who never seemed to lose his temper. I cannot remember Paul, although he often spoke with emphasis, ever raising his voice. His eyes could sometimes shift from a twinkle of amusement to an almost diabolic maliciousness, especially if he were writing a sarcastic book review. He had an arsenal of barbs handy that he particularly enjoyed discharging at pretentiousness. I have kept one of his wickedest criticisms, probably because I agreed with him so thoroughly both about the quality of the book and the character of its author. The book was *Paris Salons, Cafes, Studios, Being Social, Artistic and Literary Memories* by Sisley Huddleston, a pompous windbag with an opinion of himself as inflated as his figure. He had "consented," as he put it, to become Paris correspondent of the *London Times*, reporting the doings of the Montparnasse coterie. His stories were gossip, badly written gossip, since they consisted of long and unrelated name-dropping anecdotes. Paul finished his review by saying: "As I write this, I am haunted by the fear that Mr. Huddleston will find in it something which may be construed as complimentary to him.

He is exceptionally adroit at this sort of thing. I, therefore, publicly disavow any such intention. If I have failed to make this clear, it is the fault of my technique."

To most people Paul was kindlier than to Huddleston. Indeed he went to great trouble to help his friends and those who aroused his enthusiasm. Among these was Bravig Imbs, formerly a proofreader on the Paris Edition, whom Paul helped to write his first novel, *The Professor's Wife*. He also did all he could to win an audience for Virgil Geddes, the poet who was financial editor of the Paris Edition when I joined it. Paul printed some of his poems in the magazine *transition*, wrote a preface to his *Forty Poems*, published in Paris in 1926 by the author, and introduced him to Katharine Huntington, director of the Boston Stage Society, which led to the production of his play *The Frog* in Boston.

The most important writer Paul championed was Gertrude Stein. He devoted three laudatory articles to her in the Paris Edition, where she had not otherwise been flattered, describing her prose as "like music." He wrote: "Having stripped stories of narrative and description and purged characterization of incident, she proceeded to another refinement of her product and molded her typical situations and universal qualities into pure patterns." Paul also gave Miss Stein more concrete help. When Lee Furman, president of the Macaulay publishing firm, showed interest in bringing out *The Making of Americans* if it could be reduced to practical dimensions, Paul set to work to help shorten it. This was all the more meritorious since he had no illusions about the likelihood of its appearance. Paul was right: Though the manuscript was reduced to a mere two hundred thousand words, it was still rejected as too long.

A grateful Gertrude Stein wrote that it was Elliot Paul who had expressed the "first seriously popular estimation of her work." In *The Autobiography of Alice B. Toklas*, she said that Paul "was a new englander but he was a saracen, a saracen such as you sometimes see in the villages of France, where the strain from some Crusading ancestor's dependents still survives. Elliot Paul was such a one. He had an element not of mystery but of evanescence, actually little by little he appeared and then as slowly he disappeared."

Some of her other remarks about Paul should be seen in the context of her quarrel with *transition*. Eugene Jolas and Paul founded the magazine in 1927, shortly afterward adding Robert Sage as a third editor—all of them were on the copydesk of the Paris Edition. At the beginning *transition* published both Gertrude Stein and James Joyce, but Miss Stein's jealousy of Joyce resulted in her disappearance from its pages, for which she blamed Jolas. In the *Autobiography* she implied that Paul had been the more important of the two founders and that it went downhill when his influence weakened and her work disappeared from it. "Elliot Paul," she wrote, "slowly disappeared and Eugene and Maria Jolas appeared." This was a trifle cavalier since Jolas had been present from the beginning and it was the Jolases who found the money to finance the magazine. It was my impression that Jolas was always the dominant editor but that Paul served a highly important function in restraining Jolas' tendency to become entangled in doctrinaire ideologies, artificial theories, and empty manifestos.

Was it a reflection of Gertrude Stein's falling out with Ernest Hemingway when Paul wrote of him in the Paris Edition: "When a man is told from every side that he is natural, it makes it very difficult for him to remain so"? If this observation was a ricochet from an opinion of Miss Stein's, Paul did not join her in the denigration of a writer she had once appreciated and helped. Paul went on to say that Hemingway had managed to remain natural all the same, "but there are signs of a struggle."

Paul wrote a short story at this period that is perhaps worth calling to the attention of anthologists. "The Life and Death of Isaac Mumblo," which appeared in *transition* in, I think, 1927, was a masterpiece on a minor scale. So far as I know, it has not been reprinted since. It would probably be classed as black humor now because of its ending, a suicide, but it was gentle enough, as Paul's humor characteristically was.

On a less sophisticated level, Paul exercised this humor for a while on the Paris Edition. I suspect most of our readers didn't get the joke; the editor certainly didn't. At that time American journalism was afflicted by "Ten Questions." Every newspaper felt obligated to print daily, and every magazine weekly or monthly, a list of ten teaser questions on which readers could test their stock of information. The answers were printed upside down under the questions or on some page in the back of the publication or in the next issue, if nobody forgot to insert them. The Paris *Chicago Tribune*, obeying what must have been public demand, printed ten questions daily, cribbing them either from the home paper or from its wholly owned subsidiary, *Liberty* magazine. Unfortunately, questions compiled for people living in Chicago were often inappropriate for residents of Paris, so the luckless drudge charged with putting together our daily questions had to plow through American publications that had drifted into our office and steal a few. It was a relief to everybody when Paul volunteered to handle "Ten Questions" regularly.

He did not steal questions from other publications but made up his own. One of them I still remember was: "Q. When a bear cub is pursued through the snow by hunters, does it turn as it runs to cover its tracks? A. No, it thinks the hunters follow it by scent." Another went: "Q. Why do European people eat mussels? A. Because mussels are good to eat."

This went on for some time, delighting those readers who appreciated Paul's sense of humor, while managing editor Bernhard Ragner apparently thought our ten questions were still being culled from the home papers. He was jolted out of this belief when one of Paul's questions dealt irreverently with the Virgin Birth. Ragner knew blasphemy when he saw it and the ten questions never appeared in the Paris Edition again. Ragner was too timid to reprimand a recognized novelist or even to offend him by assigning someone else to this chore. He took the easiest way out, which was to drop the feature entirely.

Paul was also our official gourmet, always ferreting out remarkable places to eat and presiding over our private feasts. He once led a few of us to an improbable address far from the center of Paris. It looked like a typical workman's bistro and was furnished, when we arrived, with a full cast of typical workmen lined up at the bar. Paul stationed himself behind the *zinc*, shooing the chef-proprietor into the kitchen, and proceeded to serve the customers. Trying to confound him, they called for such rare drinks as *arfenarf*, which sounded like a bark but represented the French attempt to say "half and half," a mixture of light and dark beer. Paul had no trouble with their commands. Tiring of the sport in half an hour, the workmen finished their apéritifs and moved off to lunch somewhere else. We then sat down in the back room and had one of the meals of our lives.

The bill, wine included, came to thirty-five cents each. Paul explained that our host had been the chef of Marshal Ferdinand Foch. After the chef retired, he discovered that he missed his pots and pans and perhaps also the occasional rounds of applause from appreciative eaters. So he bought a place whose bar paid the bills, plus a reasonable profit, allowing him to indulge in flattering the palates of invaders from other parts of Paris, like us, since his cooking was over the heads of his immediate neighbors. He made no money on these meals but contented himself with praise and the satisfaction of work well done.

It was Paul also who organized our occasional blowouts, held after we had put the paper to bed, at a restaurant in the rue de la Huchette that squatted over a series of cellars. We used the third level below the street. The advantage of this depth was that no matter how much racket we made, nothing could be heard outside; this was an era when noise at night, officially called *tapage nocturne*, was discouraged by the author-ities. The disadvantage of the cellar was that there were even more pro-found depths, which could be reached by a spiral stairway barred only by a strand of rope. A constant temptation to bibulous explorers, the stair-way led into the Catacombs, a dangerous labyrinth to penetrate, even if we never lost a man.

For those late suppers or early breakfasts, we spirited Paul out of the office about midnight to take charge of the gastronomic operations while the rest of us remained for the last two-and-a-half hours till press time. We arrived at the rue de la Huchette a little before 3:00 A.M. and were led by Paul into our dungeon where, to my great surprise the first time I at-tended, I saw a completely bare table. A corps of waiters staggered down the stairs behind us, bearing a plank the exact size of the table. On the plank reposed the largest fish I have ever seen out of water. The beast was slid onto the table and plates, glasses, cutlery, and bottles were added. Then we settled down to a magnificent banquet. When we finally fought our way like alpinists up the stairs and into the street, we found it was broad daylight.

These parties were always accompanied by spates of group singing, unskilled but enthusiastic, usually of songs whose words would not have been welcomed in a Sunday-school hymnal. The accompaniment was provided by Paul on his concertina. He could have played the accordion too and he was a good popular-music pianist, playing occasionally at Montparnasse's Dingo Bar in the rue Delambre, just for fun. I recall that after he returned to New York, Paul played the piano for a while at Café Society Downtown.

Before his final reconciliation with the United States, however, Paul put in a stint on the Mediterranean island of Ibiza, where he had settled with a wife. This was a situation I found difficult to envisage since Paul had always seemed to me to be cut out for the role of the eternal bachelor, like Edward VII who, come to think of it, was married too. His wife was Camille Haynes, one of the long line of society editors who succeeded each other at frequent intervals in a job distinguished by drudgery and low pay. Shortly after he established himself on Ibiza, he began bombarding me with letters, urging me to join them there because they needed a fourth for bridge. This struck me as an insufficient reason. He might have won me over if it had occurred to him to tell me of some of the other charms of Ibiza, now, alas, trampled by tourism. As it was I did not discover Ibiza until shortly before the horde did, in 1958, the year of Paul's death.

His spirit was still present. When I visited Ibiza, the news got around that a friend of Señor Pol was on the island. Everybody in Santa Eulalia del Rio, the town Paul immortalized in what was probably his best book, wanted me to come for dinner. Their messages reached me on the eve of departure, when I no longer had time to go to Santa Eulalia. It was probably just as well; after Paul, I would have been an anticlimax. For the rest of the world the greatest book ever written may be *War and Peace* by Leo Tolstoy but for Santa Eulalia del Rio it is *The Life and Death of a Spanish Town* by Señor Pol.

¶

"That's Not Playing the Game"

¶

I have never come across anybody who was always right but I have on several occasions encountered people who were always wrong. One of them was Hérol Egan, sports editor of the Paris Edition, who was infallible. Whenever I was faced with a problem, I would reduce it, if possible, to a choice between two opposed alternatives. I would then ask Egan's advice about which one to choose. He was always ready with an answer and I would then do the opposite. It always worked.

Egan remained with the Paris Edition to its end, when he was certainly the editorial employee with the longest term of service. Managing editor Bernhard Ragner and Egan were both legacies of the war, drawn by it from America to a Europe they might otherwise never have seen. Ragner's history was identical with that of any number of Americans who found themselves installed in France after the war more by force of circumstances than by their own will. They had been transported to Europe by the American army, they met French girls and married them, and after the war they discovered that their wives had no intention of leaving home for an America where Indians scalped you in the streets. So Ragner stayed. Egan's story was just the opposite.

He was not brought to France by the American army but by the British army. He had not been moved like a pawn at the order of his superiors, he was a volunteer. And he did not stay because he had a wife—he was not the marrying kind. I think he stayed because he liked France and because, as our sports editor, he had a cushy job. "Cushy" is the word he might have used himself for he had come out of the British service with a vocabulary studded with Anglicisms. The actions of others were "cricket" or "not cricket." During Jules Frantz' nightly battles with Egan to get the chronically late sports page completed somewhere near its scheduled hour, Egan would assure Frantz from time to time that he was not going to "let him down." When it became evident that Egan had let Frantz down, the sports editor would advise him to "carry on" despite the problem, which would certainly be solved since Egan always "played the game." The evolution of Egan's vocabulary apparently stopped with the war since, fifteen years later, he still referred to all Germans as "those bloody Huns."

In his speech, Egan was settling the debt he owed Britain for making him an officer and a gentleman. In his native Texas, the second noun must have had a sissified connotation. Egan never told me how he, whom I had always known as a drifter with the tide, had taken the daring initiative of enlisting in the Royal Air Force before the United States entered the war in 1916. The Royal Air Force converted him into a pilot and thus into an officer and consequently a gentleman. This rank changed his world—he had become a different and a better man, transfigured first by the unaccustomed respect accorded him and later by the romantic experience of a military career, even though, as he told it to me, it fell a bit short of being a saga.

Trained in England and transported to France, Egan found himself in his first combat in a dogfight. Confused by the wheeling and whirling of the planes, he solved the problem by picking out one plane and sticking to it, releasing bursts of machine-gun fire in its direction whenever it seemed they might be useful. They were not. When the squadron landed, his commander spoke to him angrily. "Dammit, Egan," he said, "if you weren't such a bloody bad shot, I wouldn't be here. Would it be too much to ask in the future to try to identify an enemy plane instead of shooting at me? In the meantime, you're grounded."

He returned in time to join the last combat of his squadron, a bravura operation staged needlessly on the day when it was known that the Armistice would begin at 11:00 A.M. "I wanted to get one more Hun," he explained to me. If he had succeeded, it would have made a grand total of one. As it happened, the Hun got him. He was shot down, emerging unscathed from the wreckage of his plane.

The Royal Air Force, which had not done well on its investment in Egan, made one last effort to employ him usefully by assigning him to fly planes back to England. He crawled into the first one and was about to take off over the Channel when he was flagged down by an officer who felt that it would be better to refuel first. It was then decided to grant Egan his honorable discharge as soon as possible. He became, reluctantly, a civilian, but he never forgot that he was qualified to speak knowingly on military matters.

Egan's conversion to British ways had not been complete enough to blot out all his Texas attitudes, including those manifested toward people with darker skins than his own. This did not prevent him from showing cordiality to the black American boxers who fought in Paris from time to time and with whom he sometimes showed up in the office, on terms as friendly and easygoing as with any white athlete. There were other domains where he was less tolerant.

He, Frantz, and Leigh Hoffman once took their month's vacation together and toured the provinces, visiting the bordellos of the towns where they stopped. This tour proved to be monotonous since provincial bordellos turned out to be dispiritingly standardized, all organized around large and dingy rooms and large and slatternly girls. Frantz devised a means of adding a bit of interest, using a standard fixture of the provincial brothel, *la négresse*. In those days France still had an empire and three years' obligatory military service, which for almost all conscripts included some time in the colonies. So a considerable part of the male population had the opportunity to develop exotic tastes and most small-town bordellos employed a woman from the African colonies to meet the demands of its clients.

Leaving Egan in the company of Hoffman, Frantz found time each day to make a preliminary visit to the house selected for the evening, where he explained that he would later visit with a pair of friends, one of whom doted on black girls but always pretended dislike when approached by them. *La négresse*, Frantz said, was not to become discouraged by this but was to devote herself to Egan until she vanquished his resistance. There followed a series of evenings when Egan found himself pocketed by one *négresse* after another. He was, fortunately, a man who could not harbor a grudge. His attitude, when the joke was explained to him at the end of the vacation, was no stronger than mild reproach, ordinarily the closest he could come to anger.

I was once responsible for raising his hackles a bit higher, but his resentment did not last long. This incident had to do with his column.

Egan's daily column of sports chitchat and comment was born in an effort to compete with the most popular feature of the *Paris Herald*'s sports page, Sparrow Robertson's column. Sparrow, a once-famous American runner, had decided to live in Paris after age removed him from the athletic arena. His name retained enough luster that the *Herald* proposed that he write a daily sports column.

After he accepted, it was discovered that he was nearly illiterate. A few attempts to convert his prose into coherent English failed, and then an editor of genius realized that the charm of his copy lay in its badness and ordered that the column should never be edited but should be sent to the composing room exactly as Sparrow wrote it. The column became an instant success. Many *Herald* readers turned to it first to savor the mayhem it inflicted on the English language.

The topics with which Sparrow dealt, in a syntax he invented as he went along, were also unusual. He believed everything he was told and printed everything he believed. One summer a gaggle of sportswriters went to Cap Gris Nez to wait for somebody—Gertrude Ederle, perhaps?—to swim the English Channel. The attempt was postponed day after day because of high waves, crosscurrents, or other obstacles. Bored, the sportswriters amused themselves by playing an elaborate joke on Sparrow: They presented to him one of their number as an Eskimo named Itzmuk, whom they described as a spectacular swimmer as yet unknown to the public because his exploits had all taken place in arctic waters. Itzmuk, Sparrow was told, was waiting at Cap Gris Nez for favorable conditions, when he would spring into the sea and streak across the Channel with a speed that would make him an overnight sensation. Sparrow was allowed once or twice to accompany Itzmuk to the water's edge, where he inserted a toe gingerly, exclaimed, "Ugh! Too hot!" and returned to his hotel. Sparrow reported in his column about the Eskimo who couldn't swim the Channel because the water was too warm. When he discovered that he had been had, Sparrow dropped Itzmuk with the explanation that he had been having fun all along with his readers.

It was decided at Harry's Bar, a rendezvous for Americans in Paris generally and for sports-minded Americans in particular, that Sparrow was "a character." On any lively evening in Harry's, somebody was sure to shout, "Sparrow, 'Mother Dooley's Geese,'" and Sparrow would launch into his sole contribution to the performing arts. Watching him, I could never lose the feeling that he was a worn-out jockey rather than a worn-out footracer, for he had the gnomelike stature of an old jockey. He also had a nose so enormous that it seemed likely to unbalance him and throw him at any moment on his face. "Mother Dooley's Geese" was a song with interminable verses, which Sparrow delivered at the top of his lungs in a tuneless voice as he stamped up and down the center of the long, narrow room.

Egan had no performing gifts to pit against Sparrow's, unless you count his rash readiness to make speeches at public gatherings. He felt, however, that he could match Sparrow at writing a sports column. He was wrong because he couldn't write badly enough. The idea of a sports column in the Paris Edition, even though it could not hope to outdo Sparrow's in sentence structure, was not a bad one but it had one drawback—Egan had to be bludgeoned into producing it. One of Frantz' biggest problems was to herd Egan into getting his sports page done in time. This was further complicated by the necessity of wresting the sports column from him, for, however slow he might be in concocting it, Egan made it a point of honor never to send the sports page out without one. Time pressure left Egan unruffled, as did heated injunctions that he buckle down to the writing. With a slow smile, he would utter the stock formulas he employed to ward off the impatient: "Uriah the Hittite was a mighty man" or "The horse is a noble animal." When Egan's smile became a thin-lipped grin, the situation was dangerous; he could become glassy-eyed at less expense than most people, sometimes on half a glass of beer.

About half the time Egan spent at his typewriter was devoted to his pipe. Cleaning the pipe, filling the pipe, lighting and relighting the pipe were occupations so absorbing as to leave little time for other jobs. Clamping the pipe firmly between the teeth and emitting an occasional puff while fixing his gaze on the paper in his typewriter gave Egan the air of a man thinking intently, and hence working, without necessarily involving any use of his mind.

When not occupied with his pipe, Egan practiced the art of vanishing, at which he was highly skilled. One minute he would be sitting at his typewriter and the next he would be gone. If you stepped over to his desk to see how he was progressing, you would be likely to find that the sheet of paper in his typewriter had been defiled only by the title of his column and below it a single line: "By Hérol Egan." A scout would then be sent to the Chope Cadet, where Egan would be found leaning against the bar over a glass of beer. Brought back upstairs, he would sit down at his typewriter, take a peck at it, and interrupt to struggle with his pipe. Then we would realize that he was no longer there. The paper in his typewriter would now read:

By Hérol Egan

The

One evening, when Egan arrived wearing his fixed grin, it occurred to me to keep a blow-by-blow record of his activities. Each entry began with the time of the event ("8:07 Egan sits down at his typewriter") and detailed the procession of starts, stops, false starts, disappearances, and retrievals. On this night Egan returned from one of his absences about 1:00 A.M. and announced, "Well, got to finish my column"—ignoring the detail that he hadn't started it yet.

"Too late, Hérol," I said. "Your page has gone."

"You mean you sent off my page without my column?" he cried.

"The column's in," I said. "I wrote it for you."

Egan pounced on the page proof and read, in its usual place and under its usual headline, my minute-by-minute report of his night's labors under his own byline. He looked up reproachfully.

"Wave," he said, "that isn't cricket. That's not playing the game."

He was perhaps dreading the reaction at Harry's Bar, to which he went nightly after the paper was out to pick up sports gossip. He was courageous enough to make his usual visit although he may have felt some apprehension when a newsboy appeared with the paper fresh from the press. Somebody at the bar picked one up, opened it to the sports page, and began to chuckle.

"Egan," he said, "this is the best damned column you ever wrote."

Egan's broad smile reappeared. "Yeah," he said, "I didn't have anything particularly interesting to write about tonight, so I thought a little joking wouldn't hurt."

The next night his column was on time.

¶

Yolande; or, The Daily Grind

¶

The sports editor of the Paris Edition practiced one sport only: He was a sexual athlete. Egan referred to this discipline as "the daily grind," which may have been a slight exaggeration. He usually started his day—after waking, breakfasting, and dressing, in that order, for he was one of the Tribuners who lived at the Hôtel de Lisbonne and even so unprepossessing a French hotel provided its guests with breakfast in bed—by strolling over to the nearby Luxembourg Gardens, selecting one of the women sunning themselves there and leading her back to his newly abandoned bed.

Egan's technique, as he described it, seemed to be on the crude side, consisting of little more than a blunt invitation without time-wasting preliminaries. Perhaps this was the best he could manage, although his French was fluent. He was aided by his foreign accent, which was often acceptable as an excuse for violating local codes of conduct.

"Don't you ever get your face slapped, Hérol?" I once asked.

"Sometimes," he admitted as his slow grin began. "But I get an awful lot of sex."

His quest was made easy because many of the women in the Luxembourg Gardens were there for sex also. They were not professionals, just players of the same sport as Egan. Some of them would accept a present if it were offered but would not ask for one; some would even refuse one if it took the unsentimental form of money. Egan himself wanted it understood that he was not making any commitment and sometimes his largesse went no further than giving his bed-partner five and a half francs and the address of the nearby Polish restaurant that would provide a full lunch for that sum. If she had been particularly agreeable, he might devote a little more of his time to her by taking her to the Polish restaurant. This set him back roughly forty-five cents for two meals.

146

There were even times when a girl so entranced Egan that he would remain faithful to her for as long as three weeks. The girl who held on to Egan longest he met one morning in the Luxembourg Gardens, dressed in full mourning, including long veil. He made his usual approach, was rewarded with the usual response, and a few minutes later Yolande was in Egan's bedroom. When the moment to undress arrived, Yolande burst into tears.

She told her sad story. Her mother had recently died—hence the mourning—and left her penniless. She had no other clothes since her hotel had turned her out for not paying her bill and had impounded her trunk. She had agreed to follow Egan out of desperation but she couldn't go through with it. There was no future for her except in marriage but she had nothing to offer a husband, at a time when dowries were still demanded, except her virginity.

Surely Egan, an American, a member of a nation noted for its generous treatment of women, would not make her sacrifice her only asset. Would he not lend her the small sum necessary to recover her clothes? Egan was touched but broke. He promised to bail out her trunk the next payday, weeks away, and would allow her to stay in his room with her virginity intact.

Waiting for payday, Yolande ate nightly with Egan at Gillotte's, still in her full mourning. Payday came and went but Yolande did not. She had no money to move into another hotel and Egan didn't have enough to stake her to one. She was now normally dressed and it did not seem that her recovered wardrobe had been extensive. Her invariable garment was a raincoat, faded to the washed-out color of her complexion. She was still sharing Egan's bed and still insisting on respect for her virginity.

Life was becoming hard for Egan. Yolande's presence prevented him from pursuing his program of "the daily grind" at the same time he was sharing his bed with a soft body that he was forbidden to touch. He did try to touch it from time to time, but each attempt caused Yolande to leap weeping from bed and pull on her clothes. Egan would excuse himself abjectly and Yolande would finally consent to get back into bed. Egan slept badly.

Weeks later, their relations were interrupted by an accident: Yolande dropped her handbag, its contents spilled over the floor, and Egan, helping her pick them up, found a photograph of a boy who Yolande admitted was her four-year-old son. Egan reacted by suggesting that they get into bed at once and make up for lost time but Yolande dissolved into tears again and produced a second sad story. Yes, she admitted, she had lied. She was not a virgin. She had been raped at an early age and the child was the result. The experience had been so horrible that she had never again had sexual relations. Egan, a man of goodwill because he was an American, could understand that? He could and did.

Yolande continued to sleep unscathed in his bed and, worse, she became tyrannical. She was a victim of the male sex and allowed herself to take vengeance on Egan as its representative. If she wanted to change her stockings, she ordered Egan to turn his back. She made a rule that Egan had to get up first in the morning and leave the room so that she could rise without exposing herself. If he happened to look at her when she was undressing at night, there would be another storm, tears, and a threat to leave. I have no idea why Egan didn't take her up on it.

One evening I came into the office half an hour before the others because of some special job I had to do and found Egan waiting for me. He was dead drunk, the only time I ever saw him in that state.

"Waverley," he said, "friendzhip mozht zhacred thing life, agree?"

I agreed.

"I zhink no woman zhever come between men friendzh, agree?"

"Look here, Hérol," I said. "I've work to do. What are you trying to say?"

He blurted it out: "Have you been zhleeping with Yolande?"

"Me?" I responded. "With that pasty-faced, flat-chested blonde? Good grief, no."

Despite my instinctive description of Yolande, I did not know if I had convinced Egan. He ended the interrogation and stumbled toward the stairs and the Chope Cadet. Since I was not one of the Tribuners who lived at the Hôtel de Lisbonne, I was not one of those who had known for some time that although Egan wasn't making love with Yolande, somebody was. Most of them knew who, even if Egan didn't.

About nine o'clock, after the night staff had arrived and work was progressing, Egan made his second appearance, stumbling to the corner where Ragner sat. The managing editor was embraced by Egan. "Ragner," he announced, "worzh thingzh happen me tonight can happen any man. Ragner, youn I got zhtick together. Weezh 'n war. Thezh other fellerzh—zhlackers! All zhlackers!" Ragner, who was afraid of drunks, took advantage of the speech to duck away as Egan made an announcement.

"I'm goin' downzhtairs to join For'n Lezhion!" and he lurched away in the direction of the Foreign Legion recruiting office in the Chope Cadet. I have no idea whom he met there but minutes later he was back, his bearing now testifying that he was A Man Who Knew.

He stumbled around the city desk and stopped behind Swede Swenson, the commander come for Don Juan. Swenson was working with intense concentration on a story and did not look up but his neck turned scarlet under Egan's glare. "Zhwede," Egan announced, "I'll buy you drink at break." He paused a beat. "But won't drink wizh you. I only drink with zhentlemen."

I heard the full details later. Swenson's room at the Hôtel de Lisbonne was just across the corridor from Egan's. One morning after Yolande had shooed Egan out, she burst through Swenson's unlocked door in her nightgown. Tearing it off, she ripped the straps from Swede's suitcase and thrust them into his hands. "Whip me," she ordered.

Swenson was the gentlest of men but not hard-hearted enough to refuse a reasonable request by a woman. So he whipped Yolande until she signified her desire for a change in the entertainment. After that first encounter, she visited Swede's room almost daily once Egan had gone. It did not take long for the news to get around.

Yolande disappeared from Gillotte's but once or twice she and Swenson turned up in places where they would be unlikely to run into Egan. Then she was seen no more. If Swenson knew what had happened to her, he didn't say. Egan forgave Swenson. He was a quick pardoner and had besides the consolation that he could now resume his morning visits to the Luxembourg Gardens.

¶

Louisette

¶

She entered my life through a hole in the wall. The hole, about a foot square, had been cut in the partition between the office of the *Chicago Tribune* Foreign News Service and the city room of the Paris Edition. It let us pass paper directly instead of walking the forty feet that separated the doors of both offices. On my second or third day on the night staff, a pretty brunette head was thrust through this hole and turned inquiringly toward the corner usually occupied by managing editor Ragner. He was out at dinner.

It had not really been necessary for her to make sure that the coast was clear for she could have deduced it from the welcoming shouts from half-a-dozen points around the copy desk. "Louisette! Louisette!" the staff cried in joy.

Louisette seemed to be trying to plunge through the hole but thought better of this; there was a danger of becoming stuck halfway through although she was *petite*. That was the word for her, not "little" or "small." When a Frenchman describes a woman as *petite*, he usually means not only that she is small but also vivacious, sparkling, probably mischievous, and often quick at repartee. Louisette was all of these.

Having decided that the hole in the wall was not large enough, she arrived on foot in the city room, where everybody decided that it was time for a coffee break. We trooped downstairs, bearing Louisette with us. The effect was that of the inevitable scene in all musical comedies in which a female star gyrates in center stage while a male chorus dances worshipfully around her. In the theater, however, the adoring males are presumed to be revering at a distance the pure, untouchable, inaccessible goddess; it would have occurred to nobody to describe Louisette as inaccessible. She was receptive to all of us, the mistress of the Paris Edition.

I mean exactly that: not the mistress of a number of us, individually if simultaneously. Louisette was not promiscuous. She had only one lover: the staff as an entity, a corporate being. This lover happened to be a community; which one of its members represented it in its relationship with Louisette at any given time was merely a detail.

Probably this accounted for her violating what I have found to be a universal rule among women: the first night, never; the second night, it depends. Louisette went to bed with me the first night I took her out but she probably didn't think of it as a first night for I was on the staff of the Paris Edition and she had been sleeping with the Paris Edition for a long time. By joining the staff, I had acquired full rights.

I can remember only one time when Louisette stepped out of her role as comforter to all of us. She had spent the night in the Hôtel de Lisbonne, with whom I have forgotten, when Swenson dropped by early in the morning while she was still in bed with his colleague. Swenson seemed so obviously envious that Louisette's bed-partner offered his place to Swenson. "Do you take me for a whore you can pass around like a piece of property?" Louisette cried indignantly. Swede's expression changed to deep disappointment. "Never mind, Swede," Louisette said soothingly. "Just go back to your room. I'll be up in a minute."

Louisette played no favorites. Perhaps she liked some of us better than others, but she never showed it. She seemed devoid of jealousy, malice, possessiveness, and selfishness. I do not remember ever seeing her sad or depressed. She was always gay, a gaiety never forced. She simply became one with you because, being entirely at peace with herself, she was entirely at peace with everyone else. Despite her extensive sexual activity, Louisette was not a nymphomaniac. She liked to make love but it was not an obsession: What better use could be made of the evening?

No one ever accused Louisette of being an intellectual. This was one of her charms. I suppose her formal education had stopped as soon as the law allowed but her natural common sense sufficed for anything she wanted to do or be. It was true, however, that her lack of interest in all intellectual or artistic activities reduced to a minimum the entertainment you could put before her. No one would have thought to take her to a concert, much less to the opera or the ballet, nor to the theater. She would have been bored even by the popular bedroom farces of the boulevard theaters for she would have thought it silly to make so much fuss about who got into bed with whom. She did not much care for the movies either.

She was good company in large, noisy cafés, where she took immense pleasure in the spectacle provided by the other customers. She was in her element in the sort of nightclub that specialized in insulting the clients and allowing them to insult back. One thing she particularly enjoyed was to walk along the central strip of sidewalk dividing the wide boulevards, which was almost continuously occupied with traveling fairs.

It was a mistake to take Louisette into more elevated settings. When I ate with her, it was usually in Gillotte's or a similarly unpretentious restaurant or in some big brilliant café like the Coupole. Once I erred by taking her to dinner at the Chope Cadet, whose restaurant verged on the elegant and whose customers were well-dressed and soft-voiced. Louisette enjoyed the experience but some of the other diners did not. Louisette was a girl of gusto and she had a lively sense of humor. She thought many people funny, especially stuffy ones, a category well-represented in this restaurant. She confided her impressions of the other customers to me, if "confided" is the word for it. Her voice carried and, although her remarks were of a biting accuracy that would ordinarily have kept me laughing, I was embarrassed that the people she was pillorying could hear her. It was the only time she ever embarrassed me.

Completely uninterested in money, she never thought about it even when she had none. Since she had no visible means of support, there was a vague impression among the staff that somewhere in her life was an elderly gentleman who looked after basic needs. If so, he neither kept her in luxuries nor demanded much of her time since she was always with us. I never knew her family name and I think nobody else on the staff did either. Another thing none of us knew was her address although we did know she was a geniune *Parisienne*. She must have had somewhere to change clothes—she was meticulously clean and very attentive to her underwear, if only because she knew that it would frequently be on view.

I do not recall that any of us ever insulted Louisette by offering her money, and I remember her asking me for some only once and then it was a small amount: She had a toothache and no money to buy a painkiller. I once dragged her into a store to buy her a new pair of shoes but this was the extent of my generosity.

There was only one fashion in which we contributed to Louisette's support and we did not think of it in that way. Nor, I am sure, did she. She had saved us from sexual hunger and we saved her from actual hunger, even if nobody considered it to be in the nature of payment. She turned up at Gillotte's to eat with us most nights as a member of the family. Sometimes one of us invited her over and she sat down, but if nobody did, she sat down where there was an empty place and was always welcome. Nobody worried about who was going to pay her bill, least of all Louisette. If she had been taken in charge by one of us in particular, he would sign her bill with his own. If there was no volunteer, I suppose Gillotte's split the amount among us.

Often she found herself paired off with someone who had the night off, which permitted them to finish dinner in a leisurely fashion after the rest of us had returned to work. Then they might wander off together to a café terrace, and so to bed. She did not create any obligation for us to take charge of her except when we wanted to.

If Louisette was our favorite girl, she was not the only one for our dozen men—a fact symbolized at one of our deep-cellar dinners by the unusual way Elliot Paul had arranged the table. About half the staff, sitting at one end of the table, was drinking water while the upper half was drinking wine. The water drinkers had sinned. I was with the saints, drinking wine, undeservedly.

I had shared a taxi one night from the office to the Left Bank with another *Tribune* staffer. As our cab slowed from the rue Bonaparte into the place St. Germain des Prés, a young woman standing on the corner flagged us down. She shall remain anonymous although it betrays little to say she worked for the *Paris Herald*. After she joined us in the taxi, my friend threw his arm around her and drew her to him. A few blocks later I left the taxi to them and they hardly noticed my departure.

Because of this, I was sitting at the top of the table, drinking wine, while my friend was at the bottom, drinking water. You do not drink alcohol, even wine, when you have gonorrhea. The lower half of the table had been reserved for sufferers and the reason there were so many of them was the young woman in the taxi. (I learned later that there was one in our midst who should have been at the bottom of the table but who was embarrassed to admit it. He sipped some wine, knowing he would pay the price the next day. He later became a diplomat.)

The woman from the *Herald* got around. Six members of the Paris *Chi-*

cago Tribune staff, three of the *Herald*, two of the Associated Press, and one of the United Press had succumbed to her sickness before she discovered she had it.

Gonorrhea is a nasty, disagreeable, painful business. I speak with feeling on this point, for not long after that dinner, divine justice took another look at my case. Where I had picked up the unpleasant gift was not going to change anything, but I wanted to know. There were three possibilities, one of them easily dismissed. The one far above suspicion was a Swiss girl whom I had met only recently, soft-spoken, tastefully dressed, adequately educated. I had no intention of accusing her but had to tell her what had happened for her own protection. She reacted admirably, without reproaches, urging me simply to make sure I had a reliable doctor and to get cured speedily so we could resume normal relations.

The second woman was the one I suspected. She was a Spanish dancer who was performing with a not overly reputable troupe. I phoned her to ask if she might have passed the malady on to me, putting it as politely as I could. Her reaction could have blown all the fuses of France's telephone system.

There remained Louisette, with whom I had a lunch date. When I put the question, she was as indignant as she was capable of being, which was not very, and we had a pleasant lunch. I had no doubt that she was not the culprit.

The injustice of having been suspected must have bothered her, for she turned up at the office that evening to set matters straight. It happened to be my night off and it must have been Ragner's too, for if he had been there, Louisette would certainly not have jumped onto the copydesk and pulled up her clothes to demonstrate her impeccable healthiness.

"It was that Spanish girl," she charged. "She left a pair of panties in the studio once and they were dirty and yellow." Public opinion agreed with her and so did I: The Spanish dancer was convicted. A good many years later, I ran again into the Swiss woman and she confessed that it had been she who had infected me. No wonder she had been so understanding and solicitous.

After accusing the Spanish woman, Louisette was still standing on the copydesk. She had worked off her resentment and was in a good humor. In the middle of a circle of her lovers, she began pointing at each in turn and describing whatever had struck her as funny in his sexual comportment. As she ran through her catalog, I was told later, the laughter became continuous. I suspect that it was only because I was not there that I got off lightly.

The day after Louisette's show, I found a note from her tucked into my mailbox. I kept it until it had turned yellow and threatened to come apart at the folds, and then I kept a copy of it. I think it should be presented in its original language:

Mon cher vieux hibou,

Si vous saviez comme je vous aime, vous ne me tromperiez pas comme vous le faîtes avec la première femme venue au risque d'attraper une maladie et que vous pouvez me contaminer la prochaine fois que je vais coucher avec vous.

Je suis désolée, vous faîtes tellement bien l'amour que je ne pourrais jamais vous oublier.

Je pleure sur mon amour perdu toutes les larmes de mon corps.

P.S. Soignez-vous bien et je vous reviendrai.

Votre petite chose,
Louisette

In English:

My dear old owl,

If you knew how much I love you, you wouldn't betray me as you do with the first woman who turns up, at the risk of catching a disease with which you could infect me the next time I sleep with you.

I am brokenhearted, you make love so well that I can never forget you.

I weep for my lost love all the tears of my body.

P.S. Take good care of yourself and I will come back to you.

Your little thing,
Louisette

She never came back to me. My cure had barely been completed when I was promoted into the *Chicago Tribune* Foreign News Service and assigned to its London bureau. I was away for two years. When I returned, Louisette was no longer present and I was married. Some years later I learned what had become of her. She had died, it appeared, from no identifiable disease. She had simply worn herself out, still in her twenties. In that brief period she had expended all the energy allotted to her for a lifetime. She had lived herself to death.

¶

Low Blows

In 1927, when I joined the Paris Edition, there were four English-language daily newspapers published in France, whose stable American population at the time was about twenty-five thousand. Besides the Paris Edition, a subsidiary of Colonel Robert Rutherford McCormick's *Chicago Tribune*, and the *New York Herald*, a subsidiary of James Gordon Bennett's *New York Herald Tribune* (which had been unable to lengthen its name when the parent paper did since two *Tribunes* in Paris would have created vast confusion), there were the *Continental Daily Mail*, a subsidiary of the *London Daily Mail*, and the *Paris Times*, nobody's subsidiary.

We did not look on the *Daily Mail* as competition, although the *Daily Mail* thought it was and tried to woo American readers by such devices as running accounts of baseball games. Possibly some Americans did buy the *Mail* for this reason since baseball stories written by Britons who believed that baseball was a backwoods form of cricket were worth the price of the paper.

We did consider the *Paris Times* to be competition but not very serious. It hadn't the means to compete. I doubt if its existence cut at all into our circulation or into the *Herald*'s; anybody who read the *Times* was already reading one of the competitors. The *Paris Times* had been founded by an expatriate American millionaire named Courtland Bishop who had money to lose before the 1929 stock market crash. The man who was responsible for keeping this paper interesting and thus alive was Gaston Archambault, previously managing editor of the Paris *New York Herald*. He had been given leave from the *Herald* to join the armed forces in 1918 and, during his absence, Eric Hawkins, a Briton, acted as managing editor. Archambault took his job back after the war and held it until 1924, when Bishop tapped him to edit the *Paris Times*.

I disliked Archambault, who seemed to me to have a grating personality. He spoke in a rasping voice, accompanying his typically cynical remarks with a noise that was presumably intended to be a chuckle. I may have been prejudiced against him because of his sinister appearance, which was not his fault. He had lost the sight in one eye in the war, and its eyelid remained permanently half-closed. But I never heard anyone who worked for him complain about his character and I am obliged to admit that he was an extremely capable editor. The quality of the *Paris Times* proved it.

That quality had to be obtained by compensating with more brains for less money. I do not know if the *Paris Times* received any cable at all from the States, having no parent paper there to provide it. I doubt if it could even afford news agency service. Thus it had to fill its columns chiefly with material already published in other papers and could justify its existence only by making this material more interesting or delving into it more deeply or writing it better. Archambault realized that this could be achieved only by superior writers, so he spent a large part of his scanty funds to pay salaries that would attract and retain men of the caliber he needed to produce, in effect, the equal of today's weekly news magazines. He recruited some extremely able writers, among them Larry Blochman and Hillel Bernstein, both future authors, Martin Summers, later foreign editor of the *Saturday Evening Post*, and Vincent Sheehan, who worked there after leaving the *Chicago Tribune* Foreign News Service. We had a chance to assess the quality of the *Paris Times* staff when, a victim of the stock market crash, it gave up the ghost and Tom Crane came from it to us. He was one of our best men.

The roster of relatively permanent American publications, aside from the little magazines of Montparnasse, which belonged to a separate category and were usually oriented internationally, included the *Boulevardier*, a weekly or monthly, I have forgotten which, that had little success. It was the property of another expatriate American millionaire, Erskine Gwynn, and was also a casualty of the 1929 crash.

Our only real competitor was the *Paris Herald* and the battle was ferocious, knockdown journalism. I fear that as a newer, brasher, and livelier paper, we were less inhibited by scruples and delivered more low blows than the *Herald*. As befitted so venerable a newspaper—it was founded in 1887—the *Herald* was more decorous. That must have been the quality that inspired Ezra Pound, in his frequent postcards to me, to describe it regularly as "the dead-and-stuffed *New York Herald*."

We occasionally shocked it. One night, Larry Hills, the *Herald* publisher, burst into his city room, waving a copy of the Paris Edition fresh from the press. "They're crazy at the *Tribune*," he shouted. "They're stark, staring mad. They've put the word 'bordel' in a headline." So we had: The institution had been the subject of discussion at a committee meeting of the League of Nations, a respectable source if ever there was one. Still "bordel" was a hot word in those days, in French and in English. Our own printers had boggled at setting it in type until we convinced them that it meant something else in English.

We had no objection to writing lively headlines while taking care to keep unintentional innuendo out of them, a danger because of the names of some French cities. We might have been misunderstood, for example, if a headline referred to "Nancy Boys" or "Nice Boys." Nobody would be surprised today by our lighthearted headlines—one I remember was on a story about a man who had been robbed of the gold fillings in his teeth: "Thar's Gold in Them Thar Mountin's." But the *Herald* felt that these headlines stamped us as too frivolous to be trusted with the sacred role of instructing the public.

Both the *Herald* and the *Tribune* ran letter columns, supposedly written by our readers. Neither of us had a big enough circulation to assure an adequate supply of genuine letters, so we made them up. These fabricated letters usually were more sprightly than the real ones since we were, after all, professional writers and our readers mostly amateurs. We worked up some fairly heated arguments in the letters column, sometimes with one of us belaboring the letters of another, sometimes with the same man taking both sides. A redheaded rewrite man named Campbell carried on an argument with himself for several weeks on the protocol question of how a gentleman seated at a café table and encumbered by a hat, cane, and drink should juggle these when presented unexpectedly to a woman. This question drew a number of genuine letters from readers, as did one of our own letters that argued that Lewis Carroll's "Jabberwocky" ("'Twas brillig and the slithy toves / Did gyre and gimble in the wabe") was a corruption of French.

The *Herald* had an asset for its letters column that was denied to us: a pathetic query from "Old Philadelphia Lady" who was probably a member of the *Herald* staff and who wanted to know how to translate Fahrenheit into centigrade and vice versa. This letter first appeared on December 27, 1899, and by mistake appeared the next day too, inspiring the paper's unpredictable publisher, James Gordon Bennett, to order that it should be run every day. This it was, for eighteen years and five months in 6,718 editions, attracting from time to time answers so intricate that only a professional mathematician could have understood them. Three days after Bennett died, on May 17, 1918, the Old Philadelphia Lady lost her daily franchise but in my era it was still reprinted from time to time and never failed to provoke answers. The *Herald*, which by then had become the *Herald Tribune*, suspended publication when the Germans entered Paris during World War II. When it returned to activity on May 17, 1944, it celebrated by running once more the question from the Old Philadelphia Lady. The letters column got off to a good start as a new generation of writers responded. Every now and again the paper, now the *International Herald Tribune*, prints the letter still.

In our other competition with the *Herald*, the areas on which we concentrated were determined by our special function of catering to the interests of Americans living abroad. On the news in general, we ran about neck and neck except that the *Herald* had the edge in American news, transmitted directly from New York by cable. We both had the basic background service of a news agency, the Agence Havas. We ran first, and for that matter alone, in satisfying a hunger among Americans abroad for comic strips. The *Herald Tribune* in New York published none but the *Chicago Tribune* syndicate distributed to its subscribers many of the most popular comic strips, of which the sole survivor is "Gasoline Alley." We printed about half-a-dozen strips and I imagine that a considerable part of our circulation was built on them.

The most important service our two papers performed for Americans abroad and for some European readers too was to bring them stock market quotations from Wall Street. We were outgunned by the *Herald*, which received much more complete listings than we did. However our shorter list was popular with Europeans, who were then interested only in the leading American stocks and had no desire to explore a jungle of figures to find them. Next in importance was American sports news, for which there was no other source in Europe than the American papers, despite the *Daily Mail*'s efforts. The *Herald* outdid us on this one too since it received more cable, but not so badly as might have been expected. The most important part of sports news was the score, which could be transmitted without using much wordage. As the home paper maintained a stable of well-known sports writers, we could always add to the spot news of the day articles clipped from the *Chicago Tribune* when it reached us about ten days after publication.

Of great importance to both papers was society news, a fact that does not speak highly of the intellectual level of the American colony of Paris. Both papers ran a full page daily of items, rarely exceeding a paragraph in length, recording who had been received by whom, who had given bridge parties, who had entertained at lunches and dinners, and who had been invited to them. This sort of information was apparently of immense interest to a large number of our readers—not to the writers, artists, and hangers-on of Montparnasse but to the Americans of the Right Bank.

Both papers employed an editor to collect the ephemera of this society and both papers changed the editor frequently. They were fired easily in most cases since they were readily replaceable, or they quit themselves because they were bored and ill paid. There was no inducement to pay them better for they were unskilled laborers taking down over the phone the news that self-admirers gave them. It was rare for a society editor to do any genuine reporting.

The two papers would have been equals in society news if we had not had an asset that the *Herald* was never able to match. Surprisingly, it had been acquired for us by Colonel McCormick, who first instructed us to ignore the "lobster-palace Americans" and leave the reporting of their doings to the *Herald* and then, with consistent inconsistency, arranged personally for a feature devoted to the activities of the lobster-palace frequenters, both American and European. It was a column whose whole world was restricted to what was then called high society. The members looked on society reporters as servile menials begging for crumbs of gossip; the exception was May Birkhead, whose column appeared daily in our paper. She was not an outsider, permitted only grudgingly to exchange a few words with the inner circle, but a member of it. She had been on close terms with its members since birth and knew about all the skeletons in all the closets, although she was discreet enough never to mention them. Since she was always the first to be informed of impending events in high society, anyone who wanted to be up-to-date had to read the *Tribune*. We kept her column carefully aloof from the ordinary society page.

I do not know how the colonel found May Birkhead and signed her to write for us but I rather suspect that it was she who found him. I have no idea how much she was paid but it must have been too much to permit the *Herald* to hire her away. The impressive limousine in which her chauffeur delivered her copy to us nightly must have been one of the perquisites of the job. Once in a while she drove to the office herself and visited the city room, where she was a model of graciousness.

May Birkhead, the comics, and, after 1930, a more lavish use of photographs brought us readers from the *Herald* who took us as a second paper. We were the first paper only for a minority, the intellectuals of Montparnasse, who were not fervent customers of our advertisers. Both the *Herald* and the *Tribune* were local papers; the home paper had given us the official name of European Edition but we spoke of it as the Paris Edition. For both papers the largest part of the readership was in France, almost exclusively in Paris except during the Riviera season.

The American colony of Paris was an enclave in which everybody knew everybody else and wanted to know everything that happened to them, particularly if it were scandalous. Reporting of local stories was therefore one of our sharpest fields of rivalry and we were strengthened by the *Herald*, although not intentionally. Will Barber quit that paper and joined us, giving us a first-rate desk man, and Lee Dickson, his closest friend on the *Herald*, quit too, giving us a first-rate street reporter.

Dickson may have been behind one of the more bizarre incidents in the running warfare between the two papers. In any case, it was someone who had shifted from the *Herald* to us and shortly afterward ran down a good story, which he telephoned to the city desk. Unfortunately, since he had a slight load on at the time, he called not our number but the one he was accustomed to calling, that of the *Herald*.

We got our own back when the *Herald* printed a photograph showing a crowd running from soldiers who were firing into it under the headline

BREAD RIOTS IN MOSCOW, with a caption saying that starving citizens had rebelled against the Soviet government and had been dispersed, bloodily, by the army. The picture looked familiar to me and I dug into my books and found it, the frontispiece of Arno Dosch-Fleurot's *Through War to Revolution*. It had been taken a decade earlier, during the Russian Revolution. We reprinted the same photograph the next day, headed SCOOP OF THE CENTURY, giving the *Herald*'s description of it followed by the correct one. For weeks afterward, Eric Hawkins of the *Herald* never ran into me without shaking his head reproachfully and saying, "Not cricket, old boy, not cricket." In fact, the *Herald* had been the victim of an unscrupulous picture agency, which had given a new life to some of the old photos in its files by providing imaginative captions for them.

This clash between the two papers can hardly compare with our riposte to the *Herald*'s mythical story of Commander Byrd's landing in Paris when he actually came down in the ocean, from which the *Herald* must still have been smarting on January 10, 1928, when I too became a myth-maker.

Thomas Hardy, the writer, had been at the point of death for several days, and I had written a long obituary about him and had it put into type, ready to go into the paper if news of his death reached us at press time. It was just on our deadline that our cyclist courier brought me the galley proofs of *Le Matin*, a French daily newspaper with which we had an exchange agreement. In one of the galleys I found a paragraph reporting Hardy's death.

I barely had time to write an introductory paragraph, open the front page, and fill its first column with the Hardy obituary. I then walked happily home, pleased to be working for a paper where the death of an important writer justified remaking the front page.

When I entered the city room the next evening, city editor Kospoth growled at me: "Where'd you get the idea Thomas Hardy is dead?"

"It's in the *Matin*," I said.

He picked up a copy of *Le Matin* from the desk and tossed it to me. "Find it," he challenged me.

I couldn't. The *Matin* had composed an erroneous story, discovered the mistake, and killed it. There was nothing in our exchange agreement that required reporting such details.

I waited apprehensively for the London wire to open at 8:00 P.M. Not entirely to my surprise, it began: ONE WHY MUST YOU TRY TO COVER LONDON FROM PARIS QUERY WE ARE THE LAUGHINGSTOCK OF EN-GLAND STOP HARDY REPORTED BETTER THIS MORNING.

Gulping, I went on with my reading of the wire, which continued: TWO THOMAS HARDY DIED TONIGHT AT HIS SUSSEX HOME.

I dug a photo of Hardy out of the files and printed it with the caption, "Thomas Hardy, the illustrious British novelist, whose death was reported exclusively yesterday by the *Chicago Tribune*."

¶

Locusts in the Sahara

¶

A year in Paris was not the best preparation for two years in London. I rejoiced, in May 1928, at having been promoted into the Foreign News Service, where the scope was wider and the pay better, but Paris tugged at me from the other side of the Channel like urgent unfinished business. I was constantly conscious of Paris, so near in distance, so far in spirit, calling me back—especially on Sundays. The English Sunday is no longer so grim as it used to be but it was bleak indeed in those days. Every Sunday I swore I would quit and return to Paris; finally, on a Sunday in May 1930, I did.

I simply gave up my job in London and went back to Paris with no promise of employment, but I had enough sense to go to the Paris Edition office to see if there was an opening for me. There was, at the top—more exactly, one niche below the top. My departure from London had automatically made a job in Paris since everybody moved up one step all along the line. From the Paris Edition Edmond Taylor, who was night editor or news editor, second in command of the editorial organization, was moved into the Paris bureau of the Foreign News Service. I inherited his job and began the most interesting period of my work on the Paris Edition. Being a member of its staff had been fun but becoming one of those who helped direct its growth was even more fun.

A new order had set in. Six months before my return, Bernhard Ragner had been replaced as managing editor by Jules Frantz. When I replaced Taylor, a journalist of the highest quality, as news editor, Frantz and I rescued the day staff from lethargy by making Robert Stern city editor, replacing Kospoth, who did not mind. Kospoth disliked responsibility and had only wanted the job because it meant more money. There was no question of reducing his salary level and he moved on to something else, art editor perhaps.

For the first time since its carefree beginnings, the Paris Edition was organized for the exercise of serious and responsible journalism. Until that time the paper had been a masterpiece of improvisation, splendid on its good days, capable of falling on its face on the bad days. We did not lose the ability to improvise but we were now protected, by improved craftsmanship, from being a ghastly mistake on an off-day.

The new order was symbolized by a series of innovations by Taylor, Frantz, and myself. Before he moved into the Foreign News Service, Taylor started work on a tool that the Paris Edition needed: a style book, a compilation of usage, more or less arbitrarily imposed on a paper's writers and editors, to assure uniformity in the copy. When it is a case of every man for himself, the result can be the same word spelled in the American and British style—"center" and "centre," "honor" and "honour"—in adjacent headlines, giving readers the impression that the editors are unable to make up their minds. I finished the work on the style book with the aid of Taylor, who was available in the Foreign News Service office next to our city room.

The home paper had a style book, of course, but we refrained from using it since this would have committed us to variants that we felt were inappropriate to our literate readership. The colonel was an advocate of what he called "improved spelling" and ordered the use of such mildly undesirable forms as "nite" and "thru" before progressing to "thoro," "biografy," "grafic," and "frate." We were deterred from seeking guidance from Chicago by the prospect of a headline like: NITE FRATE PLOWS THRU RED LITE.

Frantz' first innovation started before I returned from London. This was the creation of a morgue, or reference library. Reference files were invaluable for a paper like ours, which, because of the high cost of cables, received the American news in skeleton form. By accumulating data on people, places, and important events, we had the means to flesh out stories. The contents of the morgue were drawn largely from newspaper and magazine clippings and included photographs, usually in the form of papier-mâché mats, or molds into which molten lead was poured to reproduce the picture.

Frantz set up the morgue primarily because he knew how useful it would be. But a basic element of his character was also involved: His affection for the men with whom he worked made it all but unthinkable for him ever to fire, or even to demote, anyone. His method was to achieve the best possible results with the material available and so he chose Leigh Hoffman to take charge of the morgue. Leigh was one of the most likable members of the staff, easygoing and tolerant, cut out to be a moderately moneyed idler, a charmer. But fate had failed to provide him with enough money for that life. Although he was willing enough, he didn't pull his weight on our copydesk—he just wasn't much good at the work, a slow writer and not a particularly readable one. He got his job through his old friend Robert Sage who, when he was an editor of *transition*, also published two or three of Leigh's poems, his only appearance in print as far as I know.

For so mild and inoffensive a person, Leigh had acquired an astonishingly belligerent mate, a Frenchwoman named Elvira, who was built something like a barroom bouncer. I once saw her rout a taxi driver with her fists. She did not interfere with his social life for we almost never saw her. She did not eat at Gillotte's with us and Leigh always seemed free to share his nights off and even his vacations with one of us rather than with her.

Leigh reveled in working on the files. We often heard him chuckling at some item, and sometimes he could not resist reading one of his better finds to us. He fed into the morgue, in addition to strictly informative material, amusing asides that made interesting reading, the sort of touch to which the *Herald* would have applied the blue pencil. When the news was heavy, Leigh remained at his typewriter but when it was light, he shifted to the files. He had enough experience as a newspaperman to know what sort of material was likely to be useful to us and under what index heading we would probably look for it, something the filing clerks who usually did this work did not always understand. You could find things fast in Leigh's morgue. Newspapers have been bought for no other asset than a well-furnished morgue. By the time the *Tribune* was sold to the *Herald*, five years of Leigh's diligence had given us a remarkably useful morgue whose envelopes filled shelves rising to the ceiling along two walls of the city room. I was sickened when I learned that all of these files were simply going to be thrown away after our purchase.

This confirmed my opinion that the *Herald* was not a wide-awake paper. Its own files were not very good. The morgue had been entrusted for a number of years to a man who never took a day off or a vacation. Nobody argued with him about this since the *Herald* editors were only too happy to have permanently in the city room a man who could produce immediately any background information. Then he died unexpectedly and the morgue died with him. He had classified all items according to his own whimsy: All political speeches were in Drawer *B*, under "Bullshit." Nobody else could solve his code.

My own innovation was put into force the first night I settled into the slot as news editor. I removed the spike from the center of the desk, where this handy tool, on which to impale any piece of paper needed for later reference, never appeared again. Until then the spike had been the real night editor. It had carried copy from the day staff, clippings from the French press, releases from the Havas news agency, stories cut from our nightly wire from London, cables from New York—all the raw material for the next day's paper spiked without order. In theory, each rewrite man picked the top story from the spike, rewrote it, and moved on to the one that now was at the top. In practice, a man who didn't relish the top story often pawed down the heap until he came to a story that interested him. Under this system, occasionally an important but difficult story that nobody was eager to tackle never got written. Or a story that had come in early and was therefore near the bottom of the pile would still be there when the deadline stopped us.

I abolished this hit-or-miss system by taking all the raw material and handing it out individually, as newspapers do today. I knew the special qualities of many of the staffers from having worked with them before I left for London, and it did not take long to learn the abilities of the others. When a story was written, it came back to me, and I marked it for the size and type of headline I thought it deserved and then gave it to the copyreader I thought likely to do the best job on it.

Making it my business to check all the edited copy that was going into the paper, except for the financial and sports pages, I was able to maintain close control of our quality. When the page proofs were spread out before me at the end of a night, I felt as if I had given birth.

Just as I enjoyed orchestrating the paper from the copydesk slot, I relished immensely the task of making up the paper in the composing room.

Usually Frantz acted as our makeup editor but I substituted for him on his weekly day off and frequently on other occasions. It made sense for the man in charge to make up the paper, at least on our small scale, where all details could be carried in a single head. The makeup editor occupies a strategic position as the last to deal with the news before the pages are finished.

Our printers were wonderfully skillful at working in a language that none of them understood. Time after time a linotype operator would come up to me with a piece of copy in his hand and ask, "Is this right?" Almost always it was not. He had recognized a typing error—which our American copyreaders had missed—by an improbable sequence of letters. I respected particularly the technical competence of the composing room foreman, a taciturn Norman named Falempin, with whom I often stepped across the street to Gillotte's for a beer while we were waiting for some vital story to emerge from the linotypes so that we could put a page together.

Falempin ran the composing room about the way I ran the copydesk, by maintaining personal control over every detail of the operation. As each piece of copy came down the chute from the city room, he allotted each headline to the printer he thought best able to handle it or to one he knew was not overloaded with work. Early in the evening, he would usually hand a story intact to a single operator but if time pressed, he would chop the copy into sections, numbering each one so that they could be assembled in the right order, and parcel them out among half-a-dozen linotypes.

The routine of the night staff was fixed by the arrival times of our leased wire from London, and our one indispensable employee was a cyclist named André who brought it to us. We leased two half-hour periods nightly on a London-Paris telegraph line. The first began coming in about 8:00 P.M., when we started work. The second installment started at 10:30, so we took our break at 10:00. The volume of copy that could be transmitted varied somewhat with the moods of the London telegraph operator, and the news itself was provided by the London bureau of the Foreign News Service. The bureau sent not only its own British news but also what it regarded as the most important of the dispatches from all other *Chicago Tribune* bureaus, including New York. Two exceptions were

Berlin and Rome, which filed directly to Chicago but were supposed to wire or phone us directly with a big story. When they didn't, we could phone them or make do with reports from Havas, which were delivered to us throughout the evening in bulging envelopes.

Transmission of news agency dispatches by telegraph, although not unknown in those days, was rare. Havas tickers did exist; they were present in most cafés and we even had one in the office; its messages, however, were usually of no interest to us since it was designed for the use of the public and yielded no information beyond stock market figures and sports scores. Straight news had to be sensational to move on a Havas ticker.

Our first cables, from the New York bureau of the *Chicago Tribune*, began to arrive after the ten o'clock break and started with the day's Wall Street figures. These were followed by the scanty quota of American news that was all our budget could afford.

André brought us all this material, shuttling between the Havas office and ours throughout the evening, calling at the main post office at the Bourse to pick up the yellow sheets of the London wire, visiting Commercial Cables for the blue dispatches from New York. (These alone sometimes reached us independent of André since late cables were phoned to us by Commercial Cables.) At the end of the evening, André had two more missions. First, he had to take a set of our galley proofs to *Le Matin* and bring their proofs back. Second, he made the rounds of all the Paris morning papers and brought us one of the first copies of each, including one from the *New York Herald*. While he was there he made it a point to slip into the pressroom and read the figure for that day's run. This was useful information that we could not have gotten from the figures the *Herald* printed. There was no Audit Bureau of Circulation then and the *Herald* in 1930 was claiming a circulation of fifty thousand and printing twenty. Modestly, we claimed a circulation of twenty and printed eight. Our advertisers believed neither paper.

One obstacle to a bigger circulation for the Paris Edition was our typographic quality. This was due to a feeling in Chicago, shared in our business office, that our front page should resemble as closely as possible that of the home paper. Aside from the fact that a paper of sixty pages can hardly furnish a valid pattern for one of twelve, it would have been difficult to find a worse example of typography to follow than the *Chicago Tribune*. Its front page looked like the crowded window of a rural general store trying to display everything it had to sell. We did not have to put at the top of the front page McCutcheon's daily cartoon, as the home paper did, probably because it often dealt with the day's news and would have been pointless when it reached us ten days later. One difficulty that was not spared us was the loss of the second column on the front page.

In Chicago, this space was occupied by a news index, useful in a big paper but ridiculous in ours. We lost the space anyway because the colonel decreed that our second column should be entirely occupied by May Birkhead's society news. I did not underestimate the value of this feature, but thought it should be elsewhere on the page, not at the top where it interfered with our display of the news.

I tried once to loosen May's exclusive right to this space, perhaps on Frantz' night off or his vacation. We were snowed under by world-shaking news and I pushed the Birkhead column a few inches down the page to run a big headline over it and across the left side of the page. She still started on the front page but finished inside. May must have cabled the colonel when she saw the paper. When I came to work the next day, there was a cable from him waiting for me: Never again, under any pretext, was May Birkhead's column to be displaced in the slightest from the ordained space. It never again was.

During one of Frantz' vacations I attacked another rule imposed on us by Chicago: Pictures should never appear on the front page. One day we had two exclusive local stories, both concerning prominent members of the American colony of Paris, with good photographs for both. I decided to break the rule and to break it hard by putting both photographs on the page. Anticipating an explosion from Chicago, I was surprised when there was none. Probably everybody had forgotten about the ancient rule. Thereafter we used photographs on the front page whenever they deserved to be there.

But I did lose the battle of the banner. Most papers believed that only a rare story deserves to be celebrated with a banner—the Lindbergh flight was a classic case. The home paper used one every day and there were people in our business office who thought we should do the same to try to boost sales. I strongly opposed the idea because an eight-column headline is typographically ugly and because, if we ran a banner every day, how were we going to play up the rare big story?

For a long time my voice was heard on this question. Frantz had brought me into the weekly conference of department heads—which I considered a waste of time and boring—because he needed moral support against the combined pressure of the publisher, the business manager, the advertising manager, and the circulation manager, all of whom regarded the news department as a barely necessary evil. Only rarely was a decision made and usually so vaguely that nobody was quite sure what it had been. Then each department head went back to his desk and ignored what had been decided.

That, at least, was how the business departments operated. The editorial department could not ignore a decision since this disdain would be obvious in the columns of the paper. So if the conference decreed clearly that the paper had to have a daily banner, we would have a daily banner.

Every week Frantz and I talked down the idea, and then I went off on vacation, leaving Frantz without a supporter. A few days later I bought the paper and saw a fat black banner across the top of the front page despite an absence of important news. The banner headlines continued every day thereafter. Imagine the malicious pleasure with which I noted, within the first two weeks of the appearance of the banner, that the biggest news it carried was that a large number of locusts were flying around in the Sahara.

¶

The Pressure Mounts

¶

The hard-drinking newspaperman is, or used to be, a stock character of fiction. Now he is being phased out of literature just as he is being phased out of life. Modern journalism is too exacting to be practiced successfully by heavy drinkers.

For members of the night staff of the Paris Edition, drinking was often a way of dealing with the pressures of work. A newspaper office is a device for applying to its staff a steadily increasing amount of pressure: Evenings begin calmly enough with, it seems, ample time to deal with the day's news. As more and more news pours in and the deadline nears, the pressure mounts. At the end, the staff is galloping and suddenly the presses start and there is nothing more to be done for the edition.

The abruptness of the change was more than our nerves could bear and the simplest remedy was alcohol. (And sometimes horseplay: We threw under the copydesk sheets of paper spoiled by stories badly begun, notes no longer needed, discarded Havas dispatches, and other inflammable debris. Occasionally a staffer would drop a lighted match into the pile and we would have to stamp the fire out. How we never burned down the building, I don't know.) But if we drank, most of it was done immediately after the paper had gone to press, not before. Once in a while we took on an alcoholic newspaperman but he usually left speedily. We ran a fast desk and a man had to be in possession of all his wits to keep up. I do not remember that any staff member had to be fired for drinking and do not even recall that anybody had to be sent home. We had five flights of stairs to climb to the city room and anyone who arrived at the bottom of them drunk was likely to stay below, continuing to drink at Gillotte's or the Chope Cadet or the Italian's or the Trois Portes. If you could get up the stairs you were sober enough not to be a nuisance.

One exception occurred early in my career. I was still on the day staff when Frantz dropped by early to pick up his mail and suggested we go downstairs for a beer. At the bar of the Trois Portes, Frantz decided not to have the beer.

"I think I'll take a Pernod," he said.

"What's a Pernod?" I asked.

"Absinthe substitute. No kick in it now. It's against the law to make real absinthe."

I had drunk real absinthe in New York, during Prohibition, without evil effect. We ordered two Pernods. The bartender placed before us a pair of large glasses, each with a finger of pale green liquid. Frantz picked up a carafe of water and filled our glasses. The pale green color disappeared as the liquid became cloudy white. The flavor was pale, a delicate breath of anise. "A lady's drink," I said to myself.

At glass five and a half, I left the café, managed to navigate the stairs, and collapsed into my seat on the copydesk. The next thing I knew I was lying fully dressed on my bed in my studio on the other side of Paris and it was 5:00 P.M. the next day.

Frantz might not have noticed that I had left. He downed his sixth Pernod and then finished mine. He went next to the Italian's around the corner, where he found a few early birds preparing for dinner with sweet Asti Spumante. Frantz joined them in their aperitifs. Then they all went to Gillotte's for dinner, at which Frantz drank his usual quota of wine. Finally he climbed the stairs to the city room, pulled out his chair in the slot, and, missing it entirely, fell to the floor, unstirring.

He was placed carefully under a table where nobody would be likely to step on him, and a sentinel was posted at the head of the stairs to listen for Ragner, who dined late. When his steps were heard a few floors below, Frantz was dragged out from under the table and put in his chair. His chin was propped on his fists and his elbows were planted on either side of the slot. The two men who flanked him braced their elbows against his. He remained that way, immobile as a block of wood, for the rest of the evening. The next day he was fine.

This was, as I say, an exception. If we had some sensational battlers with the bottle, they always seemed to be temporary staff members. A good many people learned journalism from us, probably because those with experience landed jobs with the better-paying papers like the *Her-*

ald. Sometimes we had to take any literate person available. They applied for jobs during sober intervals, usually because they had run out of drinking money, and their object was to earn enough to return to the bottle. They did not last long but they functioned well up to the moment when their lights went out.

One rewrite man whose stay with us was brief could arrive in the office showing no signs of distress until he began to type. Then, if he was drunk, he betrayed it by his typing technique. He seemed to be attached to the carriage of the typewriter: as it rattled along, he swayed with it to port and snapped back to starboard as he pushed the carriage back for a new line. There always came a moment when the carriage stopped at the end of a line but its operator did not. He followed the laws of momentum to the floor, where he stayed while the man next to him finished the story. It was always a good piece of work up to the point where oblivion occurred.

One copyreader who worked for us for a few weeks was not even slowed down by drunkenness. One evening when he was clearly feeling no pain, I played a joke on him by writing a three-page story in a single sentence and tossing it over to him for editing. He set to work and soon was shaking his head disapprovingly. "Wave," he said, "you really should learn to write shorter sentences. I'm halfway down the page and it's still the first sentence."

Getting back to work, he crossed out words here, wrote others in there, moved punctuation marks, and added capital letters. Deep into the second page, he groaned, "It's still the same sentence." When he reached the third page, he was too subdued to complain. Finishing his work, he tossed the story back to me. "There you are, and don't ever do that again."

In a masterpiece of technique, he had broken the story into neat, aligned sentences and paragraphs. He had even written a headline on it, which I couldn't have done myself—the sentence I had written had no meaning.

Besides the time Frantz and I tried Pernod, there is another exception to the rule that it was temporary employees whose drinking made problems. The other case involved Lee Dickson, the star reporter of the day staff, who violated that team's tradition by bringing in a considerable number of lively stories, often on the scandalous side.

He arrived one evening after the night staff had settled in. "I've got a story that'll bug their eyes out," he announced unsteadily before he took a seat at a vacant typewriter. He tapped away for forty-five minutes, ripped the paper from the typewriter, and gave it to the slot man.

"There's something to spice up your front page," Dickson said as he left. The night editor, busy with another story, did not look at the paper for several minutes. When he did he saw that Dickson had typed it all on a single line, without once turning up the typewriter carriage.

Despite these escapades, the single worst thing that ever happened to a staff member, permanent or temporary, had nothing to do with drink.

It involved Madison Kirby, ebullient, quick-witted, reckless Madison Kirby. Small and wiry, he had been an athlete at Stanford University, primarily a runner. Walking home at night, he would spy a line of trash cans, break into a sprint, and vault over them. Frantz said he had seen Kirby clear eight at a time. Another *Tribune* staffer told me he had walked home with Kirby one night and when they reached the Seine, Kirby had jumped in and swum across.

Kirby practiced another athletic feat, which paralyzed us with fear at first. He would have been a mountain climber if there had been any mountains handy; lacking them, he made do with the buildings in which he worked. A newspaperman who had worked with him in a skyscraper in New York told me that Kirby used to think it was fun to terrify his colleagues by climbing out a window many stories above the street, hanging by his fingers from the ledge, and laughing at their fright. Then he would brace his feet against the wall and pull himself back into the city room.

The office of the Paris Edition offered him a variant. The rear wall of the city room was all glass, a series of windows hinged in pairs with each pair opening from the center. A narrow cornice ran alongside them outside. Kirby delighted in darting out the last window on the right and inching his way along the cornice to the last window on the left, where he would reenter.

The cornice was not wide enough to take the length of his foot but it provided a toehold. There were fingerholds at the hinges and central slits on each pair of windows. At first we screamed with terror when he did his trick, pleading with him not to go out and then, when he was out, to come back in. He laughed at us. It was our terror, I think, that he found comic.

He repeated his feat often until we became used to it and reacted less violently. One night he went out the window and fell five stories to his death.

That night, the most tragic in the history of the Paris Edition, I was one of two persons in the city room who saw Kirby fall. The other was Dick Glenn, the finance editor. Everybody else in the room was either facing the wrong direction or not watching a familiar performance.

The evening was warm, so the windows stood open at both ends of the room. This may have been the reason one of the men sitting on the rim of the copydesk remarked banteringly, "Long time you haven't been out the window, Kirby." That was all he needed. With one bound, Kirby was on his chair, with another on the copydesk, across which he ran, leaped to sports editor Hérol Egan's desk, and stepped onto the sill. There was the usual chorus of "Come back, Kirby," but the cries were perfunctory: We had seen the act so often that we were no longer impressed.

After the ritual protest, everybody returned to work. Nobody watched as Kirby inched his way along the cornice and I was conscious of his shadow behind the opaque glass only because I was seated facing in that direction. He reached the far window and his fingers hooked around the jamb, where the opened windows had left a slit. At that moment I saw the window start to swing shut, moved by a breeze.

The iron frame closed on Kirby's fingers. He cried out and let go. Glenn lunged from his chair toward him, reaching across his desk. He was a heavy man and a strong one and, if he had been able to grab Kirby, might have been able to hold him. But he missed by a few inches. Then I heard the crash of shattering glass below. Kirby had gone through one of the skylights on a line of offices at ground level.

Will Barber and I rushed downstairs. With some pressmen, we ran along the row of offices shouting his name until we heard a faint answer. We broke down the door. Kirby was on his hands and knees in the middle of the floor.

"I've lost my false teeth," he said. "Find my false teeth."

Absurdly, I ran my fingers through the swamp of blood surrounding him and found the teeth. He was still on all fours. Using the broken door as a stretcher, we carried him to a delivery truck and it headed for a hospital. I ran back to the city room to take control of the situation there while Barber rode with Kirby to the hospital.

Barber's first call said that Kirby had apparently hit one of the iron bars that held the skylights in place, breaking his femur, which sheared through his thigh, severing the artery. He had lost most of his blood. A later call reported that a shattered rib had punctured a lung, which had stopped working. This was given as the cause of death, but if it had not been that, it would have been something else. Kirby had been broken to bits. Barber was weeping when he made the last call to say that Kirby was dead.

I forget now what lies I told the staff while we worked to get the paper finished for, of course, it had to come out. Only when I finally announced Kirby's death did I realize that somebody had to write the story for the paper. I asked one man to do it and he managed about a paragraph and then broke down. Somebody else tried and had to stop too. I finished it myself, the hardest story I have ever written, and telephoned it to the *Herald*. This was not the sort of news on which we wanted to have a scoop.

Then a pair of plainclothes policemen arrived, notified by the hospital. They listened to our story, then moved over to the window. One of them pointed to a fresh crack. "What happened?" he asked. "Was there a fight?" We stared at each other dumbfounded. Somebody suggested that Kirby might have kicked the window when he fell, somebody else that Glenn might have cracked it when he tried to reach Kirby. Our obvious distress convinced the police that the fall had been an accident. They left and we heard no more of them.

I finished making up the paper and joined the rest at Gillotte's. Nobody wanted to go home. Nobody felt like drinking either, but we ordered drinks all the same. Once in a while someone stammered out a banality and failed to finish it. And then somebody proposed timidly that we start a game of bridge. What can you do when you have just seen a close friend killed? We played bridge until dawn. Our hearts were not in it, but it helped a little.

¶
Zummat of That Sort

¶

The Paris Edition's book page, over which I presided for four years, was born by accident. William Lyon Phelps, venerated English professor at Yale University and a kindly soul liked by everyone who knew him, had published in *Scribner*'s magazine a list of what he regarded as the world's hundred best novels. His choices seemed to me to be so dreadful that for three Mondays in a row I had at the learned doctor's opinions with the pitiless sarcasm peculiar to very young men.

Monday was ideal for this purpose since Sunday was ordinarily devoid of news, leaving Monday's paper with plenty of space.

I needed three Mondays for I broke down Dr. Phelps' list of favorites into English books, American books, and books in other languages. Without denying that the English novel ranked high in the world of fiction, I suggested that to name sixty-five books in English and thirty-five in all the other languages showed a certain imbalance. I remarked that to name two works each by Richardson and Fielding and three each by Jane Austen and Sir Walter Scott, while omitting *Tristram Shandy*, seemed disputable. I would not want to underestimate Charles Dickens, I continued, but to list five of his books—thus crediting him with having written one-thirteenth of all the great novels in English and one-twentieth of those in the entire world—seemed to be overestimating him.

Nor would I have placed among the greatest English novels Wilkie Collins' *The Moonstone*, Charles Reade's *The Cloister and the Hearth*, W. H. Hudson's *Green Mansions*, George Bernard Shaw's unreadable *Cashel Byron's Profession*, and Richard Blackmore's *Lorna Doone*.

"It is a sad commentary on the state of criticism in the athletic states of America," I wrote, "that a gentleman respected for his critical gifts . . . should be able to sit down at his desk and, seriously, solemnly, and soberly, list *Lorna Doone* as one of the world's greatest novels. . . ."

I continued to be nasty about Dr. Phelps the following week, taking exception to his selection of sixteen American novels, more than I felt we possessed of a stature for a world's-best list. In any case I did not feel that *Uncle Tom's Cabin* or *Bob, Son of Battle* ranked with the works of Swift, Balzac, and Turgenev.

The third week brought us to Europe, where it did not seem to me the good doctor had covered himself with glory either. He could find no novel worthy of mention from Italy or Spain, not even *Don Quixote*, but named three from Scandinavia; he selected two books by Goethe, but did not seem to have heard of Thomas Mann. He played it safe on Russia, with four books by Dostoyevski, four by Tolstoy, four by Turgenev, and one by Gogol, but had more difficulty with France—four of Dumas' potboilers against two titles by Balzac, for example; Flaubert and Zola, but no Rabelais, Voltaire, Stendhal, or Proust.

The articles on Phelps touched off a voluminous correspondence with Ezra Pound, who began bombarding me with letters and postcards written in the abridged version of English he used for private messages. The first one was addressed to the editor:

> Provate and confidential and NOT for print in yr. esteemed noozpaper.
>
> Compliments to Root. Hope you give him two cols. regular at least once a week in which to take out the souls not only of Phelps but of the whole goddam series of trained lit. seals . . . AND to spit on 'em. . . .
>
> If there is any danger of the blood ole idiot's NOT receiving Root's article, PLEASE r.s.v.p. and I will take pains to send it to him with my deploments.
>
> Surely the harvest is ready and the laborers bloody few. Show this to Root. I think he cd. do a series that wd. make a book afterward. "Debunking our critics" or zummat of that sort.

Hardly had Dr. Phelps of Yale receded than Dr. Henry Van Dyke of Princeton moved into range and I loaded my blunderbuss again. Professor Van Dyke criticized the award of the Nobel Prize to Sinclair Lewis. "In *Main Street*, there is not a girl with whom one would fall in love," he wrote, using a touchstone that had escaped other literary critics.

"If Dr. Van Dyke can only enjoy books with lovable young ladies in them," I wrote, "what a lot he must miss! He can hardly read Swift at all. Laurence Sterne must be most dangerous for him, and also most of Defoe. Zola and Balzac are both full of horrors. . . . Whether Madame Bo-vary or Lady Macbeth appeal to him is a subject on which I would hardly dare to hazard a guess."

Books had now dominated the second page of the Paris Edition for five successive Mondays, so the feature became institutionalized. Nobody had set out to establish a book page but we seemed to have one. Thereafter books were granted the entire second page every Monday. This was the first time that the Paris Edition had presented a regularly scheduled book review section on the same day and in the same space, although it had always paid more attention to books than the *Herald*, which came close to ignoring them. Eugene Jolas, Robert Sage, Wambly Bald, and Elliot Paul had often written about books for the Paris Edition, Bald usually as part of his reporting on Montparnasse.

The Monday book page included reviews and more wide-ranging ar-ticles dealing with literary questions unrelated to the appearance of any specific book. Occasionally I gave books for review to other members of the staff, with my first choice usually Sage, an excellent writer who many years later brought out a successful annotated translation of Stendhal's *Private Diaries*. But usually I wrote the page myself under less-than-ideal conditions. I had time to read the books I was reviewing but not to write the reviews, so I turned them out Sunday night while sitting in the slot and directing the staff's activities as usual. This was something of a feat.

Our book page had a problem unknown to critics in the United States: getting books to review. French publishers sent us their books since we reviewed works in both languages and English publishers, after the page gained momentum, began to supply us with books too, but we were too far away from the United States to convince publishers there that we should get review copies. Then I learned that all the American books im-ported into France were handled by a single agent, who had his office above Brentano's bookstore in the avenue de l'Opéra. He began supply-ing me with new American books. My standards were more rigorous, it would seem, than those of most publishers, and a majority of the books supplied by the importer were reviewed unfavorably, even brutally. I asked him once why he continued to send me books that I often savaged. "Roast away, roast away," he answered affably. "All I know is that when

I pick up Monday's paper and see that you have written a column on a book I'm handling, I know that Brentano's will sell fifty copies. And if you give it a column and a half, Brentano's will sell seventy-five. It doesn't matter whether you've said the book is a masterpiece or a mess. Be as rough as you like, but be rough lengthily."

There were two reliable signs that the book page was being widely read. One was the amount of mail received from readers, agreeing or disagreeing with opinions expressed. The other was that unsolicited advertising began to appear on the page. Our advertising department did not at first realize that the book page gave it anything to sell, and by the time they realized it, so had their opposite numbers on the *Herald*.

Until then the *Herald* had paid little attention to books, having no book section or reviewers. When a book came along that was also news, managing editor Eric Hawkins assigned the story to a member of his staff almost at random under his theory that a book meant to be read by the general public should be assessed by a member of the general public, not a specialist. If Hawkins could find someone totally ignorant of the book's subject, so much the better. Perhaps this was a tenable theory but it translated into no readers of book articles and no advertising from booksellers.

When it was noted that the *Tribune* was attracting this advertising and the *Herald* was not, it began moving to match us, but only after a year or more, for the *Herald* was not giddily quick on the uptake. It hired Paul to lead its effort but never caught up to us in advertising or readership, possibly because it never gave him a full page to play with. We also had the advantage that our most devoted readers, the people of Montparnasse, were more literate than the *Herald*'s lobster-palace Americans.

The cafés of Montparnasse, where the *Tribune* was read, are still being written up with synthetic nostalgia by those too young to have known them and with a false tone that grates on those who did. These reports tend to focus on the Coupole, which is almost always associated with Ernest Hemingway, the symbol of the period. Hemingway must have patronized the Coupole from time to time, for he was in and out of Paris after the great days of Montparnasse were over. But he was not an ornament of the Coupole when he frequented Montparnasse because the Coupole wasn't there then.

The apogee of Hemingway's Montparnasse period might be placed at 1926, the year *The Sun Also Rises* was published; the Coupole opened on December 20, 1927. When I reached Paris that year there was a high board fence with a coalyard behind it where the Coupole stands now. Most of the people living in Montparnasse at that time resented the advent of the Coupole as the thin edge of modernism forcing its way into the comfortable, easygoing, noncommercial society of the times.

The three classic cafés of Montparnasse were the Dôme, the Rotonde, and the Select. Except for the Select, they now provide little of the atmosphere from the fabled days of Hemingway: The Dôme has been prettied up and the Rotonde half carved away to accommodate a next-door cinema. As for the carefree existence of those days, that is gone forever. The Closerie des Lilas is often spoken of in the same breath as the others but it has had its tranquility destroyed by traffic. It always stood apart from the others, in atmosphere as well as in location.

The Dôme, the Rotonde, and the Select were all at the carrefour Montparnasse while the Closerie, although not far away, where the boulevard St. Michel met the boulevard Montparnasse, was still a little farther than most Montparnassians, undistinguished by athletic prowess, cared to walk. The carrefour, or crossroads, was the mainland, the Closerie an island, a small, quiet island. It was also a place for writers—James Stephens lost the manuscript of *The Crock of Gold* there and had to write it all over again—but it was more decorous, a place reserved for established values. You were less likely to meet Robert McAlmon there than Ford Madox Ford, who was rather on the stuffy side. The bohemians of the Closerie tended to be bourgeois bohemians. When the frolickers of the Dôme, the Rotonde, and the Select turned up at the Closerie, they became quieter.

The three cafés of the carrefour maintained different moods even though their clientele was interchangeable. Indeed, on any given night, a person was likely to make the rounds of all three. The Dôme was the basic café, the all-purpose café, where the largest groups congregated, pushing tables together as more people joined. The sidewalk in front of the Dôme was more thickly populated too, by those too restless or too broke to sit down.

The Dôme was dedicated to verbal free-for-alls, so if you wanted to talk with a single friend or two or three at most, you moved across the street to the Rotonde, a notch upward in the social scale. The Rotonde was quieter than the Dôme and the food was better, although none of the three was greatly devoted to gastronomy. If you wanted to eat seriously, you could go to the Closerie but, halfway between the carrefour and the Closerie, there was a more lighthearted place with a name that would be a liability today: Le Nègre de Toulouse. At Le Nègre everybody knew everybody else, which made for a good deal of shouting from table to table and even moving about, so that waiters arrived with food to find that their customers were sitting somewhere else.

The Select was the shaggiest of the three Montparnasse cafés even when its clientele had just made port from the Dôme or the Rotonde. Arrival at the Select somehow conferred on customers an air of picturesque squalor. This made the contrast with the Coupole, almost directly across the street, all the greater. You could change worlds by crossing the street. The Coupole served as an observation post for tourists titillated by what they had read about Montparnassians but not courageous enough to mingle with them. At the Coupole they could seat themselves in brightly lighted surroundings and goggle across the way.

¶

The Great White Hope of American Literature

¶

Montparnasse in the 1920s and 1930s was, as Ernest Hemingway re-marked, full of "lady writers of all sexes." Hemingway may be presumed to have made this remark in a moment of irritation, for he numbered a good many homosexuals among his friends, among them Robert Mc-Almon, with whom he twice made the bullfight round in Spain.

I suppose there were many homosexuals in this society because Paris was so tolerant. Especially in Montparnasse nobody cared. What they did care about is illustrated in a squabble I had about McAlmon after re-viewing a book of his short stories, *The Indefinite Huntress*, on the book page of the Paris Edition. "The post-Hemingway school of writing be-lieves in stripped sentences," I wrote. "All ornamentation is ruthlessly sheared away to leave only the bare essentials. Hemingway himself seems to eliminate all indications of emotion, but the speech which he catches is so accurate and the details which he records so significant, that the underlying emotion is inevitably re-created in the reader who hears and observes the words and acts of his characters. . . . McAlmon . . . too has shorn off all the non-essentials, but it seems to me that in so doing he has cut away all the feeling as well. . . . McAlmon's stories come very close to being important and don't quite make it."

This estimate of McAlmon's writing provoked dissent from Kay Boyle, who wrote me a letter, which I printed on the book page, in which she exalted "the extraordinary debt of influence so many of [McAlmon's] contemporaries owe to him; at least a half dozen names come to mind. Because I recognize in McAlmon the sound and almost heedless builder of a certain strong wind in American letters, I can see Hemingway only as the gentleman who came in afterward and laid down the linoleum because it was so decorative and so easy to keep clean."

I answered to the effect that I was less concerned with who wrote first than with who wrote best. It was my opinion that Hemingway wrote best. It seemed to be the opinion of those who reproached Hemingway for having outwritten McAlmon that this was unfair of him.

Miss Boyle's protest seemed somewhat disingenuous. Not only did she fail to let her readers in on the secret that she herself had been instrumental in the selection of the stories published in *The Indefinite Huntress* and was therefore casting herself in the roles of both partisan and judge, but she also already knew at the time my review was published, December 1932, that McAlmon's mental disequilibrium was teetering toward paranoia, a fact of which I was unaware.

I never met Miss Boyle to my knowledge, but she must have been a woman of ardent temperament, to judge from the enthusiasm with which she championed her friends. When she described McAlmon, for instance, as "a great white god," she had clearly gone off the deep end. Miss Boyle's most conspicuous infatuation was with Raymond Duncan, Isadora's brother. She became a victim of his fake Hellenism and joined his community, whose labors served chiefly to support its guru. Once cured, she bared her own temporary gullibility and wrote a brilliant and devastating novel that should have sunk him without a trace, but it didn't. He was, I think, the only one of her false idols she ever abjured.

Despite Miss Boyle's blast, Raymond Duncan continued to recruit for his colony admiring young women, who it may be assumed had not read her book. Unabashed and unabashable, he told an interviewer on his return to Paris from a trip to New York in 1933:

I have founded a new city. It is called New Paris York and will unite the inhabitants of New York and Paris.

To the undisguised amazement of the captain, officers and passengers of the liner, I laid the foundation stone of the city's city hall, by dropping it overboard in mid-Atlantic, halfway between the United States and France. Already many prominent New Yorkers and Parisians have flocked to this new city, which is taxless, lawless, and without obligations. Each and every one of these new citizens will drop a brick or stone into the sea in mid-

Atlantic when he crosses to or from America. Thus, in time, will the new city hall rear its glorious head above the waves.

The city hall has not yet appeared above the waves and it is to be feared now that it never will, given the technical difficulty of heaving building stones from transatlantic planes.

Duncan at least kept his own head above water. Up to World War II, I used to see him from time to time, in toga and sandals, an incongruous figure in the Paris subway. That Kay Boyle could ever have been taken in by him, even briefly, did not argue well for the accuracy of her appraisals, even of McAlmon.

But I seem to have been out of tune with McAlmon's clique even when I praised him, which I did at least once, in January 1932, when I was considering the current number of Samuel Putnam's *New Review*. This was one of the most uneven of the little magazines, and I described this number, unkindly, as harboring "an undue proportion of the dry-as-dust theorists, talking a language of their own and, as a rule, laboring points that everyone else perceives intuitively, if indeed they have succeeded in getting hold of any points at all."

Then I became more encouraging: "The gem of this issue, to this reviewer's way of thinking, is the excellent story by Robert McAlmon hidden away near the back of the magazine, which succeeds nevertheless in calling attention to itself by its clarion title, 'The Highly-Prized Pyjamas.' You can safely buy the *New Review* on the strength of this story, and if you don't like anything else in this number, you still have your money's worth."

When McAlmon's collection *The Indefinite Huntress* appeared, it contained nine stories chosen by his admirers. The one point on which they all agreed, from Caresse Crosby, who published the book, through Kay Boyle to Katherine Anne Porter, was that "The Highly-Prized Pyjamas" was not worth reprinting. Apparently I could not keep in step about McAlmon.

To tell the truth, he made an unpleasant impression on me the first time I met him. He seemed to me to be unhealthy, physically and spiritually. He was cadaverously thin; when he moved his fingers, you expected his knuckles to crack. According to his mood, his eyes were either blank and vague, looking through or around you, or they were malevolent, staring you down.

I remember having written somewhere that he would probably never have been published if he had not had the means to publish himself. This was probably inaccurate, judging from the ease with which the café sitters of Montparnasse broke into the little magazines, for McAlmon was an indefatigable café sitter and partygoer. The fact remains that he *was* almost always published by himself, and even the few exceptions were the result of personal relationships.

McAlmon's first publishing effort seems to have been in 1920, when he and William Carlos Williams, both of them in Paris, started a little magazine called *Contact*. It began, of course, with a manifesto, but its real raison d'être quickly became apparent: It was to give the two partners a place in which to publish their own poems. They soon ran out of money and *Contact* disappeared, but the next year they found themselves together again in New York, where Williams introduced McAlmon to Winifred Ellerman, "a small, dark English girl with piercing intense eyes."

Miss Ellerman was visiting America with the Imagist poet who signed her works "H.D." probably because Hilda Doolittle sounded discouragingly unpoetic. Sylvia Beach was to describe Miss Ellerman later as "a shy young English girl in a tailor-made suit." She could not have been as shy as she looked. It was she, apparently, who took the initiative of proposing marriage to McAlmon—on the condition that it should not be consummated. Miss Ellerman was less enthralled emotionally by McAlmon than by H.D. What she wanted was to get out from under her bourgeois family, which would not have approved of the free life she wanted to lead, particularly with H.D.

Miss Ellerman, better known by her pen name, Bryher, defined McAlmon's job for him: He would have to accompany her from time to time on visits to her parents, to demonstrate respectability; for the rest of the time, he was to keep out of her hair. This was quite all right with McAlmon, who had no more interest in connubial life with a woman than Bryher, at that time, had for connubial life with a man.

Some writers have contended that when McAlmon accepted this arrangement he did not know that Bryher was the daughter of the British shipping magnate Sir John Ellerman, who had been described as the heaviest taxpayer in England. They are entitled to believe this if they wish.

The young couple—that is, McAlmon, Bryher, and H.D.—returned to Europe together. Late in 1921 McAlmon was back in Paris, unaccompanied by his wife, who had gone off with H.D. He had received a wedding gift of £14,000 from Sir John, the equivalent of $70,000, a fortune in those days. I believe that he also received a regular allowance. Even if he did not, he was able to direct some Ellerman largesse in directions that appealed to him. One unexpected consequence of his marriage was that Sylvia Beach's Shakespeare and Company received, as an appropriate decoration for its bookstore and lending library, a bust of Shakespeare, the gift of Lady Ellerman. McAlmon also persuaded his mother-in-law to underwrite the composer George Antheil for two years. The marriage lasted seven years, and at its breakup (for which H.D. seems to have been at least partly responsible), Sir John paid McAlmon off so handsomely that envious Montparnassians began referring to him as Robert McAlimony.

Now in the money, McAlmon was not niggardly with it. "If a man of talent needed help," the writer Morley Callaghan said, "McAlmon would help him if he could." A great James Joyce enthusiast, McAlmon subsidized him to the extent of $150 a month for a while. He paid a year's fees at a sanitarium near Bologna for the Italian-American poet Emanuel Carnevali, who was dying. He picked up the printing bill for Djuna Barnes' *Ladies' Almanac* and I seem to recall that at one time he was giving her an allowance.

His aid to Joyce went further than money. McAlmon was the top subscription agent for *Ulysses* when Sylvia Beach was preparing to publish it in 1922. He would carry a sheaf of order forms in his pocket during his nightlong vigils at the cafés of Montparnasse and, before going home to bed, would push a handful of signed subscription blanks under the door of Shakespeare and Company with a note informing Sylvia Beach that he was handing over a "hasty bunch" of subscriptions to the coming work. McAlmon's habitual use of this phrase enabled Joyce on one occasion to display more diplomacy than is usually credited to him.

McAlmon had had a book of poems, *Explorations*, published by the

Egoist Press, which could have been taken as evidence that his talents had been recognized by someone other than himself and his intimates if you didn't happen to know that it was McAlmon himself who had paid to have the book printed. This whetted his appetite to see his works in print again, and, thinking of collecting and publishing his short stories, he read them to Joyce, then receiving McAlmon's $150 monthly subsidy.

What Joyce really thought of them was his secret but he extricated himself adroitly from the need to give an opinion by suggesting that McAlmon bring them out under the title of *A Hasty Bunch*. The stories did appear to have been written on the spur of the moment and to have been left half-finished—McAlmon disliked the drudgery of correcting, revising, rewriting, or reading proofs.

McAlmon did publish the book and received at least one good review, from no less a person than Ezra Pound and in no less a publication than the *Dial*. Pound was, like Kay Boyle, an ardent advocate, always ready to take up the defense of his protégés, of whom he had many, even when the defense seemed to be difficult.

After publishing the book, it occurred to McAlmon to set up a publishing house of his own, for which he resurrected the name of the magazine he had edited with William Carlos Williams, calling it Contact Editions. It seemed to be dedicated to publishing the work of McAlmon himself and of his closest friends. His own *Companion Volume* (companion to *A Hasty Bunch*) and *Post-Adolescence* were among the early titles, followed by his novel *Village*, which was better received by the critics than most of his works. When he tired of publishing, in 1929, the last Contact book was also his own, a forty-three page poem called *North America, Continent of Conjecture*. He brought out Bryher's *Two Selves* and H.D.'s *Palimpsest* before his marriage broke up. His friends Williams and Carnevali were also represented, the first by *Spring and All*, the second by *A Hurried Man*.

Contact also published Hemingway's *Three Stories & Ten Poems*, the first of his books to be published. Another person outside his close circle whom McAlmon published was Gertrude Stein. He deserves no small credit for undertaking the immense task of bringing out the nearly thousand-page *The Making of Americans*. In the process he discovered that Miss Stein was not easy to get along with. The book finally did appear but by that time author and publisher were at loggerheads, largely on the seemingly trifling question of supplying her ten free copies. Her disapproval of McAlmon afterward was expressed in her verdict that his writing was "rather dull stuff."

By the outbreak of the war, when I last saw him, McAlmon was in bad health, already far gone with tuberculosis. When France was invaded, he crossed into Spain, then into Portugal, and sailed from Lisbon to the United States. That was the route I took too, leaving in 1940 by the last boat sent to Portugal by the United States to pick up American refugees. Although he had gone home to die, McAlmon held out for another sixteen years, until 1956, when he was fifty-nine. So far as I know, he stopped writing after he returned to the United States, although he had been, in Europe, what might be called a compulsive writer. As long as his health permitted he worked for what I find described as "the family business" in El Paso, Texas.

I do not know what the family business was, but from time to time after the war I had to endure the sneering chuckle of Arthur Moss, a malicious little man, as malicious as McAlmon ever was, who repeated to anyone who would listen: "You know what Bob McAlmon is doing now? You know what the Great White Hope of American literature is doing? He's a truss salesman." The thought seemed to give Moss great pleasure.

¶

Cost Accounting—
Eskimos, Sled Dogs, and a
Polar Bear or Two

¶

It was while Lansing Warren was acting as city editor of the Paris Edition, sitting in the slot of the big copydesk, his head bent low over a story he was editing, that a lost visitor entered the city room. "The advertising manager, please?" the visitor asked.

Lansing neither turned nor lifted his head. "Second horse's ass to the left," he answered, thus taking care of the circulation manager as well.

In fifty years of journalism, I can recall no instance of cordiality between the business offices and the editorial department, but the nadir was reached on the Paris Edition. Our editorial department regarded the business office with loathing and the business office looked on the editorial workers as parasites. The advertising and circulation departments brought money into the paper, our businessmen reasoned, and all the editorial department did was spend it. Our businessmen would gladly have dispensed with the editorial staff if the public had not demanded news in the paper. Frustrated in its desire to do without journalists, all the business office could do was underpay them.

The two birds Warren had nicked with one stone were members of the same family, Farish senior and junior, first names forgotten. Farish *père*, the advertising manager, was a sour-faced man with an aggressive manner who spoke in a growl and antagonized everyone he met. Since he clearly couldn't sell advertising himself, he was made the boss of those who could—if they tried. Farish had formed a team of unsuccessful salesmen, we thought, who had drawing accounts that were to be repaid from their commissions. They rarely earned enough in commissions to reimburse the drawing accounts, or so we believed.

Farish *fils*, the circulation manager, arrived at the office every morning riveted dutifully to his father and went home each night chaperoned in the same fashion. His conception of his duties seemed to involve a minimum of effort. I wrote him once or twice when I was on vacation to inform him that in one important resort or another the *Tribune* was unfindable while the *Herald* blossomed on every newsstand. His reponse was that I hadn't looked hard enough.

Above the Farishes was William Elsfelder, business manager and chief accountant, and above him was Jack Hummel, who was the top of our hierarchy but did not enjoy the title of publisher. This the colonel had kept to himself, just as he kept the title of editor. Hummel was known by a number of nicknames, including Give 'em Half Hummel. Most of us on the editorial staff considered Hummel the head of the business office but he was actually the head of both business and editorial departments. He was the only person I have known who habitually came in for work in the morning drunk. He usually drank at the Bohy-Lafayette Hotel because it was only a block from the office and because he didn't have to pay for his drinks there since he owned a sizable share of stock in the hotel. All *Chicago Tribune* social events that required the use of hotel space were held at the Bohy.

One evening when Hummel turned up unexpectedly in the city room he became involved in a comedy devised by us to enable our society editor, Emily Holmes Coleman, to collect what the Paris Edition owed her before she became, inevitably, our former society editor. Society editors came and went in swift succession because their wages and expense accounts were based on a complicated system and on payday the editor always discovered that the total arrived at by the business office was far lower than she expected. Most of the women, after a short or long but always heated argument, quit in disgust. Emily looked fragile but she was tough. She did not intend to quit and wanted what she felt was coming to her.

The business office countered by decreeing a lockout. The night watchman was instructed to refuse to let her in when she reported for work. We arranged to have a few editorial workers at the door when Emily arrived and, innocently, we assured the watchman that she was a member of the staff. We did not expect him to be wily and he was not. Before witnesses, he explained that he had been ordered to keep her out.

Emily had her case. Just then Hummel walked into the middle of our group, drunk, as he always was at that hour, and she had an even better case. The head of the organization confirmed her accusation that she had been locked out of work. That was not the end of our glee. Hummel tried to insult and bully her. Emily was a high-strung woman and she slapped Hummel in the face.

She was a lightweight and Hummel a heavy but his equilibrium was not all it might have been and she nearly bowled him over. His glasses fell to the floor and cracked, evidence that he exhibited a few days later when Emily sued for her money plus severance pay and Hummel filed a countercharge of assault.

The judge stared unbelievingly at the cracked glasses, the burly Hummel, and the slender Emily. "I cannot believe that madame could have done any grievous harm to monsieur," he remarked. Then he awarded her the full amount she sought.

Hers was not an isolated case. I doubt if a payday ever passed without howls of rage from someone in the editorial department—and often from several someones at the same time—who found that the amount he received was less than he believed he had earned. The most frequent causes for these discrepancies were disallowances of expense accounts or failure to pay space rates for copy not covered by our salaries or to reimburse writers for extra work taken on in exchange for extra pay. I was in permanent conflict with Elsfelder since my job often put me in the position of fighting for colleagues who had been cheated, as well as sometimes for myself.

I cannot remember any time when, in the end, the disputed amount was not paid. Despite this, the business office never acknowledged the futility of its efforts and continued to make us fight for our money. These tactics were not designed to improve morale and if the *Chicago Tribune* had been an ordinary paper, it would have lost all its best men. But the *Chicago Tribune* was not an ordinary paper. Since we did not work there primarily for the money, important as it was for us, we did not leave on questions of money. We worked on the Paris Edition because it was a club and a cult, because we liked each other, because we loved putting out the paper. So we hated the business office, refused to allow it to discourage us, and tried to have as little to do with it as possible.

Elsfelder touched perhaps his lowest level when the home paper made Larry Rue, its Vienna correspondent, responsible for a vast territory that reached into the Middle East. Larry held a pilot's license, a rare asset in those days, so the paper provided him with a private plane to enable him to cover this territory and agreed to pay life and accident insurance in case of a crash. But when the insurance company billed Elsfelder for the premium, he refused to pay it. "If the *Chicago Tribune* is going to pay the premium," he pointed out, "the *Chicago Tribune* should be the beneficiary if he's killed." Rue did not bother to argue the point. He cabled the colonel and Elsfelder was ordered to pay the premium.

Elsfelder did not have much success in protecting the *Tribune*'s treasury from the inroads of the Foreign News Service correspondents with direct access to the colonel. Even when one of them was in the colonel's bad graces, Elsfelder was unable to curb his extravagance—which was, for once, true extravagance. The man who outfoxed Elsfelder was Floyd Gibbons, the most flamboyant of the *Chicago Tribune*'s foreign correspondents.

For some reason Gibbons had annoyed the colonel, who decided to take him down a peg or two by assigning him to cover the Sahara Desert.

Gibbons was not an easy man to downgrade. He obeyed instructions and covered the Sahara by setting out to be the first man—and surely the last—to walk across the desert carrying a large American flag.

He was accompanied by a crowd of photographers and by camels. The camels were in the employ of the *Chicago Tribune* and so were some of the photographers, but not all of them. Gibbons realized that the colonel might refuse to print photographs provided by his own hirelings. But if competing news services were picturing Gibbons and Old Glory crossing the Sahara, the *Tribune* could hardly allow itself to be scooped on its own correspondent's exploit.

Those were the days of the rotogravure section. Sunday after Sunday, Gibbons strode across the sepia pages as well as the dunes, an enormous flag floating above his head against a background of Arabs and camels.

Eventually, of course, Elsfelder received Gibbons' expense account and with it the bill for the camels. This was a problem. Elsfelder frequently consulted the Cooks-Wagons Lits guide, which recorded the fares for most kinds of transport, to check on his correspondents' expense accounts, but the guide was silent about the going rate for camels. Having no idea what figure was reasonable, Elsfelder knew that whatever it was, Gibbons would exaggerate it.

The business manager began trying to catch Gibbons by comparing one expense account with the next. The arrival of each account was signaled by Elsfelder's entry into the Foreign News Service office, which had a large map of the world on its wall. Elsfelder carried calipers. With their aid, he tried to determine whether Gibbons had charged more to cover so many miles one week than he had charged the week before.

This was not an entirely satisfactory method. The Foreign News Service map was large and so was the Sahara, but even so the place the desert occupied on a map of the world did not permit adequate caliperization. Elsfelder did his best but Gibbons did better. Asked about variations in his bills for camel service, he responded with accounts of delays imposed by hills, gorges, stony terrain, and unscheduled sandstorms. He explained the difference in rates charged for lowly pack camels and racing camels.

His finest touch came in an exchange of letters with the auditors concerning a camel that had given birth. He had not only been obliged to hire another camel to replace her, he wrote, but also was entitled to no rebate for the loss of her services. In a maneuver that should have been dear to Elsfelder's heart, he explained that he had tried to claim the infant camel as the property of the *Chicago Tribune* but the law of the desert had ruled against him. He had not even been allowed a share in the mother's milk, he added. Gibbons must have been enjoying himself immensely.

Elsfelder finally gave up and paid the expense accounts in full. The colonel remained silent. Not long afterward, Gibbons left the *Tribune*'s employ. I do not know why but it must have been unexpectedly since it cut short his projected trip to the North Pole. Perhaps this was next in the colonel's program to cut Gibbons down to size and he decided to abandon it to avoid having to pay bills for Eskimos, sled dogs, and a polar bear or two.

¶

Six-Penny Stamp

¶

The colonel may have learned something from his experience with Gibbons in the Sahara but Elsfelder did not. He continued his futile skirmishes to save pennies at whatever cost, losing them all and each time coming back for more.

I knew of another example from my two years in our London bureau. The office there enjoyed a certain amount of autonomy, including a bank account large enough to cover emergencies, but each month it had to send to Paris the record of its expenditures in order to be reimbursed. One such accounting listed the purchase of a six-penny stamp on behalf of the Paris Edition.

In response, Elsfelder's auditing department sent the London office a letter pointing out that the six-penny stamp had been attached to a letter that referred both to the Paris Edition and to the Foreign News Service. So, the auditors ruled, the charge should be shared equally between the two.

The secretary of the London office thought this was rather funny and passed the letter around so we might all appreciate it. She then wrote a lengthy answer, suggesting after an analysis of the original letter's contents that it would be more equitable to charge fourpence to the Paris Edition and tuppence to the Foreign News Service. All of us read this letter too and thought it hilarious but its reception in Paris was otherwise. The auditors sent an even lengthier letter offering, in all seriousness, a counterproposal for the splitting of the six-penny cost.

Then our secretary rejected the new proposal and offered another of her own. The exchange of letters continued until our secretary tired of the business and wrote what she thought would be the last letter, pointing out that something like ten shillings in postage had now been spent to decide how to charge sixpence. In the interest of economy, she suggested, the

Paris office should charge the original stamp any way it wanted. Elsfelder instead sent her a reprimand, telling her she was incompetent to handle her job since she obviously knew nothing about the principles of cost accounting.

I was back on the Paris Edition for the next example of Elsfelder's economy. He had learned that a minute fraction of a cent per unit could be saved if he bought pencils by the boxcar. He promptly ordered a boxcar load of pencils of inferior quality. They refused to make a mark on copy paper unless the editor bore down on them, and then they broke. And so we bore down. That is why I know that a dozen men, working in their slack moments, will need three months to break a boxcar load of pencils.

In addition to the pencils, we violently opposed what we referred to as Elsfelder's New Economic Policy. We almost always ran out of money before payday and the remedy was to seek an advance. Applications were made to the cashier, a Swiss named Windblatt, who sat all day in a wire cage at the door, as motionless as a stuffed animal. Windblatt was empowered to respond to our pleas but not obliged to do so, and we usually had to argue.

I do not know why it was made so difficult, unless the office was simply reluctant to part with money. Under no circumstances were we advanced more than we had earned to date, so it was our own money we were being permitted to borrow. To borrow? Strictly speaking this was not borrowing. Perhaps Elsfelder thought of it that way, and it gave him an idea. When you borrow money, you pay interest. The business manager decreed that journalists would no longer have to wheedle or beg to get an advance. Advances became obtainable on demand—at three percent interest.

Elsfelder skipped over the detail that a lender's interest is justified by the risk he is taking, while the paper was taking no risk since we were still limited to advances no greater than the amount we had already earned. This operation must have been illegal since this was a banking operation and the *Tribune* had no authority to act as a bank. Its usury was defended on the grounds that the paper did not keep the interest in its profit-and-loss account but paid it into the nonprofit *Chicago Tribune* Social Club, in which all employees were enrolled. The idea was that whenever enough money was accumulated, the Social Club would sponsor a banquet at Hummel's Hotel Bohy, or a dance, again at the Bohy, or whatever else the business office could think up.

The editorial workers were uninterested in the activities of the Social Club and I do not know of anyone other than Hérol Egan, who loved crowds, who attended any of the functions held with our money. And it was our money because we were the sole supporters of the *Chicago Tribune* Social Club. The mentality that makes newspapermen also usually makes poor money managers, who never succeed in coming out even at the end of the month. The mentality that makes accountants sees to it that the end of the month is reached solvently.

The minor office workers, stenographers and such, were nearly all French, lived with their families, never had much money but never ran out of it, and would have thought it immoral to anticipate payday, much less pay interest for doing so. The advertising men, with their drawing accounts, already had advances, interest-free. So we put in the money and the business employees spent it.

The beneficiaries of our enforced charity were considerably more numerous than we were. Fifteen to twenty men in the city room, all of them never present at the same time, created the newspaper that supported us all. It took five times as many to handle the paperwork related to our jobs.

A visitor who made the trek from the front door past row after row of desks bordering the corridor—through the whirring of mimeographs and the crunching of adding machines—finally reached our handful of workers and asked, "What do all those people out there do?"

"They're auditing each other's figures," somebody joked. We discovered later that this was exactly what they were doing, and moreover the figures that they were auditing were imaginary. We found this out with a shock one day when we came into the office and someone else was sitting in Windblatt's cage.

It was out of the question that Windblatt was ill. He was an iron man. In all his years at the *Chicago Tribune*, he had never missed a day. By the end of the day we knew. Windblatt had been arrested for embezzlement. He had simply channeled part of the money paid into the *Tribune* into his own pocket, and he had been able to get away with it because, of all that army of business-office workers, he was the only one who was exercising any real function connected with the paper's money. It was he who supplied the secretaries with the lists of bills to be sent out, he who received and banked all the checks, he who made all the disbursements—in short, he was the only man in the office who handled any money.

When an advertiser or a newspaper distributor paid his bill, Windblatt put part of the money into the *Tribune*'s account, credited the remitter with partial payment and kept the difference. On paper, all the *Tribune*'s most important advertisers and distributors were falling further and further behind on their payments. But as long as they kept paying something, nobody in the business department wanted to annoy them by pressing for full and prompter payment. Besides, that was Windblatt's job.

He must have needed a prodigious amount of bookkeeping to manage all the accounts so that none of them seemed to be falling behind at a rate that would have jolted someone into investigating the case. Sometimes, I was told later, he would realize that a dangerous imbalance had developed for an account, and he would record a payment for it, deducting the amount from a payment made by somebody else. It was a remarkable job of juggling but he kept it up too long. The discrepancy between the amounts owed the *Tribune*, on paper, and the amounts that Windblatt reported it had received became too great. Someone was sent, without Windblatt's knowledge, to chat with a few of the largest and, according to the books, most delinquent advertisers—and the cat was out of the bag.

The *Tribune* never found out for how many years Windblatt had been milking the paper nor how much he had taken. He was the only one who knew and he preferred not to tell. No doubt the *Tribune* could have arrived at an approximate figure if it had checked with all its thousands of advertisers and distributors, but I gathered that the business office preferred not to make a public spectacle of its shame.

The editorial department greeted the news of Windblatt's exploit with an explosion of joy. We were delighted that someone had put something over on the hated business department. From an automaton without personality Windblatt was transformed in our eyes to a hero, a Robin Hood who had wrested from the rich (Elsfelder) the spoils that the rich had taken from the poor (us). We even chipped in to hire a lawyer for him, although we should have realized that he was perfectly capable of paying for his own lawyer: Although nobody knew how much he had stolen, there was no reason to believe that he did not still have his millions.

Windblatt had lived simply, well within the limits of his salary. He was unmarried, had no mistress, and did not frequent women. He neither gambled nor drank. He had no hobbies and collected nothing. The *Tribune* intimated that it might withdraw all charges if Windblatt returned the money, even a substantial part of it. He chose instead two years in prison.

I forget who got hold of him when he was released but whoever it was brought him around to have a drink with us. It was his coming-out party, so to speak. We had in mind a bit of chortling over what he had done to the *Tribune*'s business department. He turned out not to be the chortling type. In prison pallor, he sat stolidly among us and had nothing to say. He was just as forbidding, just as thoroughly closed to all human contact, as he had been when he sat in his cage and dealt our money out to us mechanically. There seemed to be only one explanation for what we were finally willing to call his crime: He had calculated that there was a certain amount of money that could be stolen and a certain amount of time that would have to be spent in prison, and that the amount was worth the time. He was no Robin Hood but just another member of the business department.

¶

The Wrong Way to
Kill a Newspaper

¶

Jules Frantz never made a visit back home to the United States from the time that he arrived in Paris in 1925 until he decided to return there for his vacation in October 1934. His absence left me in charge of the editorial department. Not long after he left, I came into the office one afternoon to find Hummel's secretary waiting for me.

"Mr. Hummel wants to see you right away," she said. I went to his office. He seemed to be sober but the hand in which he held out a piece of blue paper, obviously a cable, was trembling.

"Read this," he said. It started: HUMMEL STRICTLY CONFIDENTIAL SHOW THIS TO NO ONE ELSE.

EUROPEAN EDITION SOLD TO NEW YORK HERALD STOP, it continued. CEASE PUBLICATION WITH ISSUE OF NOVEMBER 30 STOP MAKE EQUITABLE ARRANGEMENTS WITH STAFF. It was signed MCCORMICK.

We had brought our fate on ourselves by improving the Paris Edition. I knew that the colonel had tired of the paper somewhat after the stock market crash, when it ran into the red and Chicago had to pay the deficit. I knew also that he had at least once asked the *Herald* if it wanted to buy him out. The *Herald* had answered, in effect, with a sneer, "What have you got to sell?" We had indeed had little to sell when we had a circulation of eight thousand copies versus the *Herald*'s twenty-two thousand. We had given the colonel something to sell now that we had built the paper up to twenty-five thousand while the *Herald*'s circulation remained unchanged. And so he sold us.

Sentence of death, with the execution set for a month later, is the wrong way to kill a newspaper. If the Paris Edition was doomed, why wait until November 30? Why not kill it today? That seemed to be what the staff favored. I had to fight with the editorial workers every night to get the paper out; they no longer cared whether it appeared.

I prevented people from setting fire to the morgue several times. If that great mass of paper had caught fire, the building would probably have burned down. The staff seemed to feel that this would be no great loss.

Gillotte's and the Chope Cadet profited heavily from the mood of desperation. Twice Will Barber and I wrote and produced the whole paper while everyone else was roaring drunk. The pressure relaxed a little when Frantz returned. He had cut his vacation short when he heard the news, and he reached Paris a couple of weeks later, good enough time in those days when Ohio to France was not yet a few hours' plane flight. Now there were two of us to combat the what-the-hell spirit of the staff, who believed that if the paper failed to come out it wouldn't matter. I thought it would matter. We had been given no hint what was to happen to us. Would other jobs be found? Would we get severance pay? Or would we simply be turned out and left to shift for ourselves? I felt that the business department could be counted on to take advantage of any failure on our part to produce the paper, probably arguing that we had thus forfeited our rights to compensation at the end.

MAKE EQUITABLE ARRANGEMENTS WITH STAFF, the colonel had cabled but he had not discussed the meaning of "equitable." Elsfelder, we felt, would translate the word in the lowest possible terms. Whatever other faults the colonel had, he was not stingy. But Elsfelder would almost certainly reason that the more money he saved for the paper in severance, the more grateful the paper would be. He would want to impress management in Chicago since his own position was also in doubt. He might be kept in place as paymaster for the European bureaus of the Foreign News Service, he might be given a job in Chicago, or he might simply be dropped. He set out to guarantee his future by acting as a stern watchdog of the treasury.

STAFF MAKING UNREASONABLE DEMANDS, he cabled the colonel, although I do not recall that the staff made any demands. There was no concerted action on our part. Individually, some of us may have pointed out that French law covered our case since the Paris Edition was a French corporation. Apparently the law that applied to us was considered unreasonable by Elsfelder.

This was a shift in his view: For years he had countered complaints that our wage scale was far below pay in the United States by pointing out that in compensation we were much better protected by French law. Now he seemed to feel that we should accept American practice, which then meant that we were entitled to two weeks' notice of firing. Since we had a month, he seemed to say, the paper had fulfilled its obligation. It was one thing to be fired in the United States, where other jobs were available, and another to be fired in France, where the only other employer was the *Herald*, which was fully staffed. We could not even look for other forms of work for we had no French labor permits. They were required of all working foreigners except journalists, who enjoyed special status.

French law on severance pay was generous: one month's pay for each year worked. In my case, that meant eight months' pay, but this was only the beginning. French legislators had been impressed by the hardship of working at night, perhaps because of their exposure to all-night sessions in the Chamber of Deputies. The night staff had been granted a special deduction on income taxes and, in case of firing, had the right to double the amount granted day workers. This put my payoff at sixteen months' salary. The scale mounted also in proportion to the importance of the job. As news editor, I was granted another doubling, to thirty-two months' pay. I had a secondary job, for which I was paid extra, as book critic. That counted too. I calculated finally that the *Tribune*, under French law, owed me something like three years' pay or enough to console most people for the loss of a job.

From the beginning it was obvious that the business office never considered paying us at the level the law decreed. There was not much we could do about it. Sue? If we were cut off without a penny we would be able neither to afford lawyers nor to wait for a verdict. And if we won, could we collect from a company that by then would have ceased to exist? One rumor floating around the office said that management intended to transfer, or had already transferred, the paper's funds to London, out of reach of French courts.

Although we thought it probable that some severance payment would be made, we did not know for certain. I wondered whether the business office was not keeping silent in the hope that we would fail to produce the paper one day, in which case it would have a pretext to pay us nothing.

So I continued to battle to get work out of men who didn't feel like furnishing it.

I was angry—angry at everybody. The last paper was put out on my normal night off, and I took it. Looking back now, that seems childish of me, but my resentment had been building for a month. My future was safe: I received a phone call from the United Press as soon as the *Paris Herald* published the news that it was taking us over, and was offered the job of overnight editor there. There was a catch since the United Press wanted me to start at once. So, every night during that last month, I left the Paris Edition's office after putting the paper to bed about 2:00 A.M., walked the few blocks to the UP on the rue des Italiens, and worked there until 8:00. This workload probably did not improve my temper during my nightly fights with the staff, especially as I was also Paris correspondent for the *Politiken* newspaper of Copenhagen, normally a full-time job, as well as a steady contributor to the "Periscope" section of *Newsweek*. I was making, in addition to my Paris Edition salary, $150 a week, a lot of money for those days, when it was possible to live not too badly in Paris on $25 a month.

As though this weren't enough, I had another temporary job that some of my fellow staffers knew about, which I had taken to protect them from the consequences of the *Tribune*'s disappearance on November 30.

At the end, we were notified to call at the office for our severance checks, the first hint there would be any. I arrived late and stopped at Gillotte's, where the others were relieving their tension after a month of uncertainty. On the whole, the staff was not grumbling. French legal requirements had not been fulfilled but my colleagues were more or less satisfied since any settlement looked good. The business office employees, most of whom were French and familiar with the law, may have felt more resentment than we did since they had expected to be paid off correctly. They hadn't been. So far as I know, nobody protested but forty years later I received a letter from one of the paper's secretaries, who wrote: "I was twenty-three when I began work at the *Chicago Tribune*, where I stayed fifteen years. What did I get out of it: some experience and a lot of fun. When the *Chicago Tribune* was absorbed by the *N.Y.H.T.*, what did I get: 1,000 francs ($20) as severance plus my typewriter. . . ."

Having reviewed the situation at Gillotte's, I went upstairs to see Elsfelder. He took a check from a portfolio on his desk. "We wrote a check for you yesterday. Quite a substantial check." He waved it in the air but did not show it to me. Then he returned it to the portfolio. "But today there seems to be some discussion whether you deserve so much. You will hear from us when a decision has been made."

I was not surprised, certainly not so surprised as he had been that morning when he received in his mail, as had all the other subscribers to the former *Chicago Tribune*, a new paper called the *Paris Tribune*. It was a modest publication, a tabloid with eight or twelve pages, that was announced not as a daily but a weekly. It contained articles signed with the bylines that readers of the now-dead *Chicago Tribune* had been accustomed to and it contained several of the Paris Edition's regular features. The paper killed the day before had not succumbed.

Elsfelder could hardly have had any doubts about who was behind the new paper. Although no editor's name appeared, my byline was prominent and none of the others who had signed stories would have had the means to launch a paper. The front page editorial, "The Toast Is 'The *Tribune*,'" was not signed either but the style was obviously mine:

"One month ago, *Chicago Tribune* readers—and *Chicago Tribune* writers as well—learned with amazement that two gentlemen sitting in an office somewhere across the Atlantic Ocean had signed a document that disposed of the Paris edition of the *Chicago Tribune* to the Paris edition of the *New York Herald*. The arrangement gave the *New York Herald* the right to add to its title the words *Chicago Daily Tribune*. Perhaps the public is expected to believe that the transfer of these three words is equivalent to the transfer of the newspaper that was the *Chicago Tribune*, Paris edition. The public is likely to prove obdurate.

What is a newspaper? Is it a name that can be sold for so many dollars, and does the mere printing of that name constitute the issuance of the paper? We are inclined to think that there is a great deal more to a newspaper than that, specifically that there was a great deal more to the *Chicago Tribune* than that. That paper had won itself a very considerable respect in Europe, particularly among newspapermen, who may be conceded to be good judges. They did not respect it because its name was the *Chicago Tribune*, but because the men who wrote the *Chicago Tribune* did a good job, because they developed esprit de corps and a viewpoint that, if one wanted to use big words, might be considered as approximating to a philosophy.

This the so-called owners of the *Chicago Tribune* could not sell. . . . It did not belong to them. It was more than the money they paid in salaries contracted for. America is full today of newspapers competently written, adequately edited, whose writers give their employers exactly what they pay for—and no more. Good standardized journalism, accurate journalism, uninteresting journalism. The papers of our big business era lack spark. . . . Here and there an individualistic paper remains. There are not many of them. The *Chicago Tribune* of Paris was one. . . . It died from mismanagement in the business office while editorially it was still thriving. . . .

The *New York Herald* has made no move to acquire the features that made up the *Chicago Tribune*'s personality. That was no doubt a wise decision. The two papers had different characters, and their styles would not have mixed. *Tribune* men on the *Herald* would have had to conform to the *Herald* tradition, and therefore would have been transformed into *Herald* men, of whom the *Herald* has enough already. The only way in which they could have been an addition to the *Herald* would have been to transform its character, and the *Herald* probably objects, quite naturally, to having its character transformed. There are many *Tribune* subscribers, no doubt, who might consider the change an improvement. Undoubtedly there would be quite as many *Herald* subscribers who would find it a sacrilege.

No, there is no place in the *New York Herald* for the features that had made the *Chicago Tribune* increasingly popular with Americans in Europe. Yet for these features there was obviously a demand. A flood of letters of protest poured into the *Tribune* offices when the news was known. Perfect strangers all but wept on the shoulders of *Tribune* reporters whom they encountered at odd moments, chiefly in bars, whose lachrymose effect is well known. Critics and columnists had their private mail swelled by despairing appeals from previously unknown admirers who asked pathetically where now they might read their writings.

They may read them here, in the *Paris Tribune*. . . .

This editorial seems to have moved a number of people. Will Barber had it framed and made me a present of it. When, in 1976, I regretted in print that I had no copy of it, an unknown correspondent who had preserved it for forty-two years mailed me one.

The most unbelievable aspect of this episode was that it came to most people as a complete surprise. Neither the management of the *New York Herald* nor the former management for the *Chicago Tribune* had an inkling that anything was up. Yet for the paper to appear the day after the *Chicago Tribune* disappeared, a good many people had to be in on the secret at least a week or two in advance. Not one gave it away. Those staffers whose bylines I wanted in my first issue knew, but I told nobody else on the editorial staff, particularly not Frantz, for he was supposed to be moving to the paper in Chicago and I did not want to put him in an equivocal position. To my great surprise, May Birkhead agreed to contribute society news to our first issue, although she wrote to me regretfully afterward that she could not continue because of orders from Chicago.

Something like a hundred advertisers had been approached, all of them advertising in the *New York Herald*, and none of them gave us away. Even *Chicago Tribune* circulation department employees who saw us running newspaper mailing wrappers through the paper's addressing machines night after night did not report us to their bosses. We got away with it.

The *New York Herald* had helped us. Too greedy to wait, it had already notified its advertisers that it was going to raise its rates as soon as it had a monopoly. As long as no other publication could reach the lucrative market provided by Americans in Europe, the advertisers were helpless. So we pointed out our existence as an alternative advertising medium. To daily advertisers—steamship lines, movies, and theaters—we remarked that one low-cost ad a week with us would save them money over the *Herald*'s new rates. A respectable number of orders for advertising space welcomed our first issue.

From friends at the *Herald* I learned that the first result of the appearance of the *Paris Tribune* was a bitter exchange between the *Herald* and the *Chicago Tribune*. "You sold your paper to us," the *Herald* screamed, "and it's still coming out. You've got to stop it."

"How can we stop it?" the *Chicago Tribune* asked. "We've fired these men. We have no control over them anymore."

The *Herald*, which subscribed to the United Press news service, complained to the agency about me. The United Press apparently decided that I was worth more to it than the *Herald* was but did ask me not to sign my articles in the *Paris Tribune*. I left my signature out but continued to write for the paper and to edit it.

The *Paris Tribune* lasted two months—eight issues—and achieved one of its two main goals. My first desire was to keep the spirit of the *Chicago Tribune* alive, producing a paper that depended on features and good writing rather than on news, for which we could not afford to pay. I realize today that this was an impossible objective since I didn't have the means to support the paper for very long and we had no newsstand distribution.

The second objective was to provide jobs for men who were thrown out of work. For the moment they were writing for us for nothing, in the hope that someday we would be able to pay. I fear that this too was a dream. They got paying jobs all the same, for the *New York Herald* and the *Chicago Tribune* hired my staff away. The *Chicago Tribune* took four persons either into the Foreign News Service or the home paper, the *Herald* hired four others, and the very few who remained found jobs for themselves or decided to go home while some of their severance pay remained.

There was no point in trying to continue. I gave the paper to James King, a former Paris Edition man who had rounded up much of the *Paris Tribune*'s advertising. He brought out one or two issues more but they were sorry imitations of a paper. And then there was no more *Paris Tribune*.

To my surprise, the *Chicago Tribune* eventually gave me severance pay. Elsfelder took pleasure in observing that my check would have been much bigger if I had been a good boy—how much bigger he didn't say. I suppose Elsfelder reasoned that if I accepted a small amount, I could not sue for a larger one. I wouldn't have bothered. I was satisfied with the way things had turned out. The total cost to me for having been a newspaper publisher was $100, the deficit on the first issue. The others paid for themselves. For that $100, eight newspapermen had found jobs. I thought it was cheap at the price.